Clear Pond

Clear Pond

The Reconstruction of a Life

ROGER MITCHELL

SYRACUSE UNIVERSITY PRESS

Copyright © 1991 by Syracuse University Press
Syracuse, New York 13224-5160

First Edition 1991

91 92 93 94 95 96 97 98 99   6 5 4 3 2 1

Winner of the 1990 John Ben Snow Prize, *Clear Pond: The Reconstruction of a Life* is published with the assistance of a grant from the John Ben Snow Foundation.

The paper used in this publication meets the minimum requirements of American National Standard for Information Sciences—Permanence of Paper for Printed Library Materials. ANSI Z39.48-1984. ∞™

Library of Congress Cataloging-in-Publication Data

Mitchell, Roger.
    Clear pond : the reconstruction of a life / by Roger Mitchell. —
1st ed.
      p.   cm.
    Includes index.
    ISBN 0-8156-0257-X (alk. paper)
    1. Frontier and pioneer life—New York (State)—Adirondack
Mountains. 2. Adirondack Mountains (N.Y.)—Biography.
3. Adirondack Mountains (N.Y.)—History. 4. Johnson family.
I. Title.
F127.A2M64   1991
974.7'5—dc20   90-26079
                                                               CIP

Manufactured in the United States of America

To the people of North Hudson, Blue Ridge,
and Newcomb. In part, this is their story.

ROGER MITCHELL lived much of his early life in the Adirondacks, but once he earned his Ph.D. at Manchester University in England, he moved to the Middle West. He now lives in Bloomington, Indiana, and teaches at Indiana University. He is the author of four books of poetry and numerous essays and reviews.

Contents

Illustrations

FIGURES

MAPS

Preface

Nearly a decade ago, at the age of forty-five, I decided I wanted to know something about the place where I grew up, something other than the view we had out our back window or the street on which I spent years walking to and from school. It would be another way, I realized, of finding out what I was. Which appealed to me, since I was still not sure. I no longer lived in that place and had not, in fact, gone back to visit in the twenty-five years since my family reluctantly packed up and left. Still, the place beckoned to me. More and more of the stories I told came from there, and I would routinely use parts of it—rooms, meadows, alleys, brooks—to flesh out some author's description in a book or to do my daydreaming in. Life is either hiding something from me, I thought, or trying to tell me something that I'm not hearing. And, since I couldn't go back, except as a kind of curator of my own itches, I decided that I would study the place.

So, for three years or more I read anything I could find on the Adirondacks. I was born in Boston while my father was in medical school and had lived till the age of eight in his home town—Glens Falls, New York—but it was in the Adirondacks, just outside Saranac Lake, that I tried, unsuccessfully, to be an adolescent, a boy scout, and a juvenile delinquent. It was there that I had my first date, drank my first beer, and failed my first driver's test. I've won only one medal in my life. It, too, was in the Adirondacks: first place in the Class B downhill, Lake Placid Winter Carnival, 1950. Or was it 1949? It was there, too, that I first fell in love, ruptured a kidney, and climbed a mountain in the dead of winter, not necessarily in that order.

These and a thousand other things happened with a kind of blind, ferocious intensity. My attention was consumed by my own small round of longings. In my forties, I began wondering what else had happened there. What was I not paying attention to? It was not that I had suddenly become unselfish. I hadn't. I wanted to know if anything had happened then or in the historical past that would help make sense of the most confused and delicious time of my life. Foolish longings, I suppose, but I pored over articles, poems, guide-books, diaries, travelogues, maps, memoirs, novels, broadsides, pamphlets, filled seven notebooks — all so I might write a book about things I had grown up in the shadow of but knew almost nothing about, indeed, in many cases, absolutely nothing about.

And there, somewhere in the middle of this unregulated search, looking for one sort of thing, I found another. A man. An ordinary man, about whom nothing was known. He was neither related to me nor alive in my lifetime. In fact, he was long dead and had lived in a part of the Adirondacks I had never seen. I found him in someone else's diary. The diarist had put up for a night at his cabin as he was traveling through the woods in the 1830s. It was a chance meeting, an evening spent in front of a fire, a good-bye.

Nothing is more astonishing than people; and nothing is more astonishing about people than that they are themselves; as whole and separate and mysterious as we are. Something the diarist said of this man, that the diarist could not even say of himself, made me sense the completeness and otherness of this unassuming man. Here was a man who had lived at a certain time and in a certain place, who had done with his life whatever it was he had done, and then died. No one knew the least thing about him, and even I, who have now spent years reading census reports and deed books, visiting libraries, talking with local historians, searching in the National Archives, walking up and down the places where he lived, have found neither a living descendant nor his grave. It's this very ordinariness, even anonymity, that draws me to him. I ask myself, what could be more like ourselves than this?

This is the story of my finding a man on the edge of our consciousness and of my attempts to bring him a small way back into it.

Roger Mitchell

Bloomington, Indiana
September 1990

Acknowledgments

*T*his book is little more than a tissue of acknowledgments, but I would like to give special thanks to Emily Neville, Paul Stapley, Warder H. Cadbury, Robert Johnson, Judith Roman, and to the librarians at The Adirondack Museum, The National Archives, Connecticut State Library, Indiana State Library, Connecticut State Historical Society, Keene Valley Public Library, Essex County Historical Society, New York State Library, Syracuse University, and Indiana University.

Research for this book was substantially supported by grants-in-aid from Indiana University, and *Blueline* published a version of the first chapter in its 1986 issues. My thanks to both.

Clear Pond

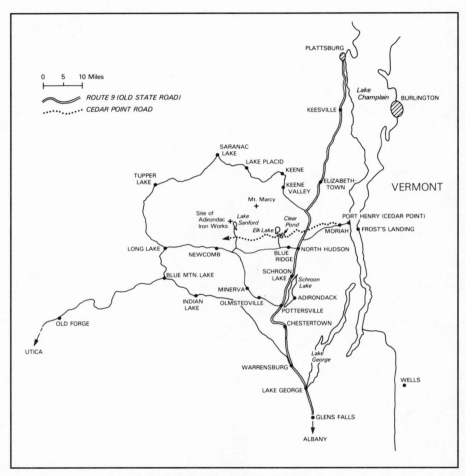

1. The Southeastern Adirondacks.

How I Came to Be This Way

*I*t was the fall of 1981, September in fact, and the west side of Blue Mountain, which I could see from my car, was flamboyant with color. The little village of Blue Mountain Lake is about as close to the center of the Adirondacks as you can get, and of course it is home to the Adirondack Museum. It was my good fortune to have the use of the museum's library for a week while I did research for a book of poems (eventually to have the uninspired but straightforward title, *Adirondack*), and I was eating a sandwich in my car out in the parking lot because the library closed between twelve and one. Usually, I took a book from the library out to the car to read during lunch, but that morning was special. I had stumbled on an interesting passage in an old diary. It did not seem to lead to a poem, but it intrigued me. It came from a diary kept by William C. Redfield. Redfield had been a member of the party that tried to climb Mt. Marcy in August of 1836 and then finally did it, the first time ever recorded, the next summer. On their way into the woods that first year, the party put up for a night at the home of a local settler. Redfield wrote in his journal for Sunday, August 14:

> Weather mild and showery. Breakfast at 7 A.M. & started for Johnsons 9 miles. Showery and at times raining very hard. Found the benefit of India Rubber Cloth. Johnsons at 10:30 and put up for the day it being the last house on the *road*—if road it can be called. Johnsons lies at the outlet of Clear Pond has been here four years with his family. Began with his hands and has built 2 saw mills himself of a peculiar construction and is said to have been offered 3000 Doll[ar]s

for his place. Has been a frost which killed the potato tops to a small extent.

Redfield had been a member of a party of geologists, led by Ebenezer Emmons, professor of chemistry at Williams College, which that morning had ridden west along the Cedar Point road away from Lake Champlain. This was the new state road built from Cedar Point (now Port Henry) into the center of a mountainous region in upper New York State, about the size of Connecticut and Rhode Island combined, where almost no one lived and where the same dense forest that Cartier had seen from as far away as Montreal in 1534 still covered the ground. White pines from this forest grew to an average height of 150 feet and were much prized by the imperial navies of Great Britain and France. It has been said that every ship at the Battle of Trafalgar was masted with Adirondack pine.

The road passed a few miles south of the McIntyre Iron Works and went to the western edge of Essex County. The state bill of appropriation had said that the road was to help settle this area, but everyone knew that it had been built through the careful lobbying of Archibald McIntyre, David Henderson, Duncan McMartin, and the other gentleman who found and instantly bought, in 1827, the largest deposit of iron ore then known in North America. They themselves had not found it, really. An Indian named Lewis Elijah had brought them a piece of the ore and had then taken them to the place where he picked it up. These gentlemen naturally wanted a road to it, or at least near it, so that business could profitably be conducted there.

The road was not more than five or six years old in 1836, but the terrain was so rough and the weather so severe that the road was little more than an elongated clearing, stumpy and uneven. If you managed to make a passable route one year, it did not guarantee that it would be there the next. Upheavals of frost, spring mud, and new growth usually meant that no road existed at all from April to June and that when things had dried out, the brush had been cut back, the potholes filled, and the rotten logs replaced, there was still the relentless jolting of the buckboard as it passed over miles of logs laid side by side, cross-ways across the right of way. It was called "corduroy." The best time for traveling on such a road was the middle of the winter. You could hitch up a team and drive a sleigh over five or six feet of snow. But you also had to put up with the temperature.

Ebenezer Emmons and his friends had breakfasted by seven o'clock at the last inn on the road. It was an all-day trip to the Iron Works, even under ideal conditions, and they were anxious to get away. It had rained much of the night, and from the look of things, it would rain more that day. A heavy rain would probably prevent them from getting to the Works that day, and a night in the forest, especially a rainy one, where one might be visited by a panther or a bear, did not seem appealing. Someone suggested that they wait until tomorrow. Someone else mentioned that there was a house on the road, about seven or eight miles away, and that the man—who ran a sawmill—and his wife sometimes put people up overnight. It was sprinkling again, but with that reassurance, they set out.

Professor Emmons and his party had no direct interest in the Iron Works. They had been commissioned by the state of New York and its governor, William Learned Marcy, to conduct a survey of the second geological district, a district large enough to contain the Adirondack Mountains and much more. Even in 1836, it was still what Thomas Pownall, the mapmaker, had called it sixty years earlier, "a broken unpracticable tract." A few settlements lay scattered around its fringes, some logging and a little farming took place toward the interior, and not much else. It was still a hunting ground for various Indian hunters and home to a few white hermits. White hunters and vacationers had not yet discovered the area except in small numbers.

Once the Cedar Point road left Cedar Point and crossed the old state road between Albany and Plattsburgh (now Route 9), where Weatherhead's inn was located, it still passed, in 1836, through dense, original forest. The roadway, that is, the entire cleared space, would have been no more than twenty feet wide. The surface of the road, logs laid side by side, kept down the mud, made passage— especially of wagons—possible, and created what were commonly known as the worst roads ever made anywhere.

Professor Emmons and his party used this road to reach the middle of the wilderness. The village there, depending on conditions, was a three days' journey in from Lake Champlain. After spending one night at Weatherhead's and another at the cabin of the local settler, eight miles further in, they went on across the Boreas River to the Works where there was a furnace, a company village

1. Theodore R. Davis's woodcut *The Corduroy, Harper's Weekly,*
November 21, 1868.

with a post office, and a farm to provide food for the men, their
families, and the animals. Though they had no real business at the
Works, it was largely because iron ore had been found in the middle
of this wilderness that the state of New York decided a thorough
survey had to be undertaken to see what else might lie hidden
beneath the trees and mountains. It was also a part of their purpose to
locate the headwaters of the Hudson River. The Erie Canal was only
eleven years old in 1836, but already concern had risen over the
declining level of water in the system. More had to be learned about
watersheds in the state if the system were to be kept functioning.

The next day the Emmons party, with guides, left the Works and
walked north toward the cluster of high mountains that lies at the
center of the Adirondack wilderness. Their guides, John Cheney and
Harvey Holt, were two of the most famous guides in the history of
this region. It would be gratifying to say that the Emmons party
strode on at the heels of Cheney and Holt and accomplished their
ambitious objectives, but weather intervened. High up among
nameless lakes, rivers, and mountains, near what is now called Lake
Colden, along the river which these geologists named the Opalescent, two days of unbroken rain drove them back. Back to the Works,
out the Cedar Point road to the log cabin of the local settler, and
thence to Lake Champlain. They would have to wait until next year.

On August 5, 1837, Ebenezer Emmons and his party, back for another try, reached the top of what was then called "the high peak of Essex." Realizing they stood on the highest ground around, they decided to name it. They named the mountain Marcy out of deference to the governor who hired them, and the region they called "the Adirondacks" in honor of an Indian tribe, by then exterminated, which they believed had once hunted there.

The Iron Works closed nineteen years later. Its owners could never solve the transportation problem. They fixed and refixed the Cedar Point road, but it would not stay fixed. By 1841 or 1842 it was practically out of use, replaced mostly by a road to the south called, then, the Carthage road. This is now the numberless road from North Hudson through Blue Ridge to Newcomb and beyond. The Cedar Point road has disappeared into the forests of second and third growth that now make up nearly all of the Adirondacks. Attempts to put a railroad through to the Iron Works failed, and though work was begun on an ingenious wooden railroad, that too came to nothing. Larger deposits of more accessible iron ore were found in other parts of the country. For many years after the mining and smelting stopped in 1856, the company hired a man, Robert Hunter, and his family to live in the village of Adirondack among the empty houses and sheds and among the stacks of unburnt charcoal. John Burroughs passed through in 1863 and brought the family its mail from the post office in Newcomb, twelve miles away. The children in the family went to school every day, walking across the grass to the dilapidating school house. They were its only students, and the oldest of them was the teacher.

The geological survey, though impressive for its energy and thoroughness, also came to little. The Adirondacks did not prove to be as rich in minerals as speculators hoped and the canals were replaced by the railroads. What the Emmons party did, however, and they did it only inadvertently, was to awaken people in the east to the fact that in their midst, not thousands of miles away in the west, lay a large, primitive wilderness.

William Redfield, a member of the Emmons party, wrote the first account of their historic climb. It appeared in the New York *Journal of Commerce* in August and September of 1837, then reappeared in the *American Journal of Science and Arts* for January 1838 and was reprinted a second time almost at once in the widely circulated

Family Magazine. The original article prompted at least one other person, Charles Fenno Hoffman, to attempt the climb that same summer. Hoffman, editor of the *New York Mirror* and a well-known Knickerbocker poet, was lame and so could not get all the way up Mt. Marcy, but he wrote of his experiences in the woods, first for his own paper, but then in the first lengthy account of vacationing in the Adirondacks, published in 1839. A trend was begun, and though there were to be sixty years of struggle between those who wanted the mountains for timber and those who wanted them for vacations, the latter finally won.

The party that set out from Cedar Point on Saturday, August 13, 1836, made history in a small way. Some of that history it intended to make; some it did not. What came to interest me was even further from the minds of Ebenezer Emmons, William Redfield, and the rest, and yet they saw it. It is really only because they saw it, or because Redfield did, that I first learned it was there. Something in the way Redfield described it made me take an interest in it.

I am not a historian, but history, it seems, is made up of notable events and successions of notable events. History is created or facilitated or, I suppose, sometimes merely endured by individuals who happen to be where it takes place. History happens to us all, and so the study of history could involve any one of us. For the most part, though, we either exist across a great gulf from history, waving to it occasionally, or are one of its random, passive agents or victims. History, as it were, knocked on Israel Johnson's door one day. That door, miles from any other door, opened perhaps the best kept secret of all human life, the life of an ordinary person. History was mildly intrigued. It had got soaking wet out in the rain getting there and had to put up for most of a day and a night in an ordinary log cabin smoking a cheroot and making small talk. It looked around and asked a few questions, and the answers it got flicked briefly into Johnson's nature and suggested, perhaps also to Redfield, that it was worth knowing more about, if more could be found out. "The last house on the *road*—if road it can be called...has built 2 saw mills himself of a peculiar construction...began with his hands." Who was this man who entertained the party that first climbed the highest mountain in the state? Who was this man who lived in the woods with his family? What sort of person is it who lives, dies, and is then forgotten? Emmons and Redfield had mountains named for them. So did the men who started the Adirondack Iron works. A painting of Indian Pass by C. C. Ingham, who made the climb in 1837, hangs in the Adirondack Museum. Cheney had a pond named for him, and his pistol is said to be in the state museum in Albany. Though unnamed, it is Harvey Holt's descendant who stands next to Old Mountain Phelps in Winslow Homer's painting, "Two Woodsmen." What of Johnson? Who was he, and what has survived of him?

❋

I had been trying to find out all I could about the first climb of Mt. Marcy when I found the Redfield notes. The library of the Adirondack Museum has the most complete collection of Adirondack materials anywhere. I knew Redfield had written the first essay on the climb, but when I discovered there was also a Redfield journal, I wanted to see it first. Johnson is called there, the first time he is mentioned, "Is." Johnson. My initial guesses were that he was an Isaac or Isaiah, but in the published essay he is called Israel. Israel Johnson. Here was a start, a whole name.

I was lucky to have the Redfield notes at all, really. They were a copy of a copy of excerpts made from a copy of the original. Charles B. Redfield, probably William's grandson, loaned his grandfather's papers to Verplanck Colvin after the latter became head of the Adirondack Survey. Colvin asked his assistant, Mills Blake, to make a copy of them. This was in 1875. On April 4, 1926, Russell M. L. Carson, doing research for his *Peaks and People of the Adirondacks*, made an excerpted copy of the Blake copy, which he then typed. It was a xerox copy of this that I read in Blue Mountain Lake, passed on by some of the most famous names in Adirondack history. And it is only in this journal, written hastily, on the spot, without thought of publication, in ungrammatical and elliptical language, that any sense of the person known as Israel Johnson comes forth.

I was curious to know where Clear Pond was, so I got out my topographical maps. Redfield said that Johnson built his house at its outlet. Today there is almost nothing on or near Clear Pond. A road runs by the west side of it between a small settlement called Blue Ridge, three and a half miles to the south, and Elk Lake, two miles to the north. The 1979 map showed eight or nine structures there, probably summer camps. The road, a "light duty" road, went right across the outlet to Clear Pond.

By the time I got around to consulting the maps, I had moved from Blue Mountain Lake to Keene Valley. I was staying for short periods of time in various places in the Adirondacks to do research and some general looking around for my book of poems. Israel Johnson was, as I said, a diversion. Any work I did on him, though interesting, kept me from doing what I should have been doing. He would not stay out of my mind, however. One day I found myself driving over the hill to Elizabethtown, the county seat. I was going to look into the land deed associated with the so-called philosophers' camp in Keene Valley, where people like William James and John Dewey came in the summer in the early 1900s to give lectures. I also wanted to know where in the valley Prestonia Mann Martin had lived, because Maxim Gorky, while staying there for several months in 1906, had written all or most of his most famous novel, *The Mother.* This is easily the most astonishing of several literary events associated with the Adirondacks. Gorky was hiding from the puritanical American press, which vilified him for living with a woman who was not his wife.

I tried looking for the property on which the "philosophers' camp" had stood, but gave that up after an hour or so. The rest of the day I spent on Johnson. Somewhere in the county survey and tax records, I was sure, would be a reference or two to Israel Johnson, the man who lived on Clear Pond in the 1830s, the man who was most likely the original settler of that land and who had been offered a large sum of money to sell it. The deed or deeds would tell me when he bought the land, how much of it he bought, from whom, for what price, and perhaps when he sold or willed it away.

The Essex County clerk's office is in the center of a complex of two-story, red-brick buildings, one or two of which are about 150 years old. Across the street is "The Deer's Head," a place that advertises itself as the oldest inn in the Adirondacks. I told the man behind the counter at the clerk's office that I wanted to check on whether a certain man had owned a certain piece of property in the 1830s. He asked, "Do you know who the current owner is?" I had no idea, of course, having only a man's name and a rough description of the land "at the outlet of Clear Pond." He said the only way of finding the original owner of a piece of land from records kept in the county clerk's office was to start with the current owner and trace the ownership back, deed by deed. Each deed would indicate when the land had been bought and from whom. He said further that if I went to the "tax map" office, they would be able to help me locate the current owner of the property, it being their business to stay in close touch with current owners.

The tax map office, with its long, broad counter for laying out maps on, was shiny new. The young man behind the counter had no trouble finding the property on his assessment maps. These are a special kind of map, very accurate concerning property lines but only sketchy when it comes to topographical details. Clear Pond was scrawled in quickly. No outlet was shown. The place where it seemed logical for it to be, however, was all owned by one person, a man named Ernst who lived in the east fifties in New York City. Most of the neighboring land was owned by Finch, Pruyn, the largest lumber company in the Adirondacks. I had copies of the relevant tax map made and copied onto it, parcel by parcel, the current owners and where, by book page and number, the county deed books recorded their purchases.

The Essex County clerk's office makes tracing land ownership by legal deed as easy as it can be made, but it took me a while to discover and understand the whole system. The deeds are all recorded and kept in a series of large books. Hundreds of them, each about two feet high and one foot wide and weighing five to ten pounds, line the walls. In them every legal land transaction ever made in the county, starting in 1800, is recorded chronologically. If you know the date of a transaction, you can go straight to the right book and page. If you don't know the date of a transaction, as I didn't, you will have rough sledding. The man in the tax office had anticipated the latter and given me the book and page number of the most recent purchase of the Clear Pond property. "Start there," he said, smiling.

I found the deed of sale right away. And right away there was trouble. The current land owner had the same name as the previous owner. Can you sell yourself a piece of land you already own? Maybe it was an inheritance sale, from father to son. I decided to ignore these early warning signs and keep going. A woman in the clerk's office showed me that each deed made reference to the book and page number of the preceding sale. This would be easy, I thought. It might take time and much lifting of heavy deed books, but it would not be complicated.

Parcels of land are identified, however, by reference to surveyor's lines and occasionally by reference to landmarks such as "pile of stones next to fence-post." The early records refer often to piles of stones and to fenceposts, but fenceposts rot, fences themselves occasionally disappear, and piles of stones are kicked or bulldozed out of the way. Because of these natural depredations, surveyors now make reference to a wholly abstract and mathematical grid of lines laid out arbitrarily over the land. A place 125 feet south of the southwest corner of lot 57 of the Essex Tract, Henry Survey, may exist, but you have to be a surveyor to find it.

There were other problems that made tracing land ownership through the deed difficult. People often split land and sell only a part of it. Sometimes they don't pay their taxes and so forfeit the land to the state. At one point, after several hours of searching, I had traced what I thought was at least part of the Clear Pond property back to an Alfred C. Chapin. The deed by which he purchased the land made no reference to a prior book or page number. I thought I must be missing something, so I read the deed word for word four or five times before it struck me as significant that Mr. Chapin was identified as "Comptroller, State of New York." To be brief, it was a tax sale. Alfred C. Chapin had, for the state, taken possession of the land because the owner has not paid taxes. He (or the state) then sold it on September 27, 1887, to John C. Hughson, who, it happened, bought thousands of acres that year by paying up other people's lapsed taxes. I remembered reading somewhere that it was a common practice among lumber speculators in the nineteenth century to buy land, clear it of all timber, and since it was then of no value, let the state seize it for failure to pay taxes.

Hours of searching through deeds, however, had led me to a dead end. The previous owner was not indicated on the Chapin deed. I must have looked helpless and dejected, because shortly after getting myself into this quandry, someone who worked in the Clerk's office asked me if I had checked the Grantee's list. I had not, of course, because I had never heard of it. As it turned out, there was both a Grantee's and a Grantor's list, one listing alphabetically all the people to whom land had ever been sold in Essex County, the other listing all those who had sold land. Both listed the book and page number of the deeds. In other words, one could go straight to the deed one was looking for. I didn't know whether to cheer or weep after all the hours of lifting huge books down off shelves, squinting through handwritten legal prose, and lifting them back up. I could have gone directly to the Grantee's list and looked for Israel Johnson. I did precisely that, right then.

The first Grantee's book covers the years 1800–1840. I turned to the J's and started running my finger down the page, and there it was. Israel Johnson. Not only was it Israel Johnson but it was also the only Israel Johnson listed in that entire period. But, there was something odd. The deed said that he had bought three hundred acres of land from Zephaniah Platt in 1803. Redfield, in 1836, said that Johnson had only been on Clear Pond for four years. Had Redfield misunderstood him? Had Johnson been fabricating a lie for some reason? Something else was wrong. The deed was for land bordering on the Schroon River, at least nine miles from Clear Pond. So, here was Israel Johnson, but he was on the wrong land. And, from what Redfield said, this did not seem to be the same person. Could a man who was old enough to buy land in 1803 have built a house and two sawmills twenty-eight years later? Maybe. Why was there no deed for the Clear Pond property in Johnson's name? I looked again, slowly and deliberately, but there was no way to avoid the conclusion: no other parcel of land anywhere in the county was ever deeded to anyone named Israel Johnson.

My battle with the deed books was inconclusive. I had found an Israel Johnson, but I had at least two reasons to think he was not the man I was looking for. Why wasn't there a deed for the property William Redfield said Johnson owned? Did Johnson not own it? If he didn't, why was he offered three thousand dollars for it? Or, I began saying to myself, what if he did own it? What if I had found the deed? What would I do with a few inconsequential facts about someone whose outline would never, at best, be more than hazy? Did I really want to waste my time trying to solve a mystery that would, in most respects, never be solved?

I spent the next several days reading in the library at Keene Valley. The library has a good collection of books on the Adirondacks donated by John Loomis. Over the years since the original donation was made, many other books have been added. I had come to the Loomis Room because they had an old county history I hadn't yet read: H. P. Smith's *History of Essex County*, Syracuse, 1885. I was reading Smith's description of the Elba Iron Works, established just outside present-day Lake Placid in 1809, when I read this:

> The land was owned by the State of New York. The settlement commenced soon after Thoon's survey [Stephen Thoon in 1806] by a few pioneer hunters. Soon after the settlement iron ore was discovered . . . . During the time the forge was in operation considerable of a settlement was made, some settlers buying their land, while many others went on the land, intending to buy at their convenience. When the settlement seemed to be in a prosperous condition, Peter Smith (father of the late Gerrit Smith), of Peterboro, N.Y., heard of this tract of land, made an examination of it, and returned to Albany and made a purchase of nearly the entire town not previously sold. The settlers sought to purchase their homes, but Mr. Smith told them the time had not come to sell this land, but he would not drive them from their homes, and when he was ready to sell, would give them the first chance of buying. But the settlers were unwilling to continue to improve their land, which might result in benefiting a stranger. Most of the people, therefore, left, and but few remained there for many years.

Israel Johnson drifted back into my thoughts. Here was a plausible explanation why his name never appeared on the Grantee's list at Elizabethtown. In 1832 or thereabouts, he might have put himself down on wild, remote land, which no one owned and which was later bought from under him. The one problem with this theory is that whoever offered him three thousand dollars for it must have thought Johnson had some legal right to it. Or, possibly, the person—maybe the real owner—might have been fair-minded and offered him the money for the improvements he had made. Perhaps, too, the comment was made idly by someone who had spent the night at Johnson's on his way in to do business at the Iron Works. Or, maybe Johnson was doing a small bit of boasting to a crowd of important gentlemen from downstate. The more I thought, the less I had.

I was at the end of my evidence, awash in conjecture, and I still had not seen the actual land. I had little or no reason to think I could find out anything more about Israel Johnson, but I thought I could at least go stand by the outlet to Clear Pond. I could look at the place where the Emmons party spent a few nights on their way into and out of the mountains in 1836 and 1837 and where they were fed and housed by a man named Israel Johnson who, if he never owned the sweat of his brow and disappeared from this life as quietly as he had come into it, owned or thought he owned property which he cleared himself and on which be built sawmills, which might have provided boards for numerous buildings in the area, buildings that no doubt have all gone the way he has.

The road to Clear Pond is unpaved, but as wide as a highway. It was newly graded, with a high crown and deep triangular ditches on both sides. Finch, Pruyn owns the land, so this road had been made for running big log trucks in and out on. The land was also posted. Every hundred feet on both sides white pieces of paper were stapled to trees. Once every half mile or so rough, single-lane tracks would turn off the main road and disappear almost at once in the woods. It was uphill most of the way, no houses or clearings, just woods.

These were recent woods. Nothing I saw from the car looked to be more than fifty years old. The land had either been logged or burnt off sometime in the recent past. I couldn't see any, but I thought that if I got out and walked around in the woods I might run into some of the old stumps. Three and four times as wide as anything growing around them, rotting, and sometimes disappearing under the brush and slash, these would be all that was left of the original forest here. Much of which, I suppose, would have been cut down by Israel Johnson or his hired hands.

Most of the country I had come through to get here looked the same way. The only way to leave Keene Valley to the south is along Route 73 over a small pass above Chapel Pond. This is a favorite take-off point for hikers either going east up Giant and Rocky Ridge or west over Noonmark toward Dix, Nippletop, and a few others. When you come down from Chapel Pond and join Route 9 coming in from Elizabethtown, you are in a different world. The large mountains are gone. All you see are hills. The trees have a mixed, scrubby look to them, and if you take Route 9 south, instead of the Northway, you enter the old eastern edge of the Adirondacks where there has been settlement since the time of the French. This is the un-Romantic Adirondacks, chosen early because it is closer to Lake Champlain and easier to farm. Now the Adirondacks are mostly given over to tourists, and they want mountain views and lakeside cottages. On Route 9 north of Schroon Lake, you don't find much of either. The little community there, North Hudson, has a few old motels, a gas station or two, a liquor store, a bar and restaurant, and a tourist attraction called Frontier Town, which the Northway was put right next to, I presume, so that the summer visitors to the Adirondacks would not miss their chance to experience a bit of the old west.

How the life got taken out of communities like North Hudson is a long, complicated story. It has happened more than once. In earlier days, the town had a large lumber business and at one time a tannery. Both these businesses folded long ago, but with the centralization of everything since World War II, towns like North Hudson no longer even have schools, markets, or hardware stores. They usually have a small "general" store—not the quaint thing seen on TV, but a store that sells milk, flashlight batteries and potato chips at high prices. If you need anything in North Hudson now, you almost always go somewhere else to get it.

To get to Clear Pond, you turn west at North Hudson toward Newcomb. The road is paved but it has no number. A cluster of houses called Blue Ridge lies three miles to the west. In the middle of it is a general store called "General Store." The dirt road up to Clear Pond is just beyond it. I had driven about three miles up this road and was beginning to think Clear Pond had been moved or drained when I started seeing it, little slivers of gray-white flashing through the trees on the right. It is called a pond, but most of us would call it a lake. In a few hundred feet, the road bent slightly to the left, and about two hundred yards up ahead I could see a house. The road came closer to the water, and as it neared the house, it passed over a small bridge. The house stood to the left of the road at one side of a large clearing. Near here nearly one hundred and fifty years before, Ebenezer Emmons and his friends stopped for a night's rest in a cabin built by a man called Israel Johnson, but I could see no evidence of it. No old road wound in from the east or west, and there was no sign of a sawmill or even of any logging, no ruins or relics, no rusted wheel. It was a typical late twentieth-century suburban house set down beside a dirt road in the forest. Whatever had happened here one hundred and fifty years before—or whoever had stood on or near this spot then and admired sawmills of peculiar construction— nothing now suggested it had ever happened.

I was more than disappointed. It is one thing for written records, kept in some distant library or clerk's office, to garble and conceal the truth. But for the land on which that truth or fact took place to do the same thing, for it to give no hint or cast no aura, seemed cruel.

I had stopped the car in front of the house and was giving myself up to such thoughts when a large collie bounded out from behind the house. Someone is undoubtedly home, I thought, and now that I've stopped and been barked at by the dog and aroused some curiosity or even fear in someone who might be sitting all alone in the shadows behind a curtain with a shotgun across her lap, I thought it best to go through with it, if only to let whoever it might be know that the man sitting in the VW Rabbit out front with Indiana license plates was harmless. I got out of the car and walked up to the side entrance. There were two men working in back of the house putting up the frame for a large shed or garage. I did not really want to ask these men my question. It suddenly seemed an idle question, a very foolish question, and they looked busy. Nothing else came to mind, how- ever. I could hardly ask them where the nearest phone booth was or if they had the right time. So, I just blurted out that I was trying to find out something about an early settler from this neighborhood named Israel Johnson. The one standing up on the roof joist almost dropped his hammer.

"This is Johnson's Clearing, right here."

There was no mistaking it. Here was something solid. Israel Johnson had been there. It was not on any of the maps, or none that I had seen, but in local memory, still alive after all these years, "Johnson's Clearing" was a real place. It wasn't a pond or a lake or a mountain or a range of mountains. It was a small clearing beside a dirt road three and a half miles off an unmarked highway, but it was named for Israel Johnson. Whoever that was.

2. "Johnson's Clearing" today.

"There were supposed to have been two sawmills here and a house at the outlet of Clear Pond. Where's that," I asked.

"That's the little brook you drove over on the other side of the house."

They had never seen any evidence of other buildings on the site, but I asked if I might look around anyway. The outlet was only a brook, perhaps three feet wide. I walked down it a ways. There were no mouldering ruins or rusted axe-heads in the woods around the clearing and nothing but trees beside the pond.

Or, not until I looked a second time. On both sides of the outlet, for a hundred feet or more both ways, running right along the edge of the pond, was an uneven but definite hummock or dike about three feet high. Maybe it was natural. It was certainly overgrown with vegetation. A few trees grew on top of it. My guess, though—or

3. The outlet to Clear Pond today.

4. "The hummock" at Clear Pond.

rather, my conviction—was that it was manmade. It had been built there to raise the water level in the pond so that the water coming through the outlet would be high enough and strong enough to power the wheel in Israel Johnson's sawmill.

There was no doubt anymore. A man named Israel Johnson had lived here. I was going to find him.

2

Knocking on Doors

*T*here was to be one more surprise that day, but it belongs to a
separate phase of this affair.

Before describing the detective work, let me explain a little more
what I was doing. It was September 1981. I had rearranged my
teaching schedule at Indiana for the fall so that I had the first eight
weeks of it free. I wanted to travel to the Adirondacks, as I said, to do
research for a book of poems. I was reading everything I could find,
but the university library was sending more and more of my
interlibrary loan requests back stamped, "Will Not Loan." I also
wanted to see things in the Adirondacks I hadn't seen when I only
lived there. It was, I suppose, an odd endeavor, but I was learning a
great deal and beginning to find things to write about, most of them
historical. The book of poems, in fact, never got beyond about 1915.

When I first stumbled on Israel Johnson, I kept trying to think of
ways to make him part of the book of poems. But he would not lie
still. Every time I thought I had his character or experience set in my
mind, a new fact would pop up. Rather than ignore it or bend it to fit
the piece of writing I had underway, I found myself wanting to
include it and, indeed, wanting to know more. It took me a while to
see that this was a separate project. One day I realized that what I was
doing was trying to leach Israel Johnson out of the obscurity of the
past and that it was this process that interested me, almost more than
the results.

I was in the Adirondacks for about six weeks that fall. I had put
my cooler and sleeping bag in the back of the Rabbit and set off for
Blue Mountain Lake. It was there I stumbled on Israel Johnson, and
for the rest of my stay in the area, more of my time was taken up with
him and less with the general project of learning about the

Adirondacks. For one thing, I had probably read enough already.
Hardly a history or a guidebook or a memoir or a gazeteer had
escaped my gaze. Thousands of things I would never read, of course.
The Adirondack bibliography and its supplement, both edited by
Dorothy Plum, listed more items than any ten people could read in a
lifetime. For another thing, the only place I was likely to find out
anything about Israel Johnson was in the Adirondacks itself. After
all, it was folk memory that had kept his name attached to the land
he had lived on and had given me the first concrete evidence of the
man.

I entered a phase that folklorists probably have a name for,
though folklorists undoubtedly do it better than I. I followed common sense when I could. Otherwise, I followed my nose. The part of
the story I am about to tell is a warning to those who wish to know
what they are ignorant of. It comes in two parts. First, go ahead; and
second, remember that you are learning even when it seems you are
not.

*

To go back to Clear Pond and the small, earthen dike erected at
its outlet, it is probably the only artifact, if that is the right word, the
only example of Israel Johnson's handiwork, left. There might be
boards in old houses somewhere that were planed in one of his mills,
but we will never be able to identify them. After I found the em-
bankment, I walked back to the car. One of the men came up to me
and told me I ought to go up to the lodge and talk to Pete Sanders.
The lodge was Elk Lake Lodge, two miles further up the road.

Both Elk Lake and Clear Pond are now part of a private forest
preserve that, from May to December, is a fishing, hiking, and
hunting resort and, through the winter, is a managed or selectively
logged forest. Peter—or as he prefers, Pete—Sanders is the manager. He is tall, genial, and quite interested in local history. The
lodge was built in 1904 when Elk Lake was still called Mud Pond.
Logging had come to be restricted by that time, perhaps because of
the fires all over the Adirondacks in 1903, which they say burned 25
percent of the timber, but certainly also because of the 1895 state
constitution, which declared the state-owned portions of the area
"forever wild." The lodge is made of logs and sits at the outlet of Elk
Lake where a log dam raises the level of the lake eight or ten feet. It

was called Mud Pond originally because, in its natural state, it was so shallow it was almost a swamp. Inside, the lodge is hung with hunting and fishing trophies. As I remember, one is a moose head, which seems odd, because the last moose in the Adirondacks was supposed to have been killed in the 1860s.

Pete Sanders understood my kind of fascination, and between farewells to departing customers, he answered my questions and asked a few of his own. When I finally mentioned Israel Johnson, he led me over to the opposite side of the room and showed me a framed photograph of a log cabin, obviously taken a long time ago.

"That's Israel Johnson's cabin. It sat right where the new house is at the Clearing."

This was indeed progress. Who were the people in the photograph, I asked? Who took it? When did they take it? Did he know anything else about Johnson or the sawmills? He didn't, but he said he had more information on the Clear Pond area in a file he kept at his home in Schroon Lake. What sort of information, I asked. He told me about a man, Thorn Dickinson, who had often come to stay at Elk Lake and who researched the route of the Cedar Point road. His unpublished essay, a copy of which I had read through quickly in Blue Mountain Lake, shows that the road passed right along the north edge of Clear Pond, not more than two hundred feet from the site of Johnson's cabin. Sanders said that if I looked carefully, I could still find some of the original corduroy. There were other papers and maps in his file on Clear Pond and if I wanted, he would bring it up the following week for me to look through.

All the way back to Keene Valley, I kept my eyes on the road while my mind spaded its new garden. Johnson's cabin (or the cabin at Johnson's Clearing) was only partly visible in the photograph. The person who took it was taking a picture of the people who lived there. Three or four plain country people stood on and off a porch, smiling at the camera. They had a frontier look to them. The photograph, though, looked to be no more than a hundred years old, and it might have been only sixty or seventy. It was a crisp, well-defined picture printed on glossy stock. If it was as much as one hundred years old, I didn't see how anyone in the picture could have been Johnson. A man old enough to have built a house and sawmills in 1832 could hardly have been alive in the 1880s. None of the people was that old. Of course, they might have been descendants.

I had no doubts any more that Israel Johnson had lived and milled on Clear Pond, so I began arranging and rearranging the information I had, to see if it might reveal other things. It was strange, when I thought of it, for someone to be milling boards in the middle of the woods. Most sawmills were built nearer the lumber markets. It was the logging that went on in the woods. Johnson, though, had not one but two sawmills nine miles into the woods along the Cedar Point road. Why was that? Once iron ore was discovered at the head of Henderson Lake in 1826, Archibald McIntyre and the other investors immediately began lobbying for a state appropriation to build a road into the area. The bill passed in 1828, and the work of surveying and building began soon afterwards. No one knows when the road was completed. It was probably used piecemeal as stretches of it were finished and may not have been open all the way to the Works till 1830. The next year or the year after, Johnson, according to Redfield, settled at Clear Pond.

It began to look like a calculated and sensible move. Johnson settled on the land almost as soon as a road was run past it. That road led to the largest iron ore deposits known at the time in the entire country. He had reason to believe, I should imagine, that prosperity would come to the area in a short time and, with it, increased settlement and a high demand for lumber. Johnson, almost certainly, was indirectly investing in—as it was called at first—the McIntyre Iron Works. It was a high, confident time to be where he was. It makes perfect sense that someone would have offered him three thousand dollars for his place. For the moment, I would ignore the fact that he didn't own it.

I had to look at the land deed again. Now that I knew more, I might see more. A day or so later when I was in Elizabethtown buying groceries, I stopped at the county clerk's office. The deed was dated April 15, 1803, and Johnson was described as being "of the Town of Crown Point." All counties in New York are divided into "towns" or townships. Crown Point is one of the towns in Essex County. The land definitely bordered on the Schroon River. There were three hundred acres of it and Johnson had paid $1,200 for it. Much as I hated to, I felt I had to give up the idea that Israel Johnson who bought land from Zephaniah Platt was the same Israel

Johnson who lived at Clear Pond. Unless, of course, late in his life he sold the Schroon River land and moved onto land that wasn't his.

In Keene Valley I was staying in one room of the Neville's huge, old summer house. It was a half mile from the post office and the grocery store, and it sat by itself in a large meadow. It had a stove and a refrigerator and a wood stove if it got chilly. I chopped my own wood. I enjoyed it so much, I split much more than I needed.

One day it started raining early in the morning, so I called Pete Sanders and asked if he had brought his Clear Pond file up to the lodge. He had, and said I could come down and look at it. As I passed through North Hudson, I thought I would check a lead I had been given the last time I was in Elizabethtown. The man behind the counter had suggested I talk to Bernard Coleman, the town assessor of North Hudson. When I got to the center of the village, I noticed a small cinder-block building on the left that looked vaguely governmental. Across the road was a liquor store and a large old wooden building that looked like a typical turn-of-the-century Adirondack hotel, with long front porch and moosehead under its roof. The sign out front said only one thing, "Liquor."

The cinder-block building had a senior citizen's center upstairs and a "Town Justice" downstairs. Both were locked. I knocked a few times, gave up, and was walking back to the car when a man in work clothes and a hunting cap came out from the back of the building rubbing his eyes. When I asked him about Bernard Coleman, he repeated the name after me and I think corrected it to "Corman." He gave me directions, but when I got there, Corman said, "Talk to Arthur Greenough. He's an old man but he has a sharp mind. And he knows about these things."

Greenough sounded like the kind of person I wanted to talk to. He had probably lived here all his life and all through it listened to the litany of comings and goings, births, deaths, marriages and calamities, and could now give a kind of condensed oral history of the place. His mind was probably where this place was most completely gathered. He would know all those things that nobody else seems to know.

The mailbox had "Greenough" on it in large silver letters. The white clapboard house, set back about fifty feet from the road, needed paint. Two cars were parked outside. I raised my hand to knock, but before I could, I was met at the door by a woman in her fifties, graying, and I began to explain that I was looking for Arthur Greenough because I had heard that he knew a good bit about local history. She interrupted and said Arthur's mind was not reliable anymore, that I could come in if I liked, but that he probably wouldn't even hear my question much less understand it. As she was saying all this, two other people about the same age appeared in the doorway. One was a woman with as dour an aspect as the first, and the other was a man wearing an adjustable baseball cap. He stood off to one side with his hands in his pockets and watched.

There are times when I wish I had never grown a beard or when I wish my license plates were in-state or that I was not driving a foreign car. This was one of those times. I sensed some kind of impatience. They made me feel, to be honest, the way I sometimes felt myself, without outside assistance. Namely, that I was wasting my time. Of course, that is my prerogative. In this instance, however, I was wasting theirs as well. Then I thought, of course, there must be a constant flow of people to this door asking a poor old man who was deaf and infirm a plague of idle questions about cousins and lumber camps and the endless trivia of life now passed. These people, who are probably his children, want the old man left in peace. They also seemed to have somewhere to get to, but I was able to mention the name Johnson and Clear Pond, and right away one of the women turned to the other and whispered something. Somebody's family on their mother's side had that name. For a moment they forgot I was there and muttered to each other, trying to figure out all the connections. Once they had, the one who met me at the door turned and announced politely but flatly: "Frieda Provoncha. Her mother was a Johnson, over in Blue Ridge." "She lives in Schroon Lake now," the other woman said. "Ask around the school. They'll know her." The old man was still standing to one side, staring at me.

I had other questions, and, to be truthful, I would like to have met Arthur Greenough, even if he couldn't have helped me. He was to die two years later. But, people are skillful at letting you know when you've asked enough questions or stayed too long. Besides, they had given me a lead. I thanked them and walked back to the car muttering, "Frieda Provoncha from Schroon Lake, Frieda Provoncha from Schroon Lake." Before I could get it written down on a piece of paper, they drove off.

I reached Elk Lodge a short while later. Pete Sanders was out of the office, but the woman sitting behind the desk knew what I was there for. She gave me the file and I went into the front room and sat on a couch under the gaze of several stuffed animals.

The file contained a copy of Thorn Dickinson's paper on the Cedar Point road. I looked through it more carefully this time, and it gave me new information about Israel Johnson, including observations on his character. These all seemed to be taken from a book called *History of the Lumber and Forest Industry of the Northwest* by George W. Hotchkiss. A xeroxed page from the book was also in the file. I read it quickly. It seemed a waste of time to copy it out because, if the book had one reference to Johnson, it might have others. I would need to look at the whole book. If I had known then that it would be several months before I would see a copy of Hotchkiss, I would have stayed there all night to copy it. The other item of interest in the file was a copy of "A Map of Township 44 . . . in Essex County Belonging to John Ireland Peter Smith of Peterboro and John Kierstad 1829." Clear Pond lies in Township 44 of the old Totten and Crossfield Purchase, and the map showed who owned which plots of land in 1829, three years after iron ore was discovered a few miles to the west. No one owned the land at the outlet of Clear Pond. John Ireland Peter Smith of Peterboro, if this was one person and not two, would also seem to have been the same person as the Peter Smith mentioned by H. P. Smith in connection with the Elba Iron Works. And, as in 1809, Peter Smith might have had a squatter on his land to whom he did not yet wish to sell.

As soon as I got back to Keene Valley, it was dinner time. I stopped at The Spread Eagle, or The Spread, as it's known, Keene Valley's only bar and restaurant. Deer season was approaching, so they already had the pipe rigged up out front for the annual "Big Buck Contest." Whoever shot the biggest buck would win a bushel basket full of hard liquor. The Spread was a family business. Mr. Auer tended bar. Mrs. Auer and their daughter-in-law cooked and waited on tables. The son, Harry, a plumber, was often there. The grandchild played in a crib that sat off one end of the bar by the door to the kitchen, and the dog had full grazing privileges of the establishment. People said his favorite beer was "Genesee." The Auers would serve anyone who came in, but it was clear they enjoyed serving people they knew best, particularly the working people of the valley. I liked to eat there because there were no frills, no little unnecessary graciousness, just plain food and low prices. Mr. Auer has since died, alas, and The Spread is no more. Remodelled, it is now called the Ausable Inn. It has a deck out front instead of the big buck rack, and they have hired a chef, no less, whose first love, understandably, is not chicken-in-a-basket with french fries.

Back at the house in the meadow, I went through the phone book looking for Provonchas. There were several, though none called Frieda. I reached a Mrs. A. Lee Provoncha who said she was Paul Provoncha's mother. Frieda was Paul's aunt, she said, and she gave me her number. Frieda was an older woman who talked as though she were hard of hearing. She was eager to talk, but she only knew her family as far back as her grandfather, Samuel Johnson, a veteran of the Civil War who lived to be ninety and made caskets. "Real wood caskets," she said, "not like today." His wife lined them. At one time, he either owned or worked at the tannery in Blue Ridge. I thanked her and hung up.

✳

I still had faith in the grassroots method of gathering information, even though it led down a number of dead-end roads. It seemed only natural to fail occasionally, and every dead end I drove down was worth the trip. Time was running out, though. I would have to go home in a week, so I started scrambling. I wanted to talk with more people in the Blue Ridge/North Hudson area.

Not, however, before climbing Gothics. It was early October, and one morning I woke up and the tops of all the highest mountains had snow on them. The snow stopped at exactly the same height on all the mountains, well above the tops of the smaller ones. This was a warning. If I wanted to climb one of the higher peaks, it had to be done soon. I thought the highest peaks, like Marcy and Algonquin, were already too high and too cold for the gear I had, so I chose Gothics. First of all, you could get to Gothics easily from the valley. Also, it was part of "The Range," a long row of mountains that ran along one side of the Ausable lakes, said to be among the most impressive lakes in the Adirondacks and not accessible or even visible unless you hike in to see them.

I packed a lunch, filled the water bottle, put an extra sweater and a flashlight in the backpack and took off at 9:00 A.M. from the grounds of the Ausable Club. On the map Gothics looked to be about seven miles from the place where I left the car. Two to three miles per hour seemed about right for the gradual approach to the mountain proper, perhaps one mile an hour up the steep grade, and then two to three again on the way down. It seemed a perfectly manageable walk for the day. I'd be back about four. As things turned out, though, with very brisk walking for the last four miles, not on a path, but on a dirt road, I just beat stony darkness at 7:00 P.M. For one thing, the trail disappeared once on the way up, so I had to do some backtracking. Once up into the snow, the footing turned tricky, especially on the way down. Then a short stretch of catwalk across an almost vertical face of rock slowed me down.

Near the top, which is really three small knobs in a line along a narrow ridge with steep fallaway on both sides, it was winter. Luckily the sun was out, but the wind was out as well, and emerging from the snow-crusted dwarf balsams onto the open rock, I thought I might be blown off into the valley, the bottom of which I couldn't see. The view was astonishing, though. Down to the left were the Ausable lakes. Off to the right were Marcy, Skylight, and Algonquin, the highest mountains in the state. To the left beyond the lakes was Dix and beyond it, out of sight, Clear Pond.

Mountain climbing is like a good meal. You spend all day cooking it and then eat it in fifteen minutes. I suppose people climb so they can stand where they can see into the distance, though much of the experience is in the effort. To see into the distance, and to do that because of long personal exertion, seems to be the whole point. Astonishment passes almost at once, just as the mind goes numb after a few minutes in front of a great painting. I've known experienced mountain climbers who spent no more than a minute or two looking at the view they climbed all day to reach. It looks like indifference, but it isn't. The mountaintop experience is instantaneous. So, they move on or sit down for a moment to catch their breath or eat an apple. I had other reasons for not lingering on top of Gothics—high wind, cold temperatures, and the long walk back—but I had all that a mountain climber can ask for in the flash of brilliant sunshine off snow, sky-swept bone bare, and the landscape rippling off into the distance as though I were the first pebble thrown into a still pool.

The next day, I drove down to Blue Ridge, the town closest to Clear Pond. I was hoping to find someone who could tell me some-

thing about local history. I didn't know where else to begin, so I went
into the general store. It was a bit bare inside, but the building had
obviously been built to be a store a long time ago. I bought a loaf of
bread to break the ice and then asked the woman behind the counter
my, by now, worn-down opening question about original settlers in
the vicinity of Clear Pond. It turned out that she and her husband
had only lived in Blue Ridge for six years. She had a heavy downstate accent. She told me, though, that the town supervisor, Mrs.
Dobie, lived right across the road.

The house she pointed to was set back off the road. I knocked two
or three times and got no response. I had no idea where to turn now.
It looked like a wasted day. I was half way down the driveway when
the door opened behind me and a short woman in slacks called out,
"Were you looking for me?" "Mrs. Dobie?" "Yes." So, I strolled back
to the house, told her what I was doing, and she invited me in. She
was supervisor for the town of North Hudson, not to be confused
with the village of North Hudson. She was quite interested in local
history and said more than once that she wished she had the time to
do this sort of thing. People were leaving, she said. She gave me the
names of several people she thought I might want to get in touch
with. Louise Hargreaves, she said, was the historian of the Town of
Schroon and knew a great deal. Then, she asked if I had seen Paul
Stapley's *Catalogue of Cemeteries of the Towns of Schroon and North
Hudson.* I said no. She took me downstairs to her office and got down
a large orange loose-leaf binder. She found Israel Johnson and his wife
almost at once. They were buried in the Schroon River Cemetery, also
known as the DeLorme Cemetery. No other Israel Johnson is listed in
the book. The entry read as follows:

Israel Johnson: b. ?   died 8/27/1835 age 76
his wife, Elizabeth: b. ?   died 10/8/1836

It was true, then. There were at least two Israel Johnsons in the
area at roughly the same time. The one buried in Schroon River was
dead when William Redfield stopped at Clear Pond in 1836. I
couldn't be sure yet, but it seemed likely that he was also the man
who bought land from Zephaniah Platt. It has been a good afternoon
already. As I left, she told me I should probably talk to Lillian

Nolette, historian for the Town of North Hudson, and Mary Bessey, town clerk of the same.

✳

I drove back into North Hudson mulling over this new information. So many other questions were raised that things seemed to blur as quickly as they came into focus. It was hard enough to find out about "my" Israel Johnson without having another one lurking about in the neighborhood at the same time. Every piece of information I had and all that I would find in the future would have to be carefully filtered. To help this process, I decided to call the one who died in 1835 "old" Israel Johnson and the one who was living at Clear Pond in 1836 "young" Israel Johnson.

Mary Bessey had a sign in front of her house. A blue Lincoln was parked in the driveway. The television was going when she came to the door. She listened to my questions but said she couldn't help because her records only started in the 1880s. Besides, she said, the new laws said you couldn't look at other people's records without their permission. It didn't seem that the law would have had any bearing on my interest, but if the records only started in the 1880s it made no difference. I thanked her and left. Just as I reached the car, though, she came striding out the door and said that Mrs. Dobie had just called to leave me a message. She thought I should also talk with a man named Raymond Duntley who lived across from the Crow's Nest. There would be a red car and a green jeep parked out in front. I made a note of it but decided to go to Lillian Nolette's first.

Every town, that is, every township, in New York State, like the courts of the old Welsh kings, has a historian. The town historian is an official of the town, appointed most likely, and is always listed with the other town officials. The job might even carry a small stipend, though I doubt it. The historian's job seems never to have been precisely defined. The few I've met seem to have made what they wanted to of the job. That can mean anything from the great blizzard of oughty-eight to last weekend's visits from the downstate relatives. The person picked for this job is usually elderly and has spent his or her lifetime in the town, listening to the elders talk about what went on in their time and watching and memorizing the events of their own. Few of them consult books. The "book" they read, and the book they in turn "write," is the book of local memory. The town historians I have met have found various ways to pass along what they learned. One had found out everything she could about her family, one of the original families of her town. Another had written some pamphlets on old buildings in the area that were about to be torn down. She took pictures of them and put those in the pamphlets, too. Another had printed a tall tale that had been popular in her neighborhood for several generations but had never been written down. The woman whose door I was about to knock on wrote a weekly column for the *Valley News* in which she told of the comings and goings of people in North Hudson.

Lillian Nolette's house sits behind another just off Route 9. It is an older house, wooden, with simple lines, a plain, pitched tin roof and a porch that faces away from the road toward the hills. It is really a back porch that has become a front porch. The house is painted dark green with white trim. By the time I walked up on the porch, she was at the door. She invited me in before she heard what I had to say. You couldn't guess it, but she is probably in her seventies, a short but substantial woman who, though she seems to limp slightly, has no trouble getting around. We sat at the table in the kitchen. Her hair was cropped below her ears in what I think of as a Dutch bob. She smoked a pipe, lived alone, as far as I could tell, and spoke the local accent as purely as anyone I have ever heard. It is hard to describe, but the general manner is dry and tight-lipped, the most obvious mark of it being the "ou" sound, where the word "round" sounds like "reeownd," or a word like "right" sounds like "ruoieet."

Miss Nolette, as I heard others call her, told me about going to work on a farm when she was seventeen. She got room and board and fifty cents a week. "Twenty-five cents for church and twenty-five cents for the movies." She had no electricity or indoor plumbing until she was fifty. At the moment, she was involved with a senior citizens' group trying to keep a shopping service going. I was told later by my landlady, a lawyer, that Miss Nolette testified in a famous murder trial a few years ago. When I asked my question, she said she really couldn't help. The town records had been thrown away, and none of the original families were left over by Johnson Pond, which she assumed was a place I would take an interest in. I had seen Johnson Pond on the map, but it was on the other side of Route 9 from Clear Pond, so I had paid no attention to it. Johnson was too common a name for me to be aroused every time I saw or heard it. By original families, it turned out that she meant families that had lived here when she was a girl. The same was true up in Pepper Hollow, she said. All the houses were owned now by people who lived downstate. She felt like a ghost in her own town. She lived alone, or so I guessed, and that she had found a way to do, but she did not like being culturally alone, keeping track of people who seemed to have lost interest in keeping track of themselves. She said I should go visit the cemetery at the top of the hill on the way to Port Henry. She and some friends had done something recently to fix it up, set up some fallen stones, maybe, or painted the fence. She said it again. I asked, "Do you have relatives there?" "Oh, no. You'll like it. It's real nice." In a way, it was her handiwork, or part of it, and she wanted me to see it. "I will," I said. "I'll go look at it right now." And I did. It was not easy saying good-bye to her, but the promise to visit the cemetery helped.

It was only half a mile away. As you leave North Hudson on the way to Port Henry, the road enters a fairly dense piece of forest. At the top of the hill on the right, quite close to the road, a small graveyard with a white picket fence around it sits in a stand of tall pines. The ground is brown with pine needles. Fifteen to eighteen stones are scattered around it as though space had been left for others to be buried there. A river rushed past just out of sight down the hill. The stones had no familiar names on them, but because I ran across his name many months later in the half-darkened microfilm room of the genealogy section of the state library in Indianapolis, I remember the gravestones of Benajah Pond and his wife. He had started a successful lumber business in the middle of the nineteenth century. Miss Nolette was right. It was a good place to be buried. On the way back to the car, I picked the shopping bag full of empty beer bottles out of the bushes and put it in the back of the car. It was also a good place to drink beer if you were underage or a good place to dump the evidence.

I had one more stop that day. Raymond Duntley lives at the north end of the village, which means, North Hudson being laid out the way it is, that he lives a mile or two from the place where the Town Justice and the old hotel with the moose head on the front porch sit across the road from one another. I found Duntley's house and walked toward the front door. It had a porch along the front and under its roof, nailed up on the outside wall, was a bear skin. Before I got to the porch, though, Duntley knocked on the window and shouted for me to come around to the side entrance. He whisked me in and shut the door quickly. It was at least eighty degrees inside, and he didn't want to lose any heat. He took me into the kitchen, and we sat down and started talking right away. He said he was seventy, though he looked younger than that. He had been a logger most of his life. He mentioned Finch, Pruyn a time or two, always calling it "Fincha Pruyn." When I asked him about the history of the area, he took out a sheet of paper and read me the names and dates of his father and grandfather. His father had worked in a coke plant and lived from 1856 to 1950. His grandfather, Lorenzo Duntley, 1826–1910, had been in a heavy artillery unit in the Civil War. Someone in the Duntley family, then, could well have lived in that neighborhood for as much as one hundred and fifty years. A few nights later, when I was looking at the topographical map, I found a Duntley Road on it that was no more than two miles from Ray Duntley's house.

I had just come in from outside, so of course I was warm, but even he was in his undershirt and socks, and he wiped his face every now and then with a handkerchief he kept clutched in his hand. I asked him about the bear out front, and he told me he had always trapped on the side, and still did. He caught mink, otter, rat (meaning muskrat), and other animals. When you used to make $1.25 to cut and stack a cord of wood, he said, you could get $12 for a mink pelt. He said there were still plenty around and started talking about places nearby that I'd never heard of. He talked about the landscape in a very localized way, as I guess a trapper would. He spoke of something called "Roger's Mash." I asked what a mash was but wasn't able to understand the answer. He talked on and on about his life, every now and then pausing to say, "if I'd only listened to my father." His father, a man who in 1950 would have remembered the Civil War, must have been filled with stories of the old days. When I mentioned the Cedar Point road, he said when he was first logging forty-five years ago, he had used part of it to get the timber out. It still had the original corduroy in places. "It was in good shape, too." He said the road crossed Route 9 exactly three quarters of a mile north of his house. East of Route 9 it was still a single-track road for a ways. He gave me very precise directions. That seemed the right moment to say good-bye, so I thanked him and left.

I would learn very little about "my" Israel Johnson by going up Route 9 and walking east along what Ray Duntley said was a piece of the Cedar Point road, but I would be able to stand on or near the spot where, in the early morning of Sunday, August 14, 1836, William Redfield, Ebenezer Emmons, and the rest mounted their wagons and horses and set out in a drizzle that would turn into a downpour and force them to spend their first night under Israel Johnson's roof.

Ray Duntley's directions were impeccable. After a long, straight stretch, the road bends slightly to the left. At that point, an almost invisible dirt road turns east into the woods. If you weren't looking for it, you could easily miss it. Even if you knew it was there, you would pay little attention to it. It disappears in a hundred feet. I parked and locked the car and started walking down it. Within fifty feet I had flushed two large birds, probably ruffed grouse. The road went into a forest of tall, shadowy white pines mixed with aspen and big-toothed aspen. The vegetation on both sides came right up to the edge of the single set of tracks. It was a tunnel, and the further I walked into it the stiller the air became. In a hundred feet or so, it was as quiet as any place I'd ever been. I kept walking and listening, long past the point where I knew I was starting to get nervous. The road turned and twisted deeper into the forest. I was walking along a remnant of the road that once went from Lake Champlain to the Adirondac Iron Works, but I was also walking into a living blankness. I turned and walked back out, briskly.

When I reached home that night, I tried calling Paul Stapley and Louise Hargreaves. Stapley had an unlisted phone. The only Hargreaves in Schroon Lake was Chester. Louise turned out to be his wife. She sounded harried over the phone, as though she'd been asked my kind of question too often. She said she couldn't see and didn't do historical work anymore. I pleaded once with her, and she kindly told me what she knew. It came out in well-worn phrases. The first town meeting in Schroon River was held at Israel Johnson's house in 1804, right across from the cemetery. He had a boy who helped him. Johnson was a loquacious man who invented things. Did she know who the boy was? Was it his son? What did Johnson invent? She didn't know the answer to any of these questions. I asked her about Clear Pond. Had Israel Johnson ever lived there, or had she ever known of another Israel Johnson? She knew nothing about Clear Pond and had never heard of another Israel Johnson, but she told me a story about the Provonchas who had lived near Blue Ridge.

The family that started Bloomingdale's department store in New York City made much of its money speculating in large tracts of Adirondack land. At one time they owned land around Blue Ridge. Bloomingdale apparently sold land to many French Canadians, including some Provonchas. The French Canadians were thought to be the best lumberjacks you could find. As Louise Hargreaves told it to me, they all thought their mortgage payments to Bloomingdale included money to cover their yearly taxes. It turned out not to be true, and all but one family was eventually thrown off its land for failure to pay taxes. The elder Provoncha of that day was so old that he was shown mercy. Either Bloomingdale paid his taxes or they were overlooked by the collectors. He was allowed to stay on his land, which is one— perhaps the only—reason why Provonchas still live in the area, a hundred or so years later. It must have been common, then, for a private individual, even the person you were buying from, to hold your mortgage. There would have been few banks, if any, north of Albany, and fewer still interested in loaning money to poor farmers and laborers.

I thanked Louise Hargreaves. The Israel Johnson she knew about seemed to have been the "old" one. I was interested to hear her use the name Schroon River. When I had lived near Saranac Lake as a boy in the late forties and early fifties, I went to an orthodontist in Glens Falls. My aunt and uncle and grandmother lived there. I would take the bus down and go to the dentist, spend the night with my relatives, and come back the next day. My teeth being my teeth, I did this many times. It was one hundred miles and took three hours. I can still recite the towns we passed through, in order: Glens Falls, Lake George, Warrensburg, Chestertown, Pottersville, Schroon Lake, Schroon River, Keene Valley, Keene, Lake Placid, Ray Brook, Saranac Lake. Schroon Lake was the rest stop, both ways. I had been poring over the maps in recent months, and it occurred to me I hadn't seen Schroon River on any of them. It was the smallest town, by far, on the whole route. It was little more than a gas station and a few houses.

But the bus stopped there, and the driver always called out, Schroon River. What I don't remember from those days, and the bus stayed on Route 9 until it turned onto Route 73 to go into Keene Valley, was North Hudson.

As soon as I got back to Keene Valley, I drove over to Elizabethtown. I thought I should visit the Essex County Historical Society, which had both a museum and a library. I was hoping to find a copy of the Hotchkiss history of lumbering. I didn't, but I found things that were at least as important.

The Historical Society is in the old Elizabethtown High School, which has carved above its two side doors, "boys" and "girls." Most of the building houses the Adirondack Center Museum, and what must have been the school library is now the Brewster Memorial Library. The person in charge of the library, I was startled to find out, was Dorothy Plum, whose Adirondack bibliographies I had been using for nearly two years. The value of those bibliographies can hardly be measured. It doesn't seem any exaggeration to say that, without them, the study of Adirondack history and culture would be almost impossible.

Dot, as her co-workers call her, is a tiny woman, quite old, who used crutches to get around. She took an immediate interest in my project. She had been a librarian all her life, and when she retired she went right back into the business. She and the others at the Brewster Library have made an excellent start on a collection of Adirondack materials. They are short of space already.

She suggested that I look through the old county history again if I hadn't since first finding out about Johnson. When I had read H. P. Smith before, I hadn't been thinking of Israel Johnson and so missed statements like, "The first town meeting in the . . . town [Schroon] was held at the house of Israel Johnson." Three hundred and fifty pages later, Smith said that the first two town meetings were held at Johnson's house. No year was given. Israel Johnson was also among "the first officers elected in the town." His post: fence viewer. It was about four years later, when I was reading Richard Bushman's *From Puritan to Yankee*, that I found out what a fence viewer was.

In the first years of settlement [the town] usually agreed to turn its whole area into pasture, fencing out the cattle from the few cultivated acres, and a common herdsman freed the inhabitants for other work. As men enlarged their own holdings, the town continued to assist those who preferred to herd their cattle privately. To decrease the length of fence, groups would cooperatively enclose a plot containing their cultivated lands so that each individual had but a fraction as much fence to maintain as he would have had alone. Though these arrangements were voluntary, the town appointed a fence viewer to warn persons responsible for faulty sections and, if necessary, to build or repair them at double cost to the delinquent.

Smith also said that Johnson had been a town supervisor in 1811. Which of the two Israels this was, he didn't say.

Dorothy Plum also showed me a county history I had never seen mentioned. It was written by a George Smith and printed as a series of newspaper articles in the *Essex County Republican* in the 1930s. It was never published as a book, but the Brewster Library had photocopied all the articles and mounted them in a large scrap book. George Smith did not know where Israel Johnson came from, but "the first town meeting was held on the first Tuesday of April 1804" at his house. He mentioned interesting facts about the town. The peak of lumbering in the town was in 1820. The First Congregational Church of Schroon was built in 1846. "The edifice cost $3,000, a large sum for that day." It was an even larger sum in 1836 when young Israel was offered the same amount for his land on Clear Pond. When Smith got to the 1850s, he said that among the "business enterprises" in the town were blacksmiths, one of whom was Israel Johnson, and shoemakers, one of whom was Paul "Provoncher," as he spelled it. Nothing in this account suggested that Smith knew he was talking about two different Israel Johnsons. I had never heard either of them described as a blacksmith.

The third and largest favor Dorothy Plum did was to ask if I had looked at the census records. I wasn't sure what she meant, so she explained that the U.S. census records, back to the first one in 1790, were all on microfilm and that if I looked in the right county for the right year, I could find where Israel Johnson lived and with whom. She said the Brewster did not have a complete set of records, by any means, but it had a good file.

I wasn't to realize this at first, but it was here that a phase of my hunting ended. The census records would tell me much more than I knew at this point and clarify many obscurities. More information would come now from books, records, and manuscripts, some of them in libraries as far away as Washington, D.C. Less would come from the landscape, though as I learned new facts, I would always test them in my mind with what I knew of the topography and climate. I had absorbed more than I knew by spending long hours over maps and walking or driving up every path or dirt road I thought might lead somewhere. Less would come from the people who lived here, too, though they were the nearest living things to my subject. In these ramblings I had heard inflections of speech, pauses, and tones of voice, the Yankee skepticism, a terseness of phrase, that must not have been far from Israel Johnson's.

I remember the day I found out who Frieda Provoncha's great grandfather was. I was running census reels through a microfilm reader in Indianapolis, looking for Johnsons in the Blue Ridge area, and I came upon her grandfather, Samuel's, father. His name was Lyman, as I remember. I thought about sending her the information, but it was months after I had talked with her, and I had no reason to think she had any interest in him. She had probably never known him. Most of us are only interested in the people we knew. Like everyone else, I had a great grandfather—several of them, in fact—but, with one exception, I don't know their names, where they came from, what they did or what they looked like. All I know about the one called Mitchell is that he was a doctor. He liked to look at the sunset, perhaps. Or maybe his favorite drink was lemonade. He married, that we know. Though who knows, maybe his unmarried "consort," as the old tombstones call them, gave birth to the man I've heard my father, only recently, call "Paddy." It's a scandalous thought, I'm sure, but what do we know about most people, even the ones we belong to?

3

Census Reels
and Tombstones

I learned in a hurry that genealogical research would be almost impossible without census records. Certain kinds of historical and sociological study would be severely crippled, as well. Yet, the census is not what we would all like it to be: an accurate, scientific measurement of the population. To begin with, it was compiled by ordinary citizens who went around knocking on doors. The people behind those doors undoubtedly did not always answer the knock. Some forgot when their birthday was or where their mother was born. Some lied. The senile and crazy had to be spoken for, which means that information about them has a chance of being invented. And, how certain can we be that census-takers walked up every hollow or back into the woods and mountains to take down the name of every trapper and hermit?

When chasing someone through the census records, sometimes the age of that person will slip, sometimes the place of birth will change, sometimes even the name. In three successive censuses, I watched a young boy's name change from Goodman to Robin to Robert. Census records, then, are best used with a mixture of caution and informed license.

The census is compiled by town or township and then assembled by county. The first six censuses, through 1840, give only one name per household, the head, who in the case of married couples is always the man. The rest of the people living in the house are only catego-rized, by sex, age, and sometimes race. There is no way to be sure, say, whether a male between the ages of sixteen and twenty-six is a son of the householder, a boarder, or a hired hand living in. The census records give us facts, but they are often so isolated from other facts, they seem like spoonsful of fog.

I took out the 1830 census first. That was the census closest to the dates I had for "my" Israel Johnson. I turned the reel to the Town of Schroon and found one Israel Johnson. He was between seventy and eighty, and he lived with a woman who was between sixty and seventy. No one else lived in the household. This must have been "old" Israel who died in 1835 at the age of seventy-six. In 1830, he would have been seventy-one. The woman must have been his wife, Elizabeth. I then looked at the 1840 census for the Town of Schroon, and there were no Johnsons at all. This made sense because Israel died in 1835 and Elizabeth the year after. But where was the Israel who lived at Clear Pond.

In 1800 there were no Israel Johnsons at all in the whole of Essex County, but on the 1810 reel I finally found what I was looking for. In the Town of Schroon, listed one right after the other, were "Israel Johnson, Jr.," and "Israel Johnson." The household of the younger had one man twenty-six to forty-five years old, two boys under ten, a woman between twenty-six and forty-five, and one girl under ten. In the household of the older, the oldest male was over forty-five; the oldest woman was the same. "Old" Israel, who died in 1835 at the age of seventy-six, would have been born in 1759. So, in 1810, he was fifty-one. So far, so good. Also living in the second household were one male under ten, two between ten and sixteen, one between sixteen and twenty-six, as well as one female between ten and sixteen and one between sixteen and twenty-six. The designation, "Jr.," I had been warned, was used for many kinds of relatedness in the nineteenth century, so I could not be sure that these two were father and son, but it was a good hunch. I was still puzzled by not having found "my" Israel in either the 1830 or 1840 censuses. As for finding neither in 1800, I remembered that "old" Israel did not buy his land until 1803. He may have moved from another county or even another state at that time.

Only one Israel Johnson lived in the Town of Schroon in 1820. He was more than forty-five and lived with a woman, also over forty-five, and one male each in the categories, ten to sixteen, sixteen to eighteen, and sixteen to twenty-six. Because the latter category included heads of families, this probably meant that one of his sons or daughters had married but not yet set up separate housekeeping. One younger woman was between ten and sixteen. There was no way to be sure which Israel Johnson this was. A man between twenty-six and forty-five in 1810 might well have passed forty-five by 1820. If he had two sons under ten in 1810, one might have been ten to sixteen in 1820. Or, one of them could have died or left home to work in a mine. I looked in every other town in Essex County. No other Israel Johnsons lived there in 1820.

I still couldn't understand why I had not found young Israel in 1830 or 1840. Then it struck me that maybe Clear Pond wasn't in the Town of Schroon, as I had assumed. I took down a copy of French's *Gazetteer* (1860), and sure enough, the current Town of North Hudson, in which Clear Pond lies, was formed in 1848, not from the Town of Schroon, but from the Town of Moriah. And there in the Town of Moriah I found him. In 1840, Israel Johnson, no "Jr." after his name, between fifty and sixty, living with one male (ten to fifteen), two females (ten to fifteen), and one female (fifty to sixty). The census reports become more elaborate through the nineteenth century, so I learned that in 1840 two people in the Johnson household were employed in "agriculture," the other possibilities being "mining," "commerce," "manufactures and trades," "navigation of the ocean," "navigation of canals, lakes & rivers," and "learned professions & engineers." Was the milling of lumber thought to be an agricultural occupation, or had Johnson stopped running a saw-mill by 1840?

Following the same lead, I found "Israel Johnson, Jr." in 1830, again in the Town of Moriah. Why "Jr.?" Because, I was almost certain, "old" Israel was still alive, and though he was living nine or ten miles away in the next town, they were neighbors and probably next of kin. In 1840 "old" Israel was dead and "young" Israel stopped calling himself "Jr." Proof of this relationship would have to wait for more evidence, though. Young Israel's family, in 1830, was a large one. The oldest male, undoubtedly himself, was between forty and fifty; the oldest female, the same. There were nine other people in the household: one male and three females under ten, one female between ten and fifteen, one each between fifteen and twenty, and two males between twenty and thirty. I checked the 1820 census again, but young Israel was not anywhere in Essex County at that time.

I started trying to fit some of these new facts together with some of the old ones. For instance, William Redfield said that in 1836 Johnson "has been here for four years with his family," the "here" being Clear Pond. At that time Clear Pond was in the Town of Moriah. If Johnson did not settle at Clear Pond until 1832, where was he in 1830? The census records say he was in the Town of Moriah. Was it some place other than Clear Pond? Or, was Johnson or Redfield being casual about his figures in 1836? In 1830 the Cedar Point road was still being built. It is possible that Johnson was "squatting" at Clear Pond in hopes of bluffing or persuading the real owner into selling to him. It is possible, too, that one or two of the men living in the Johnson household in 1830 were members of the survey or road crew. Had Mrs. Johnson started taking in boarders, and did she then need a live-in helper around the house? Were some of the people in that large household in 1830 helping Israel build his sawmills and cut timber and mill boards? It was a busy time, and all these possibilities seemed real.

In 1850 the census began recording the names of all members of a household, as well as other useful information. No Johnsons lived in Moriah that year. French's *Gazetteer* had said that the new Town of North Hudson was formed in 1848. But Israel Johnson was not there, either. He had moved into the Town of Schroon, the town "old" Israel had lived in all his adult life and the one in which he, "young" Israel, had lived at the time of the 1810 census. "Young" Israel Johnson, aged sixty-four, had moved back to Schroon, and was living with his wife, Polly, aged sixty-seven, and one other person, "Betsey" Johnson, presumably a daughter, aged twenty-four. He had become a "farmer," and the value of his real estate was given as $700. The report also says he was born in Vermont.

From Israel Johnson's age, I was able to determine that he was born in 1786. From his place of birth, I was likely to be able to find more references to "old" Israel, the man I suspected was his father. His fortunes had declined. For one thing, he was no longer living at Clear Pond. The Iron Works was to close in six years, so the promise of prosperity in the neighborhood had begun to dwindle. Israel Johnson was no longer living on land valued at three thousand dollars. In fact, he was no longer a millwright. Even in 1840, while he was still at Clear Pond, he had turned to agriculture. What happened to bring his fortunes down? Could one find out?

Early in the nineteenth century, New York State started taking censuses of its own halfway between the Federal censuses. Unfortunately, the first three or four have been destroyed. The earliest remaining New York State census is for 1855, and it has a large entry after Israel Johnson's name. He was still living in the Town of Schroon. He gave his age as seventy. This causes a one-year discrepancy with the figure given in the 1850 census, which probably has to do with his birthday and on which side of it the census was taken. It means, though, that we must say, until we know better, that "young" Israel Johnson was born in 1785 or 1786. His wife was called Molly this time, and she was seventy-three. Their child, Betsey, was thirty-one. Johnson told the census taker that he was born in "Columbia," which I suppose might be, or might have been, the name of the part of Vermont where he was born. "Molly's" birthplace is given as New Hampshire, Betsey's "Genesee." They lived in a "frame" house worth seventy-five dollars. The census form asked how many years each member of the household had resided in this town, that is, Schroon. Israel said thirteen, but Molly said seventeen. Betsey had been in Schroon "3/12" 's of a year.

Several things are implied by these figures. First, Johnson's wife had left him for a while, perhaps only to help make the transition from Clear Pond back to the Town of Schroon. It appears as though she left Clear Pond in 1838, four years before Israel, but the 1840 census indicates that there was a woman between fifty and sixty living with Johnson in the Town of Moriah. In 1840, the Molly who was seventy-three in 1855 would have been fifty-eight, which of course falls into the age range given for the woman in 1840. It could be that Molly or Polly misremembered the year she moved back to Schroon. It is also possible that Johnson's wife died and he remarried. Betsey, who was living with her father in 1850 (though an error was made in recording her age somewhere because she was twenty-four in 1850 and thirty-one in 1855), appears to have moved away somewhere between 1850 and 1855 and had only returned to the household three months before the census taker came by. And Israel Johnson, if these figures can be relied on, moved off the Clear Pond land in 1842. Why 1842?

The 1855 census went on to describe Johnson, this time as a "millwright," a landowner, and a voter. He owned twenty-five acres of improved land and seventy-five acres unimproved. The value of what he called a "farm" was $2,000, of the stock $26, of the tools and implements $10. He had plowed two acres the previous year and left two acres fallow. Twelve acres were meadow, from which he harvested five tons of hay, and from the one acre he planted in potatoes, he harvested one-hundred bushels. Not much evidence of the millwright lurks in this description, and the farm seems fairly modest. Perhaps he thought of himself as a retired millwright, a man who, though he no longer practiced the trade, had spent his most active years as one.

There we leave Israel Johnson, as far as the census records are concerned. He does not appear again, and unless he moved to a wholly new part of the state, which does not seem likely for a man in his seventies, he died before 1860. Where, I don't know. His story does not end there, however. In a sense, it has just begun.

I was not through with the census reports. Once I discovered them, I also realized that if the Brewster Library did not have the census report for a given year, the Essex County clerk's office might. For a day or two, I had been going back and forth between both places. I was even beginning to nod to all the "regulars" at the county clerk's office. One of them said to me once, as I passed him carrying thirty or forty pounds of deed books, "Isn't it fun finding ancestors?" I wasn't looking for the ancestors, of course, and what I was doing, at that precise moment, was not having fun, but I smiled and agreed with him.

It was in the county clerk's office, actually, that I found the 1855 New York State census. I think it was at about the moment or shortly afterward (when I discovered that the earlier state censuses, like the early town records in North Hudson, had been destroyed) that a kind gentleman, named Philip Sullivan, offered me help. I had seen him every time I had gone there. And heard him, too, because he was a whistler. A middle-aging man with glasses and a pleasant expression, he whistled many of the songs I grew up with, very quietly of course, but very purely. I often stopped to hear if he could get through a tricky passage from Cole Porter or Rodgers and Hammerstein, and he invariably did. He had a wonderful ear. He had a pure heart, too, because he asked me at a particularly low moment what I was doing and saw right away that I hadn't known about the county's records of wills. He went right to the directory and found three deeds having to do with one or both Israel Johnsons before I quite knew what he was doing.

The first of these, as I call them, "will deeds" is dated December 8, 1835. Old Israel Johnson had died on August 27 of that year. This deed lists his "lawful heirs" as Israel Johnson, Jr., and his wife Molly, William Johnson and his wife Euphama, and someone called Nelson Woodworth. These lawful heirs, on the date given, sold old Israel's original 300 acre purchase of 1803 to Robert D. Lindsay of the Town of Schroon for $500. The land was also in the Town of Schroon, so they sold to a friend or at least to an acquaintance. The property seems to have dropped in value by $700 in thirty-two years.

This deed would seem to establish conclusively that Israel Johnson, Jr., of Clear Pond was the son, as well as the heir, of Israel Johnson, who died in 1835 and, according to Paul Stapley, is buried in the Schroon River or DeLorme Cemetery. Nelson Woodworth brought to mind Louise Hargreave's comment that Israel Johnson had been helped by a boy. Something in the way she said it made me think the boy was not one of his sons. It could hardly have been Israel, Jr., who helped him, since he had a family and a separate household by 1810, only seven years after old Israel bought the Schroon River land. As for Nelson Woodworth, I would have to go back through the census reports to see what I could learn about him.

The second of the will deeds is dated April 6, 1837. In it Nathan Johnson of Laporte County "for himself and for James Johnson of Dearborn County and for Sally Burgess in the County of Fayette and state of Indiana," parties of the first part, and the same Robert D. Lindsay, party of the second part, came to this agreement: That for $388, the parties of the first part would release forever to Lindsay any claim they had . . . , and here the deed went into a long description of exactly the same piece of land mentioned in the first deed, namely, the 300 acres bought by old Israel in 1803.

Together, these two deeds told me who the remaining children of old Israel were, and where they lived. In the mid thirties, he had four sons and a daughter, Sally, who had married someone named Burgess. Three of his five children had moved to Indiana. They did not attend the funeral, naturally, and it wasn't until almost two years later that one of them, Nathan, came east to collect his and his brother's and sister's shares of their father's estate.

Indiana. A small door opened somewhere, at the end of a long, dimly lit corridor. At the other end of it, I could just barely make myself out knocking on a door, perhaps in Indiana, with a heavy sheaf of papers in my hand. When someone answered the door, I heard myself say, "Mr. Johnson?"

The third deed was really the first. It was dated January 1, 1816, but not recorded till June 13, 1837. In it, old Israel Johnson and his wife Betsy sold to John Metcalf of Saratoga County, for $1,384, a small piece of the original 300-acre purchase. It lay on the east bank of the Schroon River "below a sawmill commonly called Johnson's sawmill," containing about 8.3 acres "including the said sawmill, dam & privilege of said River for raising a pond & for fixing Booms when required & for floating logs & timber." Metcalf also bought from Johnson two additional acres and an access road between the first parcel and the "State Road," which in 1816 was the road that is now Route 9.

It would appear from this that old Israel, also a millwright, sold his improvements in 1816 and got out of the milling business. And, because he sold to a man who wanted to continue in the lumber business, apparently that business was still a sound one. Old Israel, then, did not lose the value of his investment, because he sold those eight to ten acres for $184 more than he paid for the whole 300. What he did for the last twenty years of his life, I had no idea.

There turned out to be one more deed, dated March 11, 1836, after old Israel's death and before Elizabeth's. Robert Lindsay paid John Metcalf $150 for the parcels he had bought from old Israel in 1816. The original 300-acre purchase was now owned by one man again.

The will deeds told me more about old Israel than about the one who lived at Clear Pond, but now that I knew they were related, news about the one was apt to be news about the other. The next thing to do, I decided, was to follow a couple of leads given by the census reports. Young Israel, in 1850, said he was born in Vermont. At the time of the first census in 1790, he would have been four or five years old. Luckily, the 1790 census for Vermont lists only one Israel Johnson in the whole state. He lived in the Town of Wells, Rutland

County. Wells turned out to be right on the New York border across from the southern edge of Lake George, only about fifty or sixty miles from the place on the Schroon River where Israel finally settled. In 1790, the Johnson household included one male sixteen years and up, including heads of families (Israel himself, then thirty-one years old), two males under sixteen (one of whom was young Israel), and three females, sixteen years and up, including heads of families. One of the latter would have been Elizabeth, old Israel's wife.

The 1800 census is slightly more involved. Old Israel is still living in Wells Town, Rutland County, but his household has grown considerably. Old Israel would have been forty-one in 1800, but among the males there is one more than forty-five and one between twenty-six and forty-five. The latter would be Israel. The same thing is true among the females. There is a woman over forty-five and one between twenty-six and forty-five. This suggests that either his or her parents had come to live with them. Whether these two older people moved to New York State with Old Israel and his family in 1803, I don't know, but they are not visible in the 1810 census report. The rest of the household in 1800 includes two males under ten, one ten to sixteen, one sixteen to twenty-six, and three females, two under ten and one ten to sixteen. Eleven people under one roof.

So, the Johnsons had come to New York from Vermont. Whether that was the place they started from probably couldn't be known, but the family was there for at least the thirteen years between the first U.S. census in 1790 and the time Johnson bought land from Zephaniah Platt in 1803. The deed between Johnson and the man for whom the city of Plattsburgh is named was dated April 15. Snow is still apt to cover the ground in the Adirondacks in mid-April, but it is just the time of year when you could begin thinking about clearing land, building a cabin and planting. Only a year after closing the deal, old Israel held the first town meeting for the Town of Schroon in his house. He was probably well known to his neighbors. His son, Israel, was eighteen or nineteen at the time, perhaps still living at home, or just beginning to court Molly, that girl from New Hampshire. The place was thick with Yankees, and getting thicker.

The last puzzle given me by the census reports was young Israel's complete absence from them in 1820. He was not to be found anywhere in Essex County. By this time, I had learned that if you looked at your information hard enough and long enough, it would usually help you out.

It was the word "Genesee" that finally wormed its way into my brain. Betsey Johnson, daughter of young Israel, told the census-taker from New York in 1855 that she was born in Genesee. I did my math and realized that she was born in 1826. Here was a part of the missing decade, now where was Genesee? A quick glance at the map showed there was a Genesee County in western New York. And there he was. Young Israel was thirty-four or thirty-five in 1820, and the Israel Johnson household in Genesee County had one male twenty-six to forth-five, two ten to sixteen, and one under ten. Five females lived there, one twenty-six to forty-five, one ten to sixteen, and three under ten. Johnson said he was engaged in manufactures, as a mill-wright would. This is the same man who in 1840 said he was "engaged in agriculture" and in 1850 owned a "farm."

Some time before 1820, then, young Israel Johnson decided to leave the Adirondacks and make his life elsewhere. His father, for whatever reason, had decided in 1816 that he should sell his sawmill. His brothers, Nathan and James, and his sister Sally's husband, had all caught a version of "Ohio fever" and gone west looking for better and cheaper land than you could find on the sandy, rocky margins of the Adirondacks. Many people were leaving the area. John S. Wright, for instance, a farmer from Saratoga County, went out to Ohio in 1818 to look for land and came back with the gloomy report that most of the good land had been bought up by land speculators. He warned against the "Ohio mania . . . so generally prevalent in the east." His *Letters from the West, or a Caution to Immigrants* was published the next year. In between his cautions, though, he mentioned the powerful reasons why a farmer would want to move out of northern New York: "The severe winters, cold and dry summers, and short crops, we had lately experienced, had their full weight and influence on my mind." He hoped to find a country that would afford the necessaries of life in abundance and "relieve us of the necessity of perpetual labor." He wished to put himself and his family "beyond the reach of grinding poverty." The last sentence of William Redfield's journal entry at Clear Pond in August 1836 was: "Has been a frost which killed the potato tops to a small extent." Mid-August, when it's apt to be sweltering in central and southern Ohio.

If George Smith was right, it was not only bad for farmers. The lumber industry peaked in 1820 in the Schroon River area. A smart lumberman or mill owner would have seen that coming. Iron ore wasn't discovered there until 1827. So, the period between, roughly, 1815, when the second war with England ended and the frontier was safe to settle in, and 1827, when iron ore was discovered, could well have been a slack, depressed time in northern New York. Betsey's age varies in the two censuses reporting it, but young Israel was in Genesee County from before 1820 to around 1826 or later. It was the next year that iron ore was found in the middle of the Adirondacks, and my guess is that, having heard about it, he thought he would go back home and try his luck there. By 1830, as we know, he was living in the Town of Moriah, most likely at Clear Pond. Apparently, he had seen enough of "the Genesee."

✳

It was finally time to leave. The first frosts had touched down in Keene Valley, and I was lighting two fires a day now in the woodstove, one to eat breakfast by before I went out for the day and one for the long quiet evening. The leaves had passed their brilliance, and the mountains now took on the iron look they have in the fall and keep till they are coated with snow. Except when it was raining or clouded over, I had the notched peak of Noonmark to look at every morning. I had forgotten what it meant to have mountains around.

I put the cooler and sleeping bag and a large sheaf of papers in the Rabbit, took my trash over to the dump, dropped the key off at the landlady's, and drove out of Keene Valley slowly on a bright, clear, day. The only suggestion of winter was the huge pile of firewood someone had dumped by the side door of "The Spread." I had one more stop to make. I drove past the entrance to the Ausable Club at St. Hubert's, up past Chapel Pond, down to the junction where Route 9 comes in from Elizabethtown, and skipping the turnoff to the Northway (I would spend enough time in the next two days being air-whacked by semis), followed Route 9 as it wound through trees on the way to North Hudson. It was time to look at the gravestones of old Israel and his wife, Elizabeth. I wouldn't learn anything from them, except where the cemetery was, but I thought I owed it to the family. By this time, I was probably the nearest thing they had to a relative. Besides, it wasn't even out of my way. I had two little boughs of white pine that I had picked off a tree at the edge of the meadow in Keene Valley.

It was called the Schroon River cemetery, so by visiting it, I would also solve the mystery of Schroon River's disappearance. I drove past the bend in the road where a piece of the Cedar Point road came in out of the forest. In three-quarters of a mile, of course, I passed Ray Duntley's house on the left with the bearskin nailed up on the front porch, the "Crow's Nest" just beyond it on the right, a big empty bar with a huge parking lot. Beyond that, the turnoff to the left toward Port Henry with the small graveyard at the top of the hill that Lillian Nolette asked me to visit. Arthur Greenough's on the right, silver letters on a silver box. A little further on, Lillian Nolette's bright tin roof. I was getting close to the center of North Hudson and so passed Mary Bessey's on the right and Bernard Corman's on the left. No one was around. I had the road to myself. Route 9 seemed like a country road rather than the major thorough-fare for north/south traffic in this part of the state from before 1800 until the late 1960s when they built the Northway. I had gotten all the way in to North Hudson. The Senior Citizen's Center was on the left, locked up tight, and the old wooden hotel with the moosehead under the porch roof and "Liquor" on the sign out front was on the right, also closed. Up ahead was the turnoff toward Newcomb, the road that has no number but goes through Blue Ridge past the general store called "General Store" and the home of Mrs. Dobie.

I almost turned. As long as I was nodding my farewells to everybody's closed front doors (there had been a frost the night before), I thought perhaps I should go out to Clear Pond. Just before the turnoff, the merest fraction of a mile from it, common sense came back. The sign said that Schroon Lake was only a few miles straight ahead. I knew, then, that Schroon River would have to be between me and it. My pace had become almost funereal, so I stepped on the gas. I passed a few more houses, a cemetery on the left, and finally I was out of North Hudson on my way toward Schroon Lake looking for the lost town of Schroon River. I drove faster, but I looked faster, too. I looked under every shrub and gave every house, every closed motel, a steady, penetrating glare. Then, suddenly, I was in Schroon Lake, speed limit thirty miles per hour. It was like a bad movie. The

5. Grave of Israel Johnson, Esq. (1760–1835),
North Hudson, New York.

case of the missing town. Up ahead was a state police headquarters.
They would be sure to know, I thought. So, I slowed down to thirty
and drove into the lot and parked.

The officer was perfectly friendly. He listened to my question, to
which I added the amusing and instructive tale of the long bus rides
of my youth in search of straight teeth. He said he never heard of it.
What about the DeLorme Cemetery, I asked. Well, he said, some
DeLormes used to live up by the cemetery in North Hudson. Where's
that, I asked. Just as you go into North Hudson, on your right.

I had looked right at it and not seen it.

On the way back to North Hudson, I consoled myself by saying
that at least I had solved one mystery. I was now sure that North
Hudson had once, and for a very long time, been called Schroon
River. I pulled into the cemetery. On the right was a large lot with
many gravestones. On the left was an equally large lot, or lawn,
really, since the grass was cut. No gravestones stood up in the latter,
only an occasional small stone sunk flush with the ground. Bunches

6. Grave of Elizabeth Johnson (1760–1813), wife of
Israel Johnson, Esq., and their daughter Elizabeth
Woodworth (1789–1813), North Hudson, New York.

of flowers scattered here and there. Most of the sunken stones and
flowers were in the near corner. I turned to the right and almost at
once found "Israel Johnson, Esq.," who died on August 27, 1835, age
seventy-six. The motto on his stone reads, "Prepare for death and
follow me."

Then, the gravestones started to speak. They had tales to tell.
Next to Israel Johnson, Esq., was the joint grave of his first wife, also
called Elizabeth, and "her daughter," Elizabeth (was she not also his?)
who was twenty-four years old when she died and the "wife of Elijah

Woodworth." Both Elizabeths died on February 8, 1813, and they share a gravestone as well as a grave, the motto across the bottom saying,

> The longest life how soon it ends
> Yet on that life eternal bliss depends

What could have happened? It was during the War of 1812, but as far as I knew, no battles took place in that area. It could have been sickness or disease. February is certainly the right time of year for flu or pneumonia. But, it was also the right time of year for a house fire. Whatever happened, I couldn't help connecting it to old Israel's decision to sell his sawmill three years later and to most of the children's willingness to move permanently away from home. Though now that I remembered it, the name Betsy had been on the 1816 will deed. So, old Israel had remarried by then, and it is likely that his new wife had something to do with selling the mill.

The gravestone also brought the Woodworth and Johnson families together. Nelson Woodworth, the odd heir to old Israel, was probably his grandson, Elizabeth Johnson Woodworth's son. Louise Hargreaves had said that Johnson lived right across the road from the cemetery in Schroon River. All that stands there now are white pines.

The other stone that I knew was there, of course, was for Elizabeth Johnson, now to be thought of as the second wife. Her stone read simply "Elizabeth, wife of Isreal [sic] Johnson died Oct. 8, 1836." She was the wife of his old age in more ways than one, because she seems to have borne him no children. In 1810, when old Israel was fifty-one, he had one child under ten, a boy. Ten years later, after his remarriage, there were no children under ten.

Next to Elizabeth, the second wife, is the grave of Elijah Woodwarth [sic] who died December 28, 1834 at the age of forty-six. He was undoubtedly husband to Elizabeth Johnson. Buried so close to the Johnsons, he seemed to be part of the family.

A few feet from these was another group of graves. The first is of Nancy, "wife of Nelson Woodworth," who died July 3, 1866 "AE 56 yrs. 2 mos. 27 ds." and next to her the graves of four of her children, all of whom died before her. Nelson is buried somewhere else.

I looked at every stone in the graveyard, hoping that Paul Stapely, the compiler of the local graves' registry, might have missed one. For a brief moment, I thought I might have found it. A small stone, perhaps twelve inches high and ten across, about six or eight feet in back of old Israel's, had on it the initials "I. J." But it was almost certainly old Israel's footstone. I walked back to the car and looked over at the other half of the cemetery. That, I presumed, is where people are buried who either can't afford or don't want a headstone. Young Israel had moved back into the Town of Schroon in the early forties, his prospects much declined, and my guess is that he died there and is buried there. I think of him lying somewhere in the middle or at the far end of that field, which they still keep mowed and, so it appears, where they still bury people in nameless graves.

I drove up the ramp onto the Northway and headed home to Indiana. Somewhere around Syracuse, as I was rushing to make the Pennsylvania border before dark, I noticed I still had the two pine twigs in the back seat. Oh, well, I thought. I'll have to come back some day. I hadn't brought enough twigs with me, anyway.

4

"A Genius
of the First Water"

*F*our or five nights later, home in Indiana, I decided it was time
to give all my facts and guesses a rough shake to see what Israel
Johnson looked like by himself.

He was born in Rutland County, Vermont, in 1785 or 1786,
most likely the oldest child of Israel Johnson, Esq. (1759–1835), and
his wife, Elizabeth (1760–1813). He had at least five brothers and
sisters: Elizabeth (1789–1813), William, Nathan, James, and Sally.
The family moved to Essex County, Town of Schroon, early in 1803,
the year that Israel Johnson, Esq., bought three hundred acres from
Zephaniah Platt. The first town meeting of the Town of Schroon was
held in the Johnson house right across the road from the DeLorme
Cemetery in North Hudson on the first Tuesday in April of 1804.
Israel Johnson, Esq., was named fence viewer for the town that day
and later held other offices, including town supervisor.

By 1810, Israel Johnson, Jr., had married a girl whose family had
come from New Hampshire. Her name was Molly or Polly, both of
which are common nicknames for Mary. Johnson set up his own
household in the Town of Schroon on land he did not own or was in
the process of buying. Of course, he might have built a house on his
father's land. We don't know what he was doing at this time. He was
twenty-four or twenty-five, and he and Polly had three small children under the age of ten, two boys and a girl. He might have been
helping his father at what had come to be known locally as Johnson's
sawmill on the east side of the Schroon River.

In 1813, disaster struck. On the same day, his mother, Elizabeth, and his sister, Elizabeth, then married to Elijah Woodworth, died. His mother was fifty-three; his sister, twenty-four.

In the next few years, the family underwent several more upheavals. In 1816 Israel Johnson, Esq., and his new wife, Betsy, sold the sawmill to John Metcalf of Saratoga County. Johnson's new wife was apparently involved in the decision to get out of the milling business. Several of his children—Israel, Nathan, James, and Sally—four of the five who lived long enough to be his heirs, caught some version of "Ohio fever" after 1815 and moved either to Indiana or to western New York.

Young Israel had moved to the Town of Alexander, Genesee County, by 1820, and there he lived with Polly, two boys and a girl, now between ten and sixteen years old, and four additional children, three girls and a boy, all under ten. He gave his occupation as millwright. He had gone there apparently because of the land boom in that part of the country. Much of the fighting in the War of 1812 had taken place in western Pennsylvania and New York, and a good many Yankee farmers who had done the fighting discovered that there was better land to the west than they and their families had been working in Massachusetts and Connecticut. A smart millwright knew that mills—sawmills and grist mills—were among the first things needed by farmers opening up new land. Johnson was in Genesee County at least until his daughter, Betsey, was born, sometime between 1824 and 1826.

By 1830, young Israel had come back to Essex County and settled in the Town of Moriah, the township in which Clear Pond lies. The Cedar Point road had been planned, funded, surveyed, and may even have been finished by that time. Johnson left the Genesee, either because his prospects were not good there any more or because, with the discovery of iron ore near Lake Sanford, he thought he would do better in Essex County. Perhaps he was motivated by feelings of family and place. His father and mother, by that time, were in their seventies and living alone.

In 1836 William Redfield found Israel in a prosperous condition on Clear Pond. He had enough of a sawmill business to keep two mills going, and he had been offered $3,000 for his property. Four years later, things had changed. The household was much depleted. Israel and Molly were both in their fifties, and they had one boy between ten and fifteen and two women between fifteen and twenty living with them. Betsey would have been fifteen or sixteen in 1840. The biggest change, though, is that Israel Johnson was no longer a millwright. He and one other person in the family called themselves farmers.

There is a further hint of trouble. In 1855, Molly told the census taker that she had moved into the Town of Schroon four years before her husband in 1838. I don't know who else the woman in her fifties living in the Israel Johnson household in 1840 could have been except Molly, but, even though she was with her husband the day the census taker came by that year, she appears to have had her eye on getting away. The milling had slowed down, if not ended, and two years later, in 1842, he himself had moved into the Town of Schroon.

Molly took him back, or there was a reconciliation of some sort, because there they were in 1850, just three of them, in the Town of Schroon: Israel, Molly, and their daughter Betsey. He again called himself a farmer.

Five years later, he was seventy. It was the last time a census taker would find him. He probably knew it, so he said he was a millwright. He hadn't been one in fifteen years or more, but that's what he had done most of his life. It was his trade and his father's trade before him. He was still living in the Town of Schroon, where his father had brought him and the rest of the family all those years ago. Fifty of them, at least. He told the census taker his land was worth $2,000. It sounded nice to say it, and the census taker would never find out he still didn't own it. It was a harmless lie. No need telling him the truth, that there might not even be enough money for a gravestone. Who'd find out, anyway? And what if they did? "Yes, well, I'm retired from milling now, but when I was on the Genesee . . . ." It was early in the day. Molly and Betsy were gone visiting a neighbor and wouldn't be back for hours.

That's what Israel Johnson looked like at the end of 1981. He would change in the next five years in more ways than I guessed possible.

*

George W. Hotchkiss's *History of the Lumber and Forest Industry of the Northwest* (Chicago, 1898) finally arrived through interlibrary loan. At first, the library could find no one to lend it. When it came, the winter was almost over. I had done almost nothing with Israel Johnson for months. Occasionally, I would brush against some fact or observation about Johnson, but I would make a note of it and put it in the file marked "IJ." I could begin to see the whole Johnson "mania" turning into a "dead clearing," as they used to call abandoned farms in the Adirondacks. The day the Hotchkiss volume came, though, the winter's lethargy dissipated at once.

Hotchkiss's book is a popular history. It deals mostly with the life and times of its author, who had wide acquaintance in the lumber business and was willing to travel. The "Northwest" of the title is the old northwest along the upper Mississippi Valley and the Great Lakes. The early lumbermen of the old northwest all grew up in the east, and when Hotchkiss stopped and talked with the proprietors of the lumber firm, Lindsay and Phelps, in Davenport, Iowa, he ran into some people who had grown up in the Schroon River area and had known Israel Johnson.

> Prominent for many years among the mill operators of the Mississippi river have been James E. Lindsay and John B. Phelps, who as Lindsay & Phelps have been for nearly forty years connected with the manufacture of lumber at Davenport, Iowa. Both of these gentlemen are natives of Essex county, New York, where Robert D. Lindsay, father of James, was for many years a lumberman and hotel keeper. James D. Lindsay was brought up in the atmosphere of the saw mill, not only that his father was interested in the business, and owned a water-power saw mill run by a "flutter" wheel, quite up to date at that time, but that a relative and neighbor of his youthful days, was proprietor of a saw mill of the type common to the day, and was the ingenious inventor who conceived the idea which culminates in the mulay saw, and gave the first real impetus to the demand for better methods of making lumber than were afforded by the cumbersome gate or sash saw.

Robert D. Lindsay was probably the man who bought old Israel Johnson's property after the latter's death. Where his sawmill and hotel were, I don't know, except that Hotchkiss called him young Israel's neighbor, "neighbor" being a loose term in the backwoods. Redfield had said in 1836 that Johnson's was the only house on the Cedar Point road between the state road (Route 9) and the Iron

Works. The only hotels or inns I know of in the area were Weatherhead's, near the junction of Route 9 and the Cedar Point road, and Root's, down near the junction of Route 9 and the road to Blue Ridge and Newcomb. The relationship between the Johnson and Lindsay families was new information. Perhaps Molly had been a Lindsay, or Elizabeth, old Israel's second wife. Of course, the biggest news was that young Israel had been an inventor, and not just an incidental tinkerer but an inventor of consequence to the lumber industry.

As promised, though, Hotchkiss had more to say about Johnson and his saw. It came in the chapter called, "The Evolution of Saw Mill Machinery."

Until about 1835 the only style of mill known to the saw mill world was that of the "gate" or "sash" as variously termed. This . . . was constructed with a heavy weigh beam across the mill, supported in its center by two heavy posts placed about six feet apart, upon which strips of maple formed slides for the ponderous gate, which was constructed with a top and bottom timber, connected by lighter posts, the upper and lower cross-beams sliding by V-shaped notches of wood (or iron) on the maple strips of the side posts. The gate was connected at the bottom by a "noddle" pin connecting with the pitman to the water wheel shaft below, and the saw was strained between the upper and lower cross beams. The weight of this gate absorbed a large proportion of the power of the water wheel, and to that extent absorbed the ability or cutting capacity of the saw.

In 1835 Israel Johnson of Clear Pond, Essex county, N.Y., conceived the idea of dispensing with the heavy gate, by suspending two iron slides from the upper, or "fender" beam, in which by a short noddle pin two sliding boxes and rocking plates were connected with the saw at its upper end, while a similar arrangement at the lower end of the saw was connected with the pitman, and by this simple arrangement the weight of a heavy gate was dispensed with, and as the "horns" or side posts, as well as cross beams, were done away with, the old farmer adopted the nomenclature of "mulay," signifying "hornless." It is said that the mill force of Mr. Johnson, consisted of a bull for hauling on logs, his young son and a small daughter being his assistants on the floor. Probably the bull having no horns gave Mr. Johnson his first idea of the name for his innovation in saw mill construction. It is related of him by an acquaintance and neighbor, Mr. Phelps of Davenport, Iowa, that he built the mill with the aid of his boy, girl and bull, that the frame was put together with trenails and dove tails locked with wooden wedges, and that with a production of 1,000 feet per day, his slabs accumulated faster than his lumber pile, so that when the slab pile became too great for comfort and convenience, he moved the mill to another location and burned the old slab pile when it had seasoned well enough to burn, moving back to his first location, when the second slab pile had reached a size to necessitate it, he having two dams located near by on the same stream. The mulay was at once appreciated as a useful innovation and it is said that Mr. Johnson soon after testing its utility made a journey to Washington to secure a patent, where he fell in with some disinterested (?)[sic] friends, who, after dining and wining him, secured his signature to an assignment of his claims and the loss of the benefits which should have accrued to him from the invention. Mr. Johnson is described as a genius of the first water, and as being as eccentric a man as is often found. He was a soldier of the war of 1812 and saw service at the battle of Plattsburg, N.Y. After the war it was no uncommon thing for him to appear at the Phelps grist mill with a bag of grain on his "drag," which was made of two (sometimes three) small poles, one end of which dragged on the ground after the fashion of the Indians, or later with a two-wheel cart, made by sawing off a six-inch block from a good sound log of three feet diameter, attached on a wooden axle, his team consisting of a cow and a bull yoked together. Being a loquacious man, and knowing every settler in the region, it was a fixed habit to stop and chat with every man he met on his seven-mile journey from his home to the mill. As described to the historian, Mr. Johnson was a typical Yankee, of the resourceful kind, often caricatured but seldom seen in later days; the type of men who have made the term "Yankee," the synonym of invention and ready resource.

What a boon the amateur historian is. While the professional historian arrays his battalions of fighting facts for the final annihilation of ignorance, the amateur, having first lit a fresh cigar, props up his feet and chats for an hour. There is no hurry to record the exact number of board feet produced in a year. The subject may be lumber, but who is to say just where lumbering begins and where it ends?

And by such willingness to stop and linger over the incidental, we get our first glimpse of the man, rather than the statistic, Israel Johnson. An inventor, at one time a soldier, a talkative man (he, too, liked to stop and chat) known to "every settler in the region," a "typical Yankee," "synonym of invention and ready resource," an eccentric. A man who, having invented a saw, traveled to Washington to register it at the Patent Office. A man with an eye for the practical and the main chance, but being likeable and "loquacious," also vulnerable. Though, who's to say? Maybe he thought his saw would be bettered right away and that no manufacturer would take an interest in it. Better to take a few real dollars today than bank on making money in the unpredictable future. Maybe he let himself be wined and dined out of his idea and then went home chuckling to himself with a few hundred dollars sewed into his coat. What better place to sell his idea than at the door of the Patent Office itself where gladhanders and leeches gathered in swarms, hoping to talk some bumpkin out of his idea.

Hotchkiss took his information from the Phelps of Lindsay and Phelps in Davenport. John B. Phelps was the son of Elihu Phelps, born just a few years before young Israel. John, then, would have been the age of Johnson's children. He would probably have known Israel only after he returned from Genesee County and settled at Clear Pond. He appears not to have known him either early or late when Johnson was living in the Town of Schroon.

As always, new information raises new questions. What was a mulay saw? The records of the Patent Office had to be checked, as well as Johnson's service record. Could I learn who Johnson had sold the patent to? Where was the Phelps grist mill that Israel lived seven miles from? Who were the "young son" and "small daughter?" The latter was most likely Betsey who, in 1832, would have been between six and eight years old.

One earlier piece of information had to be reexamined. Because some of Louise Hargreave's information was about old Israel, I had assumed it all was. Some of her information, however, coincided exactly with what Hotchkiss said of young Israel. She told me Johnson had been helped by a boy, that he was talkative, and that he invented things. She had even used the word "loquacious." These things were too close to Hotchkiss's description, which is clearly of young Israel. None of the people I had talked to in the Schroon River area knew there had been two Johnsons. Hotchkiss did not indicate he knew it, either, though it is clear he was talking about young Israel. It now seemed as though Louise Hargreave's Israel Johnson, the Israel Johnson known around North Hudson today, was a composite—one man made up out of a father and son who had the same name. It is not hard to imagine how this sort of thing could happen over the course of 125 years. It is amazing that either of them is remembered at all. As for the boy who helped Johnson, either one or both could have been helped by a boy. Hotchkiss said young Israel was helped by his son. But, then, perhaps his information, picked up in Davenport, Iowa, fifty years or so after the fact, was not "hard" information either.

5

The Road Tune

*B*y now I knew I was embarked on a long-term project. I had no method for doing what I was doing, only the desire to find things out. And, since I had to do this in my spare time and at a great distance from most of my sources, it took on a self-contained, private quality, like a secret life. It had nothing to do with my teaching or writing. It interfered with my marriage. Call it an obsession. An obsession with what, though?

Something about the remoteness and isolation of Johnson's life intrigued me, and not just the part of it that was remote because it lay scattered and buried in a dozen libraries. It seemed right for this to have happened in a wilderness and for that wilderness to have been in many ways preserved. The stands of pine and birch and maple that one could see up the valley from Elk Lake toward Marcy and Skylight or eastward toward the Dixes, even though they may be third or fourth growth, seemed a perfect commentary on the life they had come to replace—dark, darkening the land, thick, and often impenetrable.

Woods are compelling places. Even if I had not had the luck to grow up in and near this particular woods, woods would still draw me to them. The woods was our first home. Maybe we left it millennia ago, but we cling to it anyway, cut our highways through it, build our houses next to or in it, spend our vacations there. Which of us wouldn't prefer to live in the woods, as long as he had running water, TV, and a few good neighbors? "The woods are lovely, dark and deep," the man in Frost's poem says. In my etymological dictionary, *wood* is first described as an adjective for *mad*. "See Wednesday," it says, which, of course, is Wodin's Day, the day of the Norse god Wodin who lived in the great hall, Valhalla, and for whom mead was both meat and drink. The Old English *woden* is related to an archaic English word, *wood,* different from our word *wood,* meaning mad, possessed, divinely inspired. Can woods be the original haunt of the gods, the primitive Valhalla of an earlier mythology? Somebody must have thought so, to have given them such a name. "Let's take a walk through the mad, the possessed, the divinely inspired." Imagine being able to say that. Imagine being able to do it.

One day in a lull between things I needed to do and creeping boredom, while I was waiting for the next opportunity to head for the Adirondacks or for Interlibrary Loan to locate a book for me, I said to myself, if young Israel's was the only house on the only road to the Adirondac Iron Works, he must have seen a good bit of the people who worked there. So I went to the library and read through Arthur Masten's *The Story of Adirondac*—a history of the Works published in 1922—and, as I thought, he made a few references to Johnson, but only enough to indicate that a man with that name lived in the area. If Masten mentioned him, I thought, his sources might have mentioned him many more times. So, I arranged to spend a week at the Adirondack Museum in Blue Mountain Lake during the fall of 1982 to look at the Iron Works papers.

The Adirondacks are probably at their best in late September and early October. Nearly everyone has gone home. The local people seem relaxed, even relieved. The leaves are bright, the sun sharp and brilliant, and the air cools quickly if it goes under a cloud. Sudden all-day rains spread a rich gloom over the place and promise a long winter. The swimming is over, and because hunting hasn't begun, no one seems to be around.

The Village of Blue Mountain Lake has about forty or fifty houses, only a third of which are visible from the main road. Two churches, a post office, fire house, craft center, a summer store (which closed three days after I arrived) line the "main street," as well as a roadside restaurant and three or four old summer houses that were boarded up years ago and put up for sale. There's a gas station, of course, plus the motels and cottages. The latter were not exactly closed for the season, but they were not open either. Notes were taped to front doors saying Al or Marie would be back in a while. I had to knock several times, loudly, to rouse the landlady of the one I chose. She had her hair up in curlers and couldn't find the key just then, but she said I could have the nearest cabin for only $100 a week. She'd be down just as soon as she found the key (the cabin was open) to turn the water on. All the other cottages were empty.

The week in Blue Mountain Lake was simple, exhausting, and very useful. Each day I got up at daylight, had a bowl of cereal and a cup of coffee at the chipped formica table, made some sandwiches— peanut butter only, no jelly—for lunch, and drove up to the door of the museum library just before it opened at nine. The library closed during lunch hour, so I took a book out to the car, read, ate my lunch, and looked at the reds and oranges on the near shoulder of Blue Mountain itself, once called Mount Emmons. Verplanck Colvin had had twenty acres of timber cleared from its summit in the 1870s so that his survey signals could be seen at a distance. At one I went back to the library and read till it closed at five, then "home" to the cottage where I changed and ran a few miles. After a shower, I made dinner, usually out of a can, on the tiny stove, did the dishes, then read till I turned out the light. No TV or radio diluted this good, round Spartan life, and for about forty-eight hours it was exhilarating. Then I had to break out, which at that time of the year meant getting a served meal at The Lumberjack. To increase the slope of my descent from these dizzying heights, I drove halfway down to Indian Lake for a beer. Forest House is one of the original hostelries in that part of the Adirondacks, and I could sit at the bar, as I did a time or two, alone, with the barkeep's young son riding around the barstools on his scooter, and look out the window for half an hour at Route 28 on the other side of the parking lot or at the trees beyond the highway and feel I was somewhere just off the corner of Fifth Avenue and Forty-second Street. When this illusion passed, I went back to my spare cottage and slept.

The Iron Works' papers are mostly letters to and from the major investors in the company: Archibald McIntyre, New York state comptroller for many years; Judge Duncan McMartin; David Henderson, the financial expert of the group; and Andrew Porteous, the company's agent, who lived at the Works for many years and later served as postmaster at Newcomb. The letters and ledgers tell a great deal about the problems and accomplishments of this venture and about the effects its activities had on the people most deeply involved. And, since Johnson lived on the road to the Works and had various small dealings with it, the papers, as I suspected, make many references to him and provide much new information.

The Iron Works was formed after iron ore was found in October 1826, near the head of Lake Tahawus. An Indian, Lewis Elija, brought a sample of iron to McIntyre and the others involved in the struggling Elba Iron Works, just south of present-day Lake Placid. From there, Elija took these men to the place where he found the ore. In a few years, the company built a village and a furnace, hired the necessary hands, and began producing a high grade of iron. Every problem that came its way, except one, was solved. Despite yearly attempts to repair and improve the Cedar Point road, the construction of another (the Carthage) road between 1841 and 1845, and a scheme to build a railroad out from the Works, no roadway could be built to handle the volume of business necessary to sustain production, or none that would allow the company to charge a competitive price on the market. It was certainly a calamity to the company when David Henderson was accidentally killed by his own pistol in 1845, but it was the company's inability to solve the transportation problem that led to the closing of the Works in 1856. Two years before he died, in June of 1843, David Henderson wrote to Archibald McIntyre, *"I am compelled at length to consider it lost."* The cause? "The want of a good communication out." It took thirteen more years for this view to prevail, but not even a war could reverse it. Five years after it closed, the Civil War began, but the Works stayed closed for good.

The papers of the Adirondac Iron Works, then, early in the life of the company, begin humming a little tune. Let us call it The Road Tune. In time, it rose to a high, keening wail. And all the time, it sang, among a hundred other things, of the fortunes of the millwright who lived on it.

"I got a bill through the Senate last week," wrote Duncan McMartin from Albany to his wife, Margaret, on March 29, 1828, "appointing Commissioners to lay out and open a Road from Lake Champlain Westward through the County of Essex . . . with an appropriation of $6,000." (See map 2) This was a year and a half after

7. Woodcut of the village of Adirondac, from Benson J. Lossing,
The Hudson, from Wilderness to the Sea, in *The Story of Adirondac* by
Arthur H. Masten, p. 144 (Syracuse: Syracuse University Press, 1968),
by permission of the publisher.

the ore had been discovered. On April 21 the state of New York
commissioned John Richards of Caldwell, Iddo Osgood of Keene,
and Nathan Shearman of Moriah to "lay out, open and work a road,
on the most eligible route westward from Cedar Point . . . to the
west bounds of the . . . county."

Thorn Dickinson says in his paper on the Cedar Point road, "It
may be presumed that Israel Johnson and Daniel Newcomb pre-
vailed upon the Commissioners to run the survey past their doors."
This might have been true for Newcomb. David Henderson mentions
Newcomb in the letter in which he describes the ore site to McIntyre
(October 14, 1826). "The nearest house, where one Newcomb lives,
is from six to eight miles distant." It is doubtful, however, that
Johnson was there yet. To persuade the commissioners to do anything, he would have to have settled at Clear Pond in at least 1829,
perhaps even 1828. Redfield's notes of 1836 say that Johnson had
been there "with his family" for four years. Perhaps he arrived ahead
of his family, though that seems unlikely. In a frontier wilderness, all
members of a family were needed to help run a farm or mill. The

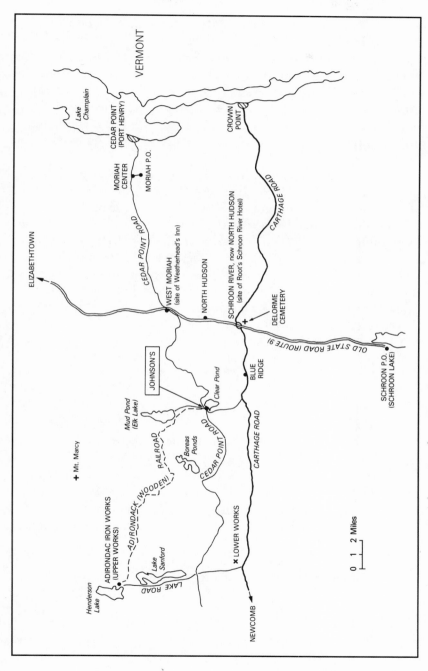

2. Adaptation from David H. Burr's "Map of the County of Essex" (1839).

census says he was in the Town of Moriah, the Clear Pond township, in 1830, but David H. Burr's *An Atlas of the State of New York* (1829), despite great detail in other parts of the state, does not show either Clear Pond or Mud Pond [now Elk Lake] on the map. The 1839 reissue, however, shows both and prints the word "Johnson's" just to the west of Clear Pond where Johnson's Clearing is today. Johnson, I think, was not there in 1829 to talk the commissioners into running the road past his door. We just don't know when he came back from western New York.

The complaints about the road begin in 1832. Duncan McMartin to his wife, May 27, 1832: "I believe he [Archibald McIntyre] did not sleep much the 1st night in the woods at the Chanta 1 mile W of Johnson's Mill (where we waited on return) . . . all our hands are disappointed in the Road, Country and particularly in the looks about the ore bed." A chanta is probably a shanty, the word most likely taken from the French Canadian "chantier," meaning log hut. The thing itself was probably a small, hastily built log cabin with several bunks in it, the kind common in lumber camps, though Theodore R. Davis's 1868 sketch of an Adirondack shanty makes it look like a lean-to. If Johnson's mill was built and working by May 27, it must have been built by at least the previous fall. On June 28, 1832, McMartin again wrote to his wife. "Yesterday I got down to Schroon in search of a Millwright. Staid at Esquire Johnson's." Stayed, in other words, in old Israel's house, he being then seventy-three, across the road from where he is buried in North Hudson. The revelation here is that as early as 1832 the Works wanted to hire its own millwright. Henderson's letter to McIntyre, September 8, 1833, says, in fact, that the village had its own sawmill. Young Israel, then, would not get a very large share, if any at all, of the Works' lumber business. It now seems doubtful if he even planned on it. Johnson's livelihood was not tied—at least directly—to the fate of the Adirondac Iron Works.

Later that year, sometime in November, Archibald McIntyre wrote to Judge McMartin about his trip out from the Works: ". . . very much fatigued when I reached Clear Pond. There we got dinner." David Henderson tells us what sort of dinner, as well as who prepared it, in a letter to McIntyre on November 18. The letter is dated, "Johnson's Clear Pond, Sunday morning 10 o'clock . . . . We

8. Theodore R. Davis's woodcut *The Shanty, Harper's Weekly,*
November 21, 1868.

have just arrived here all well. We started this morning from the
Rock Shanty at 4 o'clock—the moon shone brightly, and the sleigh-
ing proved very good . . . . We will rest here for a couple of hours—
Mrs. Johnson is providing us an excellent breakfast—fresh beef, po-
tatoes & tea, for which we are all prepared." In his diary for this trip,
McIntyre listed his expenses, one of which was "Paid at Johnson's,
Clear Pond $1."

   If the road was a "disappointment" in 1832, the winter of 1832–
33 made it even worse. It was still impassable on April 2. Archibald
McIntyre wrote McMartin that day complaining, "when will that
abominable road be in a condition to let them [a Mr. Baxter and his
family] to go in?" McIntyre repeated the phrase to McMartin in a

letter of June 6th: "The roads are abominable." The road was important enough, though, that the company resolved to keep it open the
next winter. "The road out to Clear-pond is to be kept open all
winter," wrote Henderson to McIntyre on September 14, 1833,
"from there to Moriah, will be open at any rate to draw out Johnson's
lumber." Johnson's principle business would seem to have been to
the east, though as McMartin's letter to McIntyre, October 14, 1833,
shows, the Works was not reluctant to do business with him. "I left
McIntyre [the Works] on Thursday 9 A.M. came that night to
Johnson's the next day here . . . I was forced to come express to obtain
stuff at Clear Pond Thursday I took 8 men and 2 Yoke of oxen along
to mend the road to Clear Pond   set one company at the W. end and
another E. of Boreas directed Yates to be out Friday for a load of
plank—bought of Johnson a pile of 450 bds seasoned at 5 c   100
clapboards at the same   the plk [plank?] had been turned out to
his father & by him to Stevens Foot & Co. & others."

Israel Johnson's general mode of business, then, was to log and
cut lumber on the Clear Pond property, send it by wagon load to his
father in what was then called Schroon River, who sent it (or took it)
to Cedar Point to be sold. Stevens and Foote, according to Clark
Butterfield's account in H. P. Smith's *History of Essex County* (1885),
was one of three stores in Cedar Point when he settled there in 1833,
the population of Cedar Point at the time being one hundred and
fifty.

The letters say nothing about Johnson and the Cedar Point road
for about four years after this. In that time, young Israel's father and
stepmother died, and the Emmons' party made its first attempt to
find the headwaters of the Hudson. This seems as good a time as any
to mention an undated story Henry Dornburgh tells in his book,
Why the Wilderness Is Called Adirondack. Peter Daugherty of the
Town of Minerva worked for a time as a runner or dispatcher for the
Works. One night on his way to Johnson's, he was shadowed by a
panther from the cover of the woods. Every now and then the panther
would screech at him, and not knowing what else to do, Daugherty
screeched back. It seemed to work since he made it to Johnson's
unscratched and spent the night there. "Mr. Johnson had cleared land
and built a sawmill," said Dornburgh, "it being a convenient place
for the company and their men to camp." In one of several trips

through the census reels, I found both Dornburgh and Daugherty living in the Town of Minerva in 1860. Dornburgh was then forty-two, a carpenter, born in New York. Daugherty was thirty-five, a farmer, and like a great many in those days, born in Ireland. The incident with the panther could not have taken place much before 1845. Daugherty was only twenty at the time.

At this point, I cross my path again, come back to its beginning in fact, to the first mention of Johnson I ever saw, to the fourteenth of August, 1836, when W. C. Redfield first stopped at the outlet of Clear Pond and found two sawmills "of peculiar construction" and a man who had been offered three thousand dollars for his improvements. The first "improvement," of course, was the cleared land. Add to that a house or cabin, two sawmills and probably some outbuildings. In addition to land cleared for farming and plenty of logs for milling, a steady trade of overnight travellers passed through. We now know, of course, that it was not two sawmills but two dams where the same saw could be placed and then moved when the slab pile next to it grew too large. It was peculiar in another way, too. Not an old-fashioned gate saw, this was the prototype of the muley saw, lighter and swifter, the patent for which Johnson had been wined and dined out of, just the year before.

Redfield also observed that on the fourteenth the potato tops had been frostbitten the night before. When he came back through on the twenty-third, after they had had to give up the search for the headwaters of the Hudson, his comment was terse. "Cold heavy frost and grass frozen stiff—potatoes killed—oats and Rye not yet ripe." It had been a bad growing season.

To add to the misery, the next year, 1837, a sharp depression crippled the country. Jackson and Nicholas Biddle had wrangled for a year over the Bank of the United States. Biddle wanted private banking interests to continue controlling government finances; Jackson, who won the fight, wanted the people or the government to assume a larger role. David Henderson's letters are informed and vivid on the matter and, as we might expect from a businessman, vigorously opposed to Jackson's policies.

In March 1837, the owners came up with a new scheme for solving their transportation problems. Railroads were beginning to spring up everywhere. The Erie Canal was only twelve years old, but

the new technology was beginning to make the canal obsolete.
People were experimenting, and one of the things they experimented
with was the wooden railroad, that is, the railroad made with wooden
rails. In certain situations it made sense. If you were carrying only
undamagable materials, the iron-smooth ride people preferred was
unnecessary. Also, wood was cheap and plentiful, especially in the
Adirondacks. The owners decided to build such a railroad eastward
toward the lake. It happened in an unusual way. Henderson wrote to
McIntyre on March 8, 1837: "I have always thought that wooden rail
roads in wilderness countries might be used to great advantage, ever
since I heard Johnson talk on the subject—and to say the least of it
he has proved himself a *practical* man."

Three or four years later, after I had put myself in touch with
Warder Cadbury, author of the introduction to the reissue of
"Adirondack" Murray's *Adventures in the Wilderness*, he came across
a letter in a library in Albany, from McIntyre to James Hall, and sent
me a copy of it. It is dated Albany, September 6, 1837.

"After you left us, we sent Yates & Holt to explore for a route for
a road from our works to Clear Pond, and I rejoice, that they have
found a good one. When Henderson and I returned home, we came
out that way, camped out one night with Holt & Cheney, and were
well pleased with the route.

"We have become converts to Johnson's wooden railroad system,
and we have contracted to have one made from our works to the East
River, at once, and propose to continue it to Johnson's, and perhaps
afterwards (in connection with others) to Lake Champlain."

Not only was Johnson the inventor of a particular kind of saw, he
had other good ideas and, in the eyes of those who ran the Adirondac
Iron Works, sound judgment. It wasn't until 1839 that the Adirondack
Railroad was incorporated, with a capital of $100,000, but in certain
crucial respects it was the creation of Israel Johnson. Johnson's role in
this venture is not mentioned by Arthur Masten, but Johnson was so
deeply involved in it that he made a model of the railroad near his
home so others could see how such a thing might work. I discovered
this by accident.

One day it occurred to me that many of the early travellers to the
Adirondacks must have used the Cedar Point road and perhaps even
stayed at Johnson's house. I had read most of them before Johnson

ever entered my mind, but rereading them I found in Charles Fenno Hoffman's *Wild Scenes in the Forest and Prairie* (1839) the anonymous Israel Johnson and his amazing model railroad.

Hoffman was a well-known editor from New York City who set out to climb Mt. Marcy almost as soon as he read Redfield's account of the first ascent. In early September 1837, he travelled up the Cedar Point road from Lake Champlain, and leaving the Schroon River near Weatherhead's inn, plunged into the forest. "Our road," he said, "was the worst I ever saw, except a *turnpike* through the bed of a mountain torrent, which I once travelled in eastern Kentucky. But stony declivities, stumps, quagmires, or fallen trees, had no terror for [the driver of the buckboard] . . . . Such was the road . . . that as it slammed about among trees and logs, the motion of our vehicle was as much lateral as forwards, and we were several hours in making the first eight miles." The Road Tune here turns operatic.

> Accomplishing this stage at last . . . we came to an opening in the forest, where, upon the bank of a lake, in the midst of a clearing of about a hundred acres, stood the log-cabin of a settler, at which we stopped to dine. The lake, or pond, as the people call it, was a limpid pool upon the top of a mountain, or rather an immense globular hill, flattened at the top like an old-fashioned goblet, and surrounded with mountain peaks and from which it stood wholly isolated. Upon the outlet of this lake was a sawmill and here we saw a model of a wooden railroad, contrived by a forester who has never seen a specimen of either [either wooden or iron railroad, I suppose], but whose ingenuity has found a field for its exercise, even in the depths of the woods.

Johnson's name is never mentioned, but this was his place and ingenuity was his most evident quality. If this isn't convincing, Henry Dornburgh says flatly, "The road was projected by Israel Johnson and they intended to build it to the state road [Route 9] leading from Glens Falls to Elizabethtown." Burr's 1839 atlas showed the railroad completed from the Works east to Clear Pond, but in fact only three miles of it were ever built. It was then abandoned. Like the sawmill patent he was persuaded to let go of, the Adirondack Railroad project came to nothing for Johnson, as it did, of course, for the Works.

One note to Hoffman's description: he is the first to tell us how large a clearing Johnson had made. Today, Johnson's Clearing couldn't be more than an acre or two.

In August 1837, when Redfield wrote his articles for the *New York Journal of Commerce* describing the climb of Mt. Marcy, he had much less to say about Johnson. But, when he said that "the road on which we travelled is much used for the transportation of sawed pine lumber from the interior," he was essentially describing the nature of Johnson's business. Johnson was the only person living on the road between the Works and Weatherhead's. "Much used" suggests he did a brisk business. That business was specifically in "sawed pine lumber," and it was all sent "from the interior" toward the settlements along Lake Champlain, not toward the Works. The other pertinent fact in Redfield's article was that "in the large township of Moriah, as we were informed, [were] more than sixty saw mills." With so much competition, it is little wonder that in the 1850 census Johnson should have called himself a farmer. Though it may not have been the competition that forced Johnson out of lumbering. Hotchkiss reported that in 1855 in the Schroon River area material for flooring and siding had to be purchased as much as fifty miles away, "so little pine timber could now be found in a neighborhood prolific with excellent pine timber but a comparatively few years before."

Starting in 1839 and continuing for about five years, the Iron Works' papers are fuller and more detailed than usual, owing, I think, to increasing anxiety among the original investors. By 1839 they had been in business for over ten years and still not begun making money. Detail amplifies, too, because in these years the company had hired Andrew Porteous as its agent at the site. Porteous was hard-working and scrupulous, more so than most of the people he was forced to deal with, and he kept in close contact with the men who hired him. The road was only one of many things to oversee at the Works. The farm, company housing, the smelting furnace, charcoal pits, the sawmill, and the mining itself all had to run smoothly and economically. He had to handle labor disputes and occasionally contract with local residents—among them Israel Johnson—for specific jobs.

On the twelfth of June, 1839, McIntyre wrote to Porteous, this time with news about the newly incorporated wooden railroad.

"Since leaving you, Mr. Henderson and I have agreed to employ Mr. Harris to survey the Rail Road from the Works to Johnson's, and he accordingly returns immediately to perform that service." Mr. Harris went right to work because on July 3 Henderson wrote Porteous, "I suppose Harris is still on the Survey between the East River and Johnson's."

Plans for building the railroad were in motion by that September because Henderson wrote Porteous on the fourteenth that "As there is some doubt whether Mr. Holt can get the number of hands wanted for the road making, W. Root says that he would have no objection to repair by contract the road between Johnson's & the Boreas River." Terms were not reached with Root, however. McIntyre wrote to Porteous on the twenty-seventh: "I regret that Root did not go in and contract on reasonable terms to repair the road from Johnson's to the Boreas."

In the same letter a new confusion arises, concerning roads in the area. McIntyre wanted to send in some dressed hogs for the employees' Christmas dinner in 1839. There seems to have been a choice of local contractors to haul them in, and that choice implied, as well, a choice of roads. "If the road from Johnson's to Weatherhead's direct [the Cedar Point road] will be the one you will use next winter [a phrase that implies a choice of roads], I will of course send to Weatherhead's, unless indeed, you should contract with Root, in which case I would send the pork to him." Weatherhead's, as we know, was at or near the intersection of the Cedar Point road and the old state road (now Route 9) [see map]. If Root is the man who started Root's Tavern, his establishment was about four miles south in what was then known as Schroon River near the junction of the old state road and the road that now goes west to Newcomb and Long Lake. The latter road goes through Blue Ridge, and just beyond Blue Ridge lies the current road north to Clear Pond. At Clear Pond, this north-south road crosses the path of the Cedar Point road, now lost and buried in the woods.

Here, at last, is my question: Is it possible that by 1839 a road had been developed by settlement west from Root's along the Branch—that part of the Schroon River itself west of Root's—toward Blue Ridge and from there north to Johnson's and the Cedar Point road? If so, there would have been, for a space of six or seven

miles, from the old state road to Johnson's, a choice of roads, one used
by Weatherhead, the other by Root. It was that part of the Cedar
Point road, from Weatherhead's to Johnson's, that had given the
company their greatest miseries. They would have cheered at a choice
of roads, which I think is precisely what McIntyre did when he wrote
Porteous on October 12. "I am pleased that you have contracted with
Root to haul in your provisions, etc., next winter—it will relieve you
from some trouble. I hope you have also before now agreed with him
for repairing the road from Johnson's to the Boreas [i.e., west toward
the Works]. If you have not, and cannot, the road will not be repaired
this season I fear." McIntyre no longer needed to worry about the
road between Johnson's and Weatherhead's because, if my guess is
right, Root was using a different road, made by settlement and
clearing, to get to Johnson's. Further, I think this is how the Carthage
road, or a part of it, was started, the first state appropriation for
which would be made two years later in 1841. Luckily for Johnson,
the main road to the Works still went past his door, but in a few
years, say by 1845, the Carthage road would be complete and the
main thoroughfare between the old state road and the Works would
be three miles to the south of Clear Pond, where the road from North
Hudson to Newcomb is now. To add to his worries, Johnson would
find himself increasingly cut off from those around him. Imagine
running a truck stop on Route 36 in eastern Colorado and then
having Interstate 80 put in five miles to the north.

I'm not sure what this new information implies about Johnson
other than a willingness, which may have been a need, to do other
work than lumbering. It was only eleven years later that Johnson

Root, it appears, was not the only person who sought to contract
with the Works on "unreasonable terms." The taint of unreasonable-
ness even reached Johnson. "It appears to me," wrote McIntyre to
Porteous on October 30, 1839, "that the price now demanded by
Johnson for Coaling ought not to be given." Coaling is the making of
charcoal from wood, and in those days involved digging pits and
tending hot, smoky fires for hours on end. It was a messy business.
When Thomas Wentworth Higginson came in from Lake Champlain
in 1859 to visit John Brown's widow, he remarked that every other
face was blackened from work in the iron mines while the rest were
blackened from work in the charcoal pits.

described himself to the census taker as a farmer, and this may be a sign of the shift.

Johnson drove a hard bargain, though. The Works met his price for coaling. McIntyre to Porteous, November 27: "As you say (I make no doubt) it will be cheaper to pay Mr. Johnson $4 than to pay nominally less to others who would run in our debt. The price is high, and yet we must submit to it for the present, at any rate—and I am upon the whole pleased that you retain Mr. Johnson . . . . There is no doubt some truth in what Johnson says about the timber in a dense, damp, original forest, not producing as much coal as in many other situations, and something too may be owing to the ground for covering. But I cannot believe the difference is half what he makes it." McIntyre, accordingly, urged Porteous to look for another collier.

An undated letter from Porteous to McIntyre, probably written in the winter of 1839–1840, partly concerns plans for building the wooden railroad. More important, it reveals a little of the tension at the Works between employer and employee, tension which Johnson could not avoid. "Regarding the Causeway Mr. Holt thought he could make it through to the River [probably the East River] in a State fit to receive Rails but in doing that it would take him and nine hands all the Season. He thought he might be able to do a little towards fixing part of the road to Johnsons, we have bein at work makeing the bridge across the marsh and have got it nearly across." McIntyre's letter of January 22, 1840, seems to be an answer to this one. He begins by quoting a letter Henderson had recently written to him: "The common corduroy roads where the sticks are placed in a slovenly manner on the soil merely to keep horses and wagons from sinking into it [are] . . . worse than the very worst by-roads in Great Britain." Henderson has had enough of the Cedar Point road and all roads like it. He is anxious for the railroad to be finished. However, he does not feel that Holt—and he later identifies him as the famous guide, Harvey—is the man to build the causeway. He calls Holt "A most slovenly workman," whose crew will simply be his friends from Keene from whom he will get little work. When McIntyre finally stops quoting Henderson's letter, he tells Porteous to decide for himself whether Holt or someone else would be better suited for the job. Later, though, McIntyre advised against hiring Holt. It is perhaps too bad we don't have Harvey Holt's view of this matter.

In the middle of the summer, relations between Johnson and the Works, or perhaps only those between Johnson and Porteous, came to a head. McIntyre wrote to Porteous on July 28, 1840:

> I was not at all disappointed to learn of the elopement of the Villain Wooden; but if your ideas of Johnson should prove correct, I must confess that I shall be sadly disappointed. But I shall entertain better hopes of Johnson until compelled to think otherwise by some positive unjust act on his part. You, of course, are in possession of facts and circumstances with which I am unacquainted—and the idea you have formed of the man may be correct, altho' I hope you may be mistaken. Is he bound to deliver Coal at the Coal House or at the Pit? If at the Pit, and so is my recollection of the matter, it appears to me there is no reason why he should not drive the Oxen out—for his work for the oxen will be done when his Pits are fit. You have been so annoyed with rogues that I am not surprised that you should become somewhat suspicious of any one you have to deal with. But let me beg of you not to suspect without cause, nor to believe all that Tale Bearers say. Some may have construed wrongly the expressions of Mr. Johnson or even added to his words.

This letter suggests that there was some sort of difference between Johnson and Porteous, perhaps aggravated by pressures on the company to find cheaper labor and materials.

The next day Porteous wrote to McIntyre about this whole business. The letter reads so much like the letter McIntyre was responding to above that I wonder if it wasn't misdated.

> I do not know what to think of Johnson he has been saying to some of them that he will go away this fall from this place, and wont be back in the country again he has formerly bein a Sailor and intends following it again, I am beginning to fear his honesty for two reasons he is beginning to be discontented, and thinks he has little chance of making much and dont care wethere he continues ore not he also Talkes of Driving the ore team out as soon as he has done setting the wood which will be before any Coal is delivered, if he does try ore if he is allowed to send out the team it will then be a bad debt, and if prevented from sending out the team it will then be the ground of dispute which he will quit the job on, and either

way seams to me intended for a cheat, as if he gets the oxen sold I
believe he will then give it up and what will there be left to lay
hold on There will be nothing . . . You will be surprised at what I
say about Johnson I hope it will not turn out so bad as I dread.

McIntyre and the other gentlemen in the business had a high opinion
of Johnson, and Porteous knew it. Johnson knew it, too, I imagine,
and he may not have been afraid to trade on it a little. He made
Porteous squirm a bit. He didn't like the man for some reason,
officiousness perhaps. And that story of returning to the sea, at age
fifty-five? Probably invented to keep Porteous off balance. Porteous
would complain to McIntyre, Johnson knew that. And he guessed
that McIntyre would tell Porteous to pay him what he wanted.

Still, 125 years later, Porteous would have the last word. "The
difficulty with him, Seams to be his hired help taking more to keep
his house etc. then he expected, I thought he had a great Chance to
do well." Indeed, Johnson seems to have had opportunities, a lively
practical imagination, numerous skills, even influential contacts, but
the evidence is beginning to explain something we already know,
that he did not come into either wealth or prominence. His lumber
business was flagging. Perhaps he had logged all the land he had
access to. He had turned toward the Adirondac Iron Works for odd
jobs to supplement his income and there he seems not to have gotten
along with the company's agent. Even one of his admirers, Archibald
McIntyre, thought he asked too high a price for coaling. Many factors
would have affected the fortunes of someone like Israel Johnson, and
we see only a few of them. Even so, Johnson wanted more from life
than he got, and it was in these years, the late 1830s and early 1840s,
that the strains of aspiration began to show.

The road problems continued. The railroad was only begun in
1840, so the Works continued to rely on the existing corduroy roads.
By December of 1840, the stretch of the Cedar Point road between
Johnson's and Weatherhead's had been all but abandoned. McIntyre
wrote Porteous the day before Christmas, "I regret that they [the
Town of Moriah, most likely] did not make or repair the road from
Weatherhead's to Johnsons—but I apprehended that their promises
would end as they have done . . . Whatever I may send on this winter
shall be sent to Root's house, as you advise." Thorn Dickinson, in

fact, conjectured that "most of the road through the mountain country between Weatherheads and the Hudson River [which is several miles west of Clear Pond] appears to have become impassable prior to 1841, when the Legislature provided for a new highway from Carthage . . . to Lake Champlain."

Winslow C. Watson, the early historian of Essex County, says that the Carthage road was built under acts of 1841 and 1844 but was only "gradually built by an application of specific road taxes." Which sections were built first is not clear, but on April 10, 1841, McIntyre wrote to Porteous,

> It seems you are completely blocked up yet with snow, and that there is no getting as far as Johnson's except on snow shoes . . . There is a bill which has passed the Senate, and is now in the house of Assembly, for making a road from Carthage in Jefferson County to Long Lake, and thence to Lake Champlain in Moriah or Crown Point. It has been said that a route can be had from the head of Lake Sanford, or near our Works to the bridge over Lake Delia. If that be the case, we know that the route Eastwardly from our works is the best, and we ought therefore to take measures to have this route adopted in place of the one now used a mile below the outlet of Lake Sanford. I wish you would speak to Cheney about this, and request him to examine and look for such a route, so as to be able to point it out to the Commrs. when they shall lay out the road.

One runs the risk at this point of getting lost in a maze of roads. So many people have complained about the Cedar Point road, which in 1841 is barely more than ten years old, that various alternatives have been proposed and tried. I have already suggested that a road of sorts was made by gradual settlement along The Branch. Traffic from Lake Champlain at this time seems to have come in from Cedar Point on the original road until it reached the old state road (Route 9). Then, instead of continuing west to Johnson's, it turned south until it came to Root's Tavern where an uncommissioned road went west along The Branch. This uncommissioned road would almost certainly have turned north or northwest near Blue Ridge toward Clear Pond. If it hadn't, Johnson would have had no way out except along the now abandoned piece of the Cedar Point road between his cabin and Weatherhead's Inn.

One last item for 1841. McIntyre to Porteous, June 19: "I advised old Mr. Johnson to be employed to put up the Brick Machine. When I so wrote, it had escaped me that Mr. Durand was still at the place, or I would not have done so—for he could have done the business well enough." Johnson, now thought old, tried his hand at many things, among them making bricks. There are no items for 1842 in the Iron Works' papers, the year Johnson later (1855) told the New York census-taker that he had moved into the Town of Schroon.

Altogether the Iron Works's papers suggest that everything was not going well for Johnson. He was not able to rely on his lumber business alone to support himself. He took an assortment of odd jobs at the Works—clearing land, coaling, carpentry—but does not seem to have done as well there as he might have because of Porteous's suspicions of him. It is Porteous's comments, in fact, that most stick in the mind. "I thought he had a great Chance to do well." "He is beginning to be discontented." Add to this Henderson's comment to McIntyre, January 3, 1843: "The year 1842 has perhaps been one of the gloomiest, so far as business and pecuniary matters are concerned that has occurred in this country for a quarter of a century." Six months later, Henderson would finally confess to McIntyre, "I am compelled at length to consider it lost." The Iron Works itself was teetering in 1842, and tremors of that must have been felt in the community of dependents that had grown up around it. Perhaps Johnson did move away in 1842. It was a difficult and transitional time for him and the Works.

Henderson visited the Works in June 1843 but found the roads in their usual state. He wrote to McIntyre on June 18, warning him not to come up. "Robertson & I with a buckboard started off to Johnson's at 4 P.M.—John Cheney being with us.—Robertson took to bed on our arrival at Johnsons [was Johnson still there in June 1843?], having a very bad head ache and being all out of sorts.—It poured down all day on Friday at Johnsons so we could not start—as we were so much under the weather in the way of health.—We left Johnsons (yesterday) Saturday morning at 1/2 past 5 and got to the land at 1/4 past 1 o'clock—but I never saw the road so wet and miry. . . . You talked something of coming in here when we were in Albany, but much as I would like to see you here, it would <u>not be at all prudent</u> for you to come, for the roads are in a very bad state indeed." This, remember, was a new road.

Six days later, Henderson decided that the entire venture had failed. He wrote his gloomy conclusions to McIntyre on the twenty-fourth. "My only hope has been, that if two fires could be <u>profitably</u> carried on here, to assist in keeping the place alive, and sending the iron out by sleighing, and getting a character for its quality in the market—that then the place would have a chance of being taken notice of by capitalists. The Want of a good communication out, however, is against this." Despite his final thought ("<u>I am compelled at length to consider it lost</u>"), Henderson stayed with the company until his accidental death two years later. There is no mistaking his mood, however; and there is no mistaking his explanation for the company's failure. Bad roads. By this time, the wooden railroad had come to nothing, abandoned after three miles.

Considering Henderson's gloom, McIntyre had all the more reason for going up to the Works to look things over, as he did at the end of September, when the roads were dry and the air crisp. He seems to have written no letters on this trip, though he did keep a journal. It is called "Journey to Adirondack commenced Sept. 20, 1843." Two entries are of interest. "Fri. 22. A fine morning and therefore we started for Adirondack [from Root's] at 7 O'clock, where we arrived at 7 P.M." The second is the entry for October 4th: "Altho it rained this morning and threatened to be a rainy day we left for home at 1/4 before 8 O'clock, and we reached Root's at 1/2 past 7 P.M." McIntyre's journey from Root's followed the Carthage road to the Clear Pond road, took that north to Johnson's where it joined the piece of the Cedar Point road that went west to the Works. The return journey was the same in reverse. Neither going in nor coming out did he mention Johnson.

In various small ways, the Iron Works' correspondence has suggested that Johnson and McIntyre had more than a business relationship. Henderson admired his ingenuity and his practicality. McIntyre seems almost to have been fond of him. So, the silence was puzzling. Perhaps Johnson had moved from Clear Pond in 1842, and McIntyre drove past an abandoned mill and farm. These conjectures were abruptly stopped, however, by a last-minute discovery.

My week at the Adirondack Museum was coming to an end. I did not have time to read all the Iron Works' papers, so as the week wore on, I began selecting things on the basis of catalogue descriptions. As time was running out on Friday afternoon, very close to five o'clock, I opened one more folder and found this letter from McIntyre to Porteous, dated November 17, 1843, one month after McIntyre's trip to the Works. "Johnson sent some money by me on my return from Adirondack to pay to Gerrit Smith on his farm. I sent it to Smith, who sent me a contract in duplicate to Johnson, which I enclosed on the 24th October to Johnson, and requested him to sign and send me one of the copies of the contract—which he neglects to do. I wish you would send word by someone to Johnson, not to neglect any longer to write me and return the contract. Smith deserves more attention. He has behaved very liberally to Johnson."

McIntyre had not only stopped at Johnson's, but he was also made an intermediary in a land agreement between Johnson and a man who turned out to be the famous abolitionist, philanthropist, and land reformer, Gerrit Smith. Smith was to become a confidential friend of John Brown's. He sold Brown the land on which he is buried. Smith owned hundreds of thousands of acres in New York state and gave much of it away to the needy, including runaway slaves. It was now clear that he and Johnson had dealings with one another. If a contract between the two could be found, many questions would be answered, specifically, what land Johnson was on and how long he was on it. Perhaps, too, I might find out why Johnson's name never appeared on the Essex County Grantor's list.

The story pieced together out of the Adirondac Iron Works' papers is both Johnson's story and the story of the Works. Both are sketchy, admittedly, but clear as well. In some sense, sketchier yet, the Iron Works' papers tell the story of this entire region's one chance to enter the mainstream of American culture. In the 1830s, those who thought about these things were confident that within a few years northern New York, like most of the rest of the country, would be logged clear and covered with productive farms, canals, railroads,

NIPPLE TOP.   DIX'S PEAK.   McCOMBE'S MOUNTAIN.

9. R. C. Taylor's 1842 woodcut *View from Clear Pond,*
from Ebenezer Emmons, *Geology of New York,* Part II
(Albany, 1842), p. 27.

factories, and cities. Nowhere is that vision more clearly stated than
in Ebenezer Emmons's reports to the Assembly of New York on the
survey he was conducting for the Second Geological District.

In the third annual report, dated February 1, 1839, Emmons
said, "The location . . . of the Adirondack [*sic*] iron works in the heart
of this district, is a matter of great interest to the public, forming the
nucleus of a great establishment, which will in a few years change the
entire character of this region." "On a partial view of this subject," he
says in his fourth report, "it might appear that a distance of 40 or 50
miles from water-carriage to the great markets, would be an important objection to an establishment which involves in its very nature
the transportation of heavy articles. When we further consider,
however, that such are the improvements in the construction of
railroads and canals, and that scarcely any part of the country is

inaccessible by the one or the other of these modes, the objection vanishes: and the only inquiry remaining is, whether the vicinity of the proposed establishment abounds in the necessary articles required for its successful operation." To Emmons, of course, it did. With the transportation problem hypothetically solved, the ore lying open to the air (hence no need of costly and dangerous underground mining), limitless water power, and "an unbroken forest" to provide charcoal for smelting, Pittsburgh seemed just around the corner. "It would be easy to demonstrate," he said, that the great vein of ore above Lake Sanford "cannot be exhausted for centuries." To be sure, Emmons felt that the region would "undoubtedly in a few years become a favorite place of resort to persons of leisure," and he hoped, too, "that the policy will no longer prevail of converting, indiscriminately, products of the vegetable kingdom, so slow of growth, into ready cash, by the unsparing axe of the husbandman." Still, it was a vision of what his (and our) age called progress that he had in mind for the area.

Emmons spent a number of years on his survey and often travelled past Israel Johnson's door. He probably spent several nights in his house. The reports contain a number of incidental references to Johnson or to Johnson's. For instance, it was Johnson who told Emmons about snow on Mt. Marcy in the summer of 1837 ("large banks of snow remain on Mt. Marcy until the middle of July, or until the 17th, as was observed by Mr. Johnson at Clear Pond, this last year.") But no detail is more interesting than the sketch, "View from Clear Pond," made by R. C. Taylor and printed in *Geology of New York, Part II* (1842). Neither Johnson's mill nor his house are shown, but the labors of his "unsparing axe" are quite visible. Of course, it has all grown back now.

6

I Find a Footprint

S pending a week in a library is a bit like spending time at the bottom of a well. As elated as I was at my discoveries, I was glad the week was over. A mass of undigested notes, copied quickly in pencil, filled my notebook, but before I could think of looking through them and figuring out what they meant, I needed air.

I drove from Blue Mountain Lake up to Keene Valley and asked my landlady of the previous year, Emily Neville, if she would let me stay in the big house in the meadow again, this time for ten days. She agreed. In ten days I would get the chance to do some snooping in Elizabethtown, revisit Clear Pond, and maybe climb a mountain. It turned out to be two mountains: Noonmark, the mountain framed in the south window of the big house, and Algonquin, the second highest mountain in the state, once called MacIntyre in misspelled memory of Archibald McIntyre. The climb up Algonquin actually turned into a long, hectic scramble in some impressively bad weather over that mountain plus three others clustered close to it: Wright, Boundary, and Iroquois. I did not get out of the woods until two hours after dark.

After several days of walking and climbing, I spent the last bit of time I had in Keene Valley going over my notes on Johnson. Taken together, all of the references to him in the Iron Works' correspondence gave me the sense of a hard-working but luckless man who turned to various kinds of odd jobs to supplement his income. For a time this was in milling boards, but later it seems to have been farming. All this time I had presumed that Johnson switched from milling to farming because his milling business failed, but that may not have been so. His father had sold his mill in 1816, nineteen years before he died, and Johnson's plan from the start may have been to clear land first for the lumber and then to farm it. The only way to mill all your life was to speculate in land, and that Johnson seems not to have had the wherewithall, or perhaps the urge, to do. He may have wanted to farm all along. The arguments against this are that he was a skillful and inventive millwright and, at the end of his life, when he was obviously no longer a millwright, he told the census-taker he was.

Even if Johnson intended to be a farmer, his life was not easy. He seems to have been disappointed, as Porteous said. Odd-jobbing need not be the sign of his frustration. Everyone who lived in the Adirondacks worked at a variety of things, forced to do so, really, by the severe weather. If you were a logger, you cut in the winter and drove in the spring. That left the summer and fall for hunting and guiding or perhaps a bit of farming. If you were a farmer, the growing season was so short that the yield would barely sustain your family without hunting, logging, or guiding on the side. In 1859 Higginson found John Brown's family so poor that they had no money; they made or grew everything they needed. I should imagine that few householders did just one thing.

I suspect the distrust that grew up in Porteous's mind about Johnson was not connected to the decline in Johnson's prospects. Porteous, after all, was a boss, a man with large revenues at his disposal, charged to go out among the local populace and hire people for as small a wage as conditions would allow. The people of Schroon and Minerva and Keene Flats were smart enough to see that the Iron Works was at a disadvantage in hiring. Few people were willing to work in a wilderness where the winters were long and cold. The labor pool was small, and naturally people held out for higher wages than the Works hoped to pay. From the beginning McIntyre and the others had had a labor problem, and it led, as we've seen, to a number of exasperated and disgruntled remarks from nearly everyone involved. Wooden, whoever he was, may have been a "villain." Harvey Holt may have been a "slovenly" workman. And Israel Johnson may have tried to cheat on his coaling contract. But we hear only one side of the issue, and I think it is a side predisposed to find fault with people who did not leap at the prospect of working for the Adirondac Iron Works on the company's terms.

The day came when I had to leave the Adirondacks. The quickest way home to Indiana is down the Northway to Albany, west on the New York Thruway to the Pennsylvania line, past Erie, toward Cleveland, south to Columbus, and west to the Indiana line, a route that must be very close to the one taken by Israel Johnson's brothers and sister when they went west looking for fresh prospects right after the War of 1812. I stopped at the DeLorme Cemetery in North Hudson to look at the graves again, then went across the road and wandered around in the woods, trying to imagine exactly where "old" Israel's house and sawmill might have been. Each little flattened space in the trees seemed plausible.

The New York Thruway runs right past Batavia, and Batavia has been, almost since the beginning, the county seat of Genesee County. I had not done a small errand there the year before. I can't remember why, some blindness to be home, I suppose, some stupor of the highway. This time, though, I made sure I would need gas out in western New York.

Batavia is like a great many towns and cities through central New York, only smaller. It is less populous and less prosperous than it used to be. Houses that were once large and fashionable are now only large. It is a constant challenge to the current owners to keep them in fresh paint, decent repair, and heat. Many are now subdivided. A surprising number have woodstove pipes sprouting through the roof, a stack of wood on the front porch, or sheddy additions to the original structure. Cars are sometimes parked on the lawn, not old cars particularly, but run-down cars. American cars that few people want anymore because they use too much gas and that, because of this failing, rarely seem to be washed.

At the county clerk's office, it took no more than five minutes to find out that no one named Israel Johnson had ever been grantee or grantor to a deed of land and either a mortgagee or a mortgagor. I put my customary question to the man behind the counter, and he told me that at one time in the early 1800s a company called the Holland Land Company had owned nearly all of Genesee County. This was a land-speculating company. Young Israel most likely saw their bill or heard it read from a pulpit and decided to come west. But, as in Essex County, he owned no land.

I asked, too, about the Town of Alexander, because the 1820 census had said Johnson lived there. The man said it was just a few

miles south of Batavia. He gave me a list of all the town clerks and
town historians in the county, with names and addresses. The
Alexander town historian was named Lucy Gilhooly.

Alexander is a small village (founded 1802), really no more than
an extended crossroads. The country between it and Batavia is farm-
land, and I should guess most of the people, one way and another,
still farm. It is just off Route 20, which used to be the main road
between Buffalo and Albany but now seems like a picturesque back
road.

Lucy Gilhooly lives in an old farmhouse. About three miles out
of town, it stands well back off the road called Gilhooly Road, in fact.
A barn and one or two outbuildings stand near it. No one has farmed
the property in years. The man who greeted me was tall, perhaps in
his sixties, pleasant and courteous. He showed me into the living
room, asked me to sit down, and then went through a door into a
darkened room. He spoke in low tones to someone, and then came
back and said she'd be right out.

I couldn't get a very good sense of the layout of the room, there
were so much old furniture, stacked magazine, and cardboard box
about. It was a cross between a house, a warehouse, and a museum.
The man disappeared, not into a room, but behind a partition. Lucy,
in the meantime, rattled around in a room that must have been her
bedroom. I had wakened her from a nap, so I was preparing my best
speeches of apology when out she hopped, bright and cheerful, on
one leg. She, too, seemed to be in her sixties and though somewhat
disheveled from sleep was instantly interested in Israel Johnson and
was handing me faster than I could look at them old atlases and odd
compilations of data, asking me if I couldn't find Johnson's name in
them. I didn't, of course, but not wishing to appear ungrateful, I
managed to look hopefully through the index of an old school
encyclopedia for a minute or two. Slowly, though, we slid around and
faced one another and talked about what she really knew, which was
a lot, and what we both knew interested us; namely, what the old
people did and where they came from.

Her grandfather, Michael, came over from Ireland during the
potato famine. A large, framed picture of him sat on the couch. Her
father was born in 1867, and his name was Gilhooly, as well. I assume
that meant she was unmarried, and the man behind the partition—
who went out after twenty minutes or so —was probably her brother.

Here they were, the last of the Gilhoolys, living in the old Gilhooly farmhouse, on Gilhooly Road. She told us the story of her recent accident, how she'd been walking across a rotted catwalk that gave way. The injury was so severe or the doctoring so bungled that they'd had to amputate. She was learning a whole new way of life on crutches.

She had been a schoolteacher, and if I'm any judge of these things, a good one. Since taking on the job of town historian, she'd written some pamphlets and flyers on old buildings in the area and odd bits of local history. One of the pamphlets she gave me included a sort of historical credo, which began, "We believe Alexander . . . ," and then listed forty or fifty of the most random facts ever assembled. Such as: "To have mail service by pony express in 1826," or "To have an Opera House [where Jenny Lind once sang]," or "To have Wild Lady Slippers," or "To have received a telegram from P. T. Barnum in 1850." Other phenomenal facts included the town's having had at one time two railroad stations, "a woman high school principal," and having been "smart enough to save its beautiful little town from a state highway." I guess I do know why, but it sounds better to say, I don't know why we all aren't living in Alexanders and being taught by Lucy Gilhoolys.

She had me sign her book, a big bound ledger, and said if she ever came across this Israel Johnson, she'd write. She said I should go over and look at the free cemetery. I didn't know what a free cemetery was, so she told me: a piece of land donated (and here she gave me a name and a date) so the poor could have a place to be buried. The date was too recent, so I knew there was no need to go over there. But, my mind went back to the DeLorme Cemetery, with its obvious opulence on one side and poverty on the other. Of course, it would take money to be buried in a cemetery, and a headstone would add to the expense. I now knew that young Israel was not well off at the end of his life. Somehow I felt sure, when Lucy Gilhooly told me about the free cemetery in Alexander, that I would never find the grave of Israel Johnson, Jr.

I did a little more than say hello and good-bye to Lucy Gilhooly, with a few thousand words in between. I never will see her again, and I knew that when I sat in that great, cluttered farmhouse of hers, looking for Johnson's name—not pretending, but really looking for it—in a hundred-year-old, one-volume world encyclopedia. But we were interested in the same things, even though they weren't exactly the things I came looking for. I hardly know what they were, in fact. Maybe the prevention of the passing of the past, the slowing down of time. Maybe just good conversation. Her leg was beginning to bother her, so I tore myself away and drove off toward Pennsylvania, Indiana, Israel Johnson, and home.

Three miles south of Alexander, I passed through a little place called Attica. Why do I know that name, I said. I discovered why, south of the village, when we passed a huge penal institution almost hidden in the trees off to the left. The pictures of the rioting prisoners, masked, draped in blankets, pleading for decent treatment, are still vivid in my mind. What year was that?

*

Back in Bloomington, at the first opportunity, I went to the library to look up Gerrit Smith. Octavious Brooks Frothingham published the first biography of him in 1877. The only other one was by Ralph Volney Harlow, published in 1939. Harlow's had fuller notes and other scholarly apparatus, so I learned from it that the Syracuse University library had the major collection of Smith's papers. I wrote them, describing the reference I had in Archibald McIntyre's letter and then went on to say, "What I am hoping to locate among the Smith papers is some record of a contract he had with Israel Johnson (b. 1785 or 86, d. after 1855), which would tell me where the land was, how extensive it was, and so forth. Of course, I would be interested in any and all references to Johnson in the Smith papers, though I don't expect there to be very many."

Two weeks later a letter came from the George Arents Research Library at Syracuse University, and through the generosity of Mr. Edward Lyon, I made my biggest discovery to date. "It is a pleasure to tell you," he wrote, "that the Gerrit Smith Papers contain material relating to Israel Johnson." There were no letters by Johnson, but there were five letters between McIntyre and Smith that mentioned him, plus an "agreement" between Smith and Johnson, dated April 1, 1843.

Nearly three weeks went by before the xeroxes arrived, and when they did I went straight to the agreement. These papers would be filled with interesting new information, but nothing would equal the sight—even on a xerox copy—of Israel Johnson's signature. I joined

10. Land contract between Gerrit Smith and Israel Johnson of Clear Pond. Courtesy of Syracuse University Library.

the long list of people who have felt like Robinson Crusoe when he discovered there was other life on his desert island.

Because Smith did so much land business, the contract is a printed form filled in with specific details of this agreement. "It is agreed between Gerrit Smith [even Smith's name is printed] of Peterboro, Madison County, and Israel Johnson as follows. Dated April 1, 1843." Archibald McIntyre's letter to Porteous concerning this contract was written November 17, so Johnson had been dragging his feet for nearly eight months.

> The said Smith covenants to convey by Warantee [*sic*] Deed to the aforesaid Johnson provided he shall pay as below, the following described land, viz: Subdivisions One & Three of Lot Twelve in Township 44 Totten & Crossfield." The agreement goes on to say that Johnson binds himself to pay four hundred dollars for it, "in the following, viz: The sum of fifty dollars he pays in hand. The balance, viz: $350 he hereby covenants to pay in ten equal payments computing from this day together with the interest to be paid annually on the 1st April computing from this day upon the whole amount remaining unpaid from year to year, and also pay all taxes and assessments upon said premises subsequent to Oct. 1st, 1831 viz. the date of his former & now canceled contract.

Johnson, then, had had an earlier contract. We knew he had been on this land—land we can now identify exactly—since the late twenties or early thirties. It now appears that his original purchase (though perhaps it was only a "prior" agreement) was October 1, 1831.

The first letter, from McIntyre to Smith, October 10, 1843, makes Johnson's plight fairly vivid.

> On my return from a visit to Essex County [which must be the one referred to in the journal, "Journey to Adirondack"] I called on poor old Israel Johnson, who purchased a lot of land from you or your father, and on which he resides. [N.B. His statement to the New York census taker in 1855 that he had been in the Town of Schroon for thirteen years appears to be wrong. He was still at Clear Pond in October of 1843.] He handed me $32, which is all that the poor man could just now scrape together to pay you on account of the first payment of $50 which you required to be paid by the 1st of November. This sum I have deposited to your credit

in the N.Y. State Bank, and I enclose a certificate of deposit. [I assume this $50 is the amount Johnson should have paid at the time of the agreement, April 1. He or someone else seems to have persuaded Smith to wait until November 1 for it.]

Besides the money Mr. J. also handed me two letters from you, one of which was addressed the 23d March last to Joseph Frost, Esq. and the other, dated 19th April 1843, to Mr. J. himself. [I wrote Edward Lyon right away to see if these two letters were among the Smith papers. He wrote back saying no, but he sent copies of some account sheets he had found since first writing.] He expressed a warm and sincere gratitude for your kindness to him and for the liberal terms of payment you granted him, and also his great regret that he had it not in his power to remit you the entire $50 required by the 1st of November. But he had no more now, and he was afraid, because of his necessities, that he could not pay any more before next Spring. If you will favor him until then he will be enabled from the sale of lumber to pay at least the balance of the $50 or first payment. [Johnson, then, was still selling lumber in 1843.]

Allow me to plead for this poor old Pioneer [an acknowledgment, if we needed it, that he was the first settler on his land]. He has suffered immense hardships and privations hitherto, but has now so much land handsomely cleared as will enable him and family to live in comparative comfort; and his Sawmill will enable him to pay you for the farm. I sincerely believe that he will hereafter be able to pay up the installments as required.

I perceive by your letter to Mr. Frost, you say, that upon Mr. Johnson's paying the $50, you will send him a contract. Although he had paid but $32 yet I beg you will forward to me a contract for him, which I will send him. Please at the same time to inform me where Mr. J. must make his payments. It will be a convenience to him to make them to Mr. Frost, but if you desire it he will make them here [Albany].

The terms of payment you indicate in your letter to Mr. Frost are certainly very liberal. They are, you will recollect, as follows: "The remaining $350" (that is after $50 shall have been paid) "to be paid in ten equal installments from 1st next month" (April) "with annual interest."

Joseph Frost, whoever he was, seems to have acted as intermediary or agent between Johnson and Smith. At the time of McIntyre's visit to the Works in September, Johnson had not made his first payment and so Smith had not sent the contract. What then appears to have happened is that Johnson asked McIntyre to intervene on his behalf. McIntyre was an influential man, and Johnson knew he thought well of him. Johnson must have made a similar plea to Frost but apparently failed to persuade him. McIntyre's letter brought an immediate response from Smith. Smith's letter is dated October 14, 1843.

> What you say of 'poor old Israel Johnson' goes straight to my heart—and, in addition to my former relinquishment of a part of his debt, I call the $32 pd. now, as $50 pd. 1st April last—It does us no hurt to extend a helping hand now & then to our less favored brethren.
>
> I enclose you a Contract & Duplicate for Mr. Johnson. When he shall have signed them, he will please return me one of them. Mr. Johnson must make his payments either at my office, or at N.Y. State Bank Albany.

What the "former relinquishment" was, I can't be sure, but Smith's generosity toward Johnson is clear. It would account for McIntyre's tone to Porteous when he wrote, "Smith deserves more attention. He has behaved very liberally to Johnson." This letter was written November 17. Johnson, however, had already signed and returned the contract because the next day, the eighteenth, McIntyre wrote to Smith: "I have at length received from Johnson a copy of your contract with him, executed on his part, and I hasten to return it to you. The old man resides some ten miles of very bad road from the P.O. and, no doubt, but seldom sends to it, which accounts for the delay. In his letter to me covering the contract, he desires me to express to you his sincere gratitude for your kind liberality towards him, and that he will not fail to exert himself to fulfil the contract." A postscript follows: "Johnson writes that the snow is now two feet deep at his place."

The other papers from the Syracuse library are ledger entries and accounts. One of them, however, clears up the mystery of the "now cancelled contract" referred to in the 1843 agreement. Gerrit Smith had his wealth from his father, Peter Smith. After a brief partnership with John Jacob Astor, Peter Smith accumulated enormous land-holdings, mostly in New York. After his wife died in 1819, he turned over his fortune to his son, Gerrit. Within a year or two,

however, he began amassing a second fortune, again in land. It is
from this second group of landholdings that Israel Johnson appears
to have purchased his land in 1831. Peter Smith died in 1837. I say
that Johnson "appears" to have purchased land then because in "Peter
Smith's Executor's Book, 1837–47," among the Peter Smith Papers
at Syracuse, there is this slightly hesitant entry: "Oct. 1, 1831. It
appears that on the day aforesaid Peter Smith and John Kiersted
contracted to sell to Israel Johnson Subs. numbers one & three in Lot
number twelve, of Township 44 Totten & Crossfield—195 Acres."
The "consideration" was $330. Then follows a list of payments and
interest accruals through 1839. A note to the side says, "Kiersted has
released to me [Gerrit, presumably] his interest in this contract and
the land described in it." In all those years, as shown below, Johnson
made only one payment: $156.20 in September of 1833. Peter Smith
did not even require a down payment.

Consid. $330.

Oct 1st 1833	Int[erest]. 2. yrs.	46.20
		376.20
Sept. 18, 1833 by 156.20 + .97		157.17
		219.03
Oct. 1st 1834	Int. 1 yr.	15.33
		234.36
Oct. 1st 1835	Int. " "	16.41
		250.77
Oct. 1st 1836	Int. " "	17.55
		268.32
Oct. 1st 1837	Int. " "	18.78
		287.10
Oct. 1st 1838	Int. " "	20.10
		307.20
Add for [error & int ?]		1.36
		308.56
Oct. 1st 1839	Int. 1 yr.	27.60
		336.16

A large **X** is drawn through the last two numbers.

It took Gerrit Smith years to settle the complicated affairs of his
father's estate, so it was not until 1840 that the accounts for this

property showed up in his "Land Book H." This time the language was more definite: "Oct. 1, 1831 P. S. & J Kiersted contracted to Israel Johnson Subs. 1 and 3 of Lot 12 T. 44 Totten & + field. Kiersted has released to G. Smith—195 A. Consideration $.330—Sept. 18, 1833 pd. 156.20."

Oct. 1. 1840			Balance	$353.28
"	" 1841	Int. 1 yr.		24.73
				378.01
"	" 1842	" " "		26.46
				404.47
April 1, 1843		Int.		14.16
				$418.63

Johnson had told Redfield in August 1836 that he had been at Clear Pond for four years, and the date of the original contract supports that. If Johnson bought the land on October 1, 1831, it is doubtful that he could have built a cabin for his family before bad weather set in. As a millwright, he might have spent part of that winter logging his property while his wife and children lived else-where. The spring of 1832 is the most likely time for Johnson to have moved his family into a finished cabin, which would have been only a little more than four years before Redfield and the Emmons party paid their first visit.

The next entry in Smith's "Land Book H" is only partly legible. It explains the terms of the new contract. "Oct. 13, 1843, I receive from A. McIntyre a [letter?] informing me that he has deposited $32 in [Bk? Probably "Bank"] to my [?] for Mr. Johnson—He [speaks?] of the poverty of Mr. Johnson—& [?] he [three or four illegible words], I credit the $32 for [?] as $50 for 1st Apl last—& I call the debt & ints but $400 as of 1st last April—I send Mr. McIntyre a Contract for Mr. Johnson." Smith's letter to McIntyre of the next day, October 14, mentioned a "former relinquishment" of Johnson's debt. I don't know what that would be if not a reduction of the total debt from $418.63 to $400.00. Smith's additional generosity was to allow $32 to stand for the first $50 installment due him.

The account continues and, with swiftness and clarity, tells exactly what happened to Israel Johnson's land.

Statement—

April 1 1843	$400—	
[balance?] $32 int	50—	
	$350	payable in 10 equal payts. with int.—

| April 1. 1844   Int. 1 yr. | 24.50 |
| | 374.50 |

Feb 10 1844   Recd. in letter
from Mr. McIntyre Cert. of
Dept $22

[Postage office?] .25	
$21.75 + .22	21.97
	352.53
May 22. 1844 [by?] $52—51	51.49
	301.04

Sept 17 1844	
by deposit $22—71	21.29
	279.75

Johnson made three payments in 1844, totaling $94.75, reducing his debt to $279.75. Though two of these payments were made after April 1, the next entry in the books—$279.75—is dated April 1, 1844. Whatever else this might be, I think it is another favor shown to Johnson because it credits him with payments earlier than he made them and so reduces his interest debt. The entries continue.

Apl. 1. 1844 Amt.	$279.75
" " 1845 Int.	19.58
	299.33
" " 1846 "	20.95
	320.28
Nov. 25 1846 Int	14.55
Certif. of Clerk	.25
	335.08

Nov. 23 1846 I & my wife convey by Warr. Deed to Joseph Frost in Consid $400—[?] subject to [taxes?] from Oct 1 1831.

And so the account was closed. Not able sufficiently to reduce his debt to Smith, Johnson lost his land to Joseph Frost after living on it for fifteen years (1831–1846). Frost had acted as Smith's agent for years and must have known Johnson's difficulties in making payments. I wanted to believe that Frost might have bought the land for Johnson, but there would have been no need to pay more than $335.08 to do that. Besides, few people would have had that much money to give away. It looks very much as though Frost simply bought what Johnson finally could not pay for and then evicted him. Smith's patience probably ran out, and he told Johnson he was going to sell the land if he didn't pay for it. Johnson panicked. He made three payments in a single year. Had Smith told him to get busy or else, and then after two more years of no payments—1845 and 1846—told his agent in those parts, Joseph Frost, that he would like to find a buyer for Johnson's land? Perhaps. And getting the news first, did Frost get there first? Or, indeed, did Frost plant the seed in Smith's brain and subtly ease Johnson out of his land? After all, $400 for 195 acres of land, largely cleared, was a good price. In 1843 Smith had offered the Iron Works tracts of uncleared land neighboring Johnson's for almost eight times that price. True, McIntyre thought the price too high, but he was not outraged by it.

The papers at the Syracuse library held another secret. In 1834 Johnson and two other people, Increase Wyman and R. D. Lindsay, bought lot 13 of Township 44, the lot immediately to the north of Clear Pond. Here is the entry from Gerrit Smith's "Great Book 2nd (oversized vol. 79)":

Nov. 1. 1834

It appears that on this day Peter Smith and Jna. Kiersted Cont. to sell to Inc. Wyman, Is. Johnson and R. D. Lindsay Lot 13 To. 44 in Totten & Crossfield—Consid. $869.25   1159 A.

Aug. 31. 1833	by $119.95	Kiersted has released his Int. to me. [Gerrit] —
May 30 1839	by $200.00	Aug. 13 1840 The Comp.
July 1 1840	by bal. of $500	Cert. for above Lot is this
after $277.45—		day assigned to Isaac
Aug. 13 1840	by $675 in full	Frink & Truman Safford.

In 1834 Johnson expanded his business. Or, more accurately, he went into business. He was not just going to clear his land so he could then farm it. He went into partnership with two men and bought additional land, which they would log, or have logged, and from those logs produce boards at Johnson's mill. He made the leap from being a millwright to being a lumberman. What his share of this venture was we don't know, but it is the best evidence yet of what Porteous called, six years later, Johnson's "great Chance to do well." When Redfield met him in 1836, Johnson would have been at the height of his expectations, with two mills going, his property valued at three thousand dollars, well thought of by the people at the Iron Works, and so on. The great crash of 1837 must have affected him in some way, and we know that by 1840 he was grumbling and discontent. He had missed his "great Chance," and, as he told the census-taker that year, he was not a millwright but a farmer. The son of his friend and business associate, R. D. Lindsay, would move to Iowa in a few years and start the lumber firm of Lindsay and Phelps, but Johnson was too old for that sort of thing in 1840. By 1843 McIntyre was calling him "poor old Israel Johnson."

❋

Considering the importance of Smith to Johnson, I thought I should go back and look more closely at the two Smith biographies. Neither tells us anything directly about Johnson, but near the beginning of Frothingham, there is mention of an "Esq. Johnson." It is in the chapter on Peter Smith and comes from one of "two little pocket journals . . . written rudely in pencil, containing notes of journeys northward from Albany, in the summer and autumn of 1822." This would have been three years after Peter Smith lost his first wife, at a time when he was beginning to build his second fortune in landholdings, most of which were in northern New York. "Esquire Johnson" is most certainly the father of the Clear Pond millwright, who, at this time, was in western New York. Like his son, Esquire Johnson seems to have taken in boarders. Here are Peter Smith's entries for September 8 and 9:

> Sept. 8, Sunday. Have not had a comfortable night, spirits too much agitated this morning; intend going to meeting at——five

and a half miles north [near Weatherhead's, I would guess]; may the perturbations of my mind be allayed! May I hear attentively and profitably!

Monday morning, Still at Esq. Johnson's; am not very well; mind is much perplexed regarding concerns here. Heard two sermons yesterday, from Rev. Mr. Comstock; the one in the afternoon was funeral sermon, a daughter of Mr. Catlin about——yrs. of age, had died suddenly—croup I expect.

Israel Johnson not only bought his land from Peter Smith, but Peter Smith had also, nine years earlier, stayed in his father's home. Johnson may have been out in the Genesee in 1822, but when it came time to buy land in 1831, he probably had private information on what land was available. When I wrote the Syracuse library again to see if they had Peter Smith's two pocket journals, Mr. Lyon had to report that the one mentioning the stay at old Israel's could not be found and so "must be assumed to be lost."

Johnson's name, then, does not appear in the land records of Essex County because he never finally owned the land he lived on. Had he been able to pay his debt to Smith, as Joseph Frost was with one payment, he would have received a warranty deed for the property and so had his name added to the Grantor's list in Elizabethtown. We can now be fairly certain, as well, that Johnson moved off Clear Pond, out of the Town of Moriah and into the Town of Schroon in 1846, where again he lived on land he was never able to own.

The Smith Papers also clear up some of the uncertainties raised by the census reports. Johnson must have been on the land through 1844 when he made nearly $100 in payments. It is possible he moved before the sale to Frost, though it would not seem likely so soon after making such large payments. By 1850, of course, Johnson had moved to the Town of Schroon, and "Johnson's Clearing," as the Cedar Point Road reverted to forest and the Iron Works closed down and a semblance of the original wilderness returned, became a name, the source or reason for which disappeared even from those who knew the name and used it. The photograph hanging on Pete Sanders's wall would have been taken forty or fifty years after Johnson left the property and probably long after Joseph Frost was buried. It is undoubtedly the way of these things, but over his fifteen-year stay at Clear Pond, Johnson made payments totaling $285.17 on property that was originally offered him for $330 and still wound up $335.08 short of being able to call it his.

7

Israel Johnson Speaks

I srael Johnson and people like him are little more than traces of themselves. They can't be found, really. It's like trying to see goldfinches when you hear them flying overhead. You have to learn to look ahead of the thin little four-note warble, and then, if you're lucky, you get to see a few scattered specks dipping in flight as they disappear into the air they came from. My best hopes for "finding" Israel Johnson were to find a grave and a living descendant.

I may be morbid, but I like graves. Here lies so-and-so or, at least, the bones of so-and-so. More important, someone put them there. Someone thought enough of so-and-so or of some propriety of life and death to put so-and-so in the ground where he belongs. If we must die and disappear, we can at least wave a small stone flag at the sky on the way down. Though I rather like the gesture of my ancient, distant cousin, Mary Bray, who had herself (her ashes, that is) scattered. That was the word used, *scattered*, though I suspect they were *dropped* or *dumped* or simply *thrown* into the Delaware River. If that. It's too painful to think the probable truth, that they were just washed down the drain at the mortuary. I don't inquire too closely into these practices for fear of learning the truth.

Defying death is an old art. "Do not go gentle," "Death, be not proud," and so on. It's the natural, romantic, all-boy thing to do. But the ones who invite the reaper in for tea and scones or who go for a ride in his (her?) slick black Lambretta leave my jaw a little slack.

As for living descendants of Israel Johnson, I thought one of them at least might have a whole history, maybe a photograph, a few choice memories, a story of the life. Which, of course, might or might not be true to the facts, but would be true in the other and, I'm tempted to say, better way.

In the meantime, I had a small handful of leads given me by my meager sources. George Hotchkiss, for instance. He mentioned a thing called a mulay saw and said it had been invented or patented by Johnson in 1835. Two questions came up right away. What was (or is) a mulay saw, and would the U.S. Patent Office have a record of Johnson's patent for it? It didn't seem that answers to either question would get us terribly close to the person, Israel Johnson, but with so little evidence, I couldn't turn my back on anything.

I went to the library and found some books on milling and logging. Hotchkiss had described the mulay saw as an improvement on the "gate" or "sash" saw, and had done so, as I remember, in language I could barely understand. ("The gate was connected at the bottom by a "noddle" pin connecting with the pitman to the water wheel shaft below," and so on.) I was sure this language made sense, but only to a lumberman.

It seemed necessary, first, to find out what a "gate" saw was. What was Johnson improving? And, the best source of information I could find was Oliver Evans's *The Young Mill-Wright & Miller's Guide* (Philadelphia, 1795), a book Johnson might well have known. It was exactly what I thought it would be: a simple, clear manual—with pictures. Evans was extremely, not to say painfully, thorough. He built the sawmill from the ground up, beginning with long chapters on mathematical and physical principles. So thorough was he that at one point he explained that the first effect of the mechanism of a sawmill was "to move the saw up and down," a movement one might have taken for granted. All one had to bring to this book was literacy and great patience. At the end of the book was a drawing of a sawmill, with all working parts in place, and seven pages of precise prose describing the size and function of every part. The drawing [see illustration 11] is a "perspective view of a saw-mill, shewing the foundation, walls, frame." Once Evans had described every part of the mill in detail, his description of the mill operation was brief and straightforward.

> The sluice drawn from the penstock 10, puts the wheel 11 in motion —the crank 12 moves the saw-gate and saw 9 up and down, and as they rise they lift up the lever 2, which pushes forward the hand-pole 3, which moves the rag-wheel 5, which

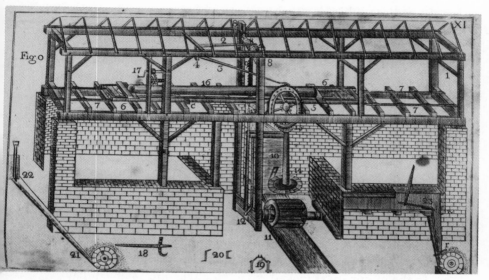

11. Illustration from Oliver Evans, *The Young Mill-Wright & Miller's Guide* (Philadelphia, 1795). Courtesy of Lilly Library, Indiana University.

gears in the cogs of the carriage 6, and draws forward the log 16 to meet the saw, as much as is proper to cut at a stroke. When it is within 3 inches of being through the log, the cleet C, on the side of the carriage, arrives at a trigger and lets it fly, and the sluice-gate shuts down; the miller instantly draws water on the wheel 14, which runs the log gently back, etc. etc."

These words describe the production of one board. The log must now go "gently back" and be run past the blade again to produce a second board. The log must be put on the carriage in the first place, of course, and it must be cut a certain length, as well, so that it will fit on the carriage. Because it starts as a tree, it must be cut down and trimmed and hauled to the mill. And, logs being more or less round, it is necessary to make roughly four cuts per log to square it. These cuts produce the almost useless but immense piles of "slab" next to the mill. The only way to get rid of them, apparently, was to burn them. Some of the slab must have been used for heating and cooking in the miller's cabin, but slab piles at a busy mill grew at a furious rate. Johnson apparently solved this problem by moving the mill away from the slab pile and setting it up at a different place on the river. When the second slab pile grew too large, he would move the mill back to the first site. Each time he moved the mill, he would burn the slab.

One problem with this kind of mill was that the crank moving the saw blade had to move the large "gate" or "sash" as well. In the drawing, that is the board at the top of the blade that steadies it between the two "fender beam (8 and 8). If the mill was twelve feet wide, the gate was nearly as wide. Every time the crank lifted the saw, it lifted that heavy board as well, so a good part of the water energy was being thrown away on moving it. How Johnson would solve this problem, I would have to wait and see, but Hotchkiss had already told me that he had "conceived the idea of dispensing with the heavy gate."

In the meantime, I looked around for a definition of a mulay saw. A. R. Reynolds, in *The Daniel Shaw Lumber Company: A Case Study of the Wisconsin Lumbering Frontier* (1957), said in a note:

> To make a sash saw, lumbermen first set up two upright parts [Evans's fender beams] connected at the top by a cross beam. They next set a saw blade between the upper and lower cross pieces of a heavy, wooden, rectangular frame, called the sash or gate. This rectangular frame held the blade rigid and assured a straight cut. The entire frame or sash moved up and down in grooves cut on the inner sides of the two upright parts. The saw cut only on the downward motion. The great weight of the frame required a large amount of power to operate it. They muley [*sic*] saw was identical in principle, but the blade was inserted in a lighter frame and so required less motive power.

Robert F. Fries in *Empire in Pine: The Story of Lumbering in Wisconsin 1830–1900* (1951) said nearly the same thing: "the early mills all used saws of this type [gate saws]. Its chief disadvantage was that because of its massive frame it took an undue amount of power to overcome friction. To a certain extent this difficulty was obviated before 1840 by the adoption of the muley [*sic*] saw, which operated exactly like the gate saw but had a lighter framework and hence could be operated at the same speed with less power." Bryan Latham wrote the nearest thing I could find to a history of milling, but when, in *Timber: Its Development and Distribution: A Historical Survey* (1957), he reached the mulay saw, he was talking about an improved, modern version of it.

> A simple type of frame saw much favored in the U.S.A. to supply rough-hewn lumber was the so-called "Mulay-Sawmill." This saw consisted in principle of an unstrained vertical saw mounted at the bottom end on guides to which a connecting rod was attached, while the upper end of the saw was similarly mounted on guides to a light cross-head. These guides could be so regulated in regard to the size of the log that very little of the saw was exposed . . . . The makers, Messrs Chandler and Taylor of Indianapolis, claimed that it cut smooth and even lumber, leaving no "stub shot," and would saw logs up to 4 ft. in diameter.

A great distance lay between Johnson's invention and the machine produced by Chandler and Taylor. The frontier miller who operated his mill with the aid of a bull and a small girl would have seemed strange indeed on the factory floor in Indianapolis. And yet, for all that difference and the passage of time, the invention by that frontier miller was still vital to the lumber industry as recently as the 1950s. "So highly esteemed was the lumber from this machine," wrote Latham, "that it commanded a superior price."

When I finally went to the state library in Indianapolis, I found a copy of *A Digest of Patents, Issued by the United States, From 1790 to January 1, 1839,* published in Washington in 1840. A bound book, it is a list of inventions, their inventors or patentees, the patentees' residences, and the date the patents were issued. The inventions themselves are grouped by "classes," class fourteen being "Lumber, including Machines and Tools for Preparing and Manufacturing, such as Sawing, Planing, Mortising, Shingle and Stove, Carpenters and Coopers Implements," and under this cumbersome heading were two pages of inventions described simply as "saw mills," including one in 1811 by our friend, Oliver Evans of Philadelphia.

"Israel Johnson Jr." appears on this list, not once, but twice. He appears a third time, in fact, in the description of another patent. On February 8, 1826, Johnson, a resident of Villenova, New York, was

issued a patent for a "saw mill." On September 28, 1827, Anson B.
Graham of Lee, Massachusetts, was issued a patent for a "Saw mill,
(improvement on Johnson's)." Finally, on May 7, 1829, Johnson was
issued another patent for a sawmill, this time as a resident of Moriah,
New York. I went immediately to the desk and asked for help, but
was told I would have to write to Washington for copies of the
patents themselves.

George Hotchkiss said that Israel Johnson had "conceived the
idea of dispensing with the heavy gate" in 1835, but it looks as
though he had had the idea sooner. Villenova, it turns out, is in
Chautauqua County, the westernmost county in the state. In 1826
Johnson was no longer in the Town of Alexander, Genesee County, as
he had been at the time of the census in 1820. While in western New
York in the 1820s, he apparently moved about. The interesting
information, though, was that Johnson was back in Essex County in
the spring of 1829. The residence listed is Moriah, but I would
assume, as with the 1830 census, that Moriah is the Town of Moriah,
not the village of the same name three or four miles west of Cedar
Point (Port Henry). Clear Pond was in the Town of Moriah at that
time, though we can't assume Johnson was there till he purchased his
land from Peter Smith in 1831. Where he was from the spring of
1829 to the late fall of 1831 or spring of 1832, we can only guess. As
we can only guess when he returned from "the Genesee." Our
guessing, however, can now be narrowed.

A few weeks later, a large canister arrived in the mail. Inside were
several oversize xeroxes and a letter. The xeroxes included the "Letters Patent" of February 8, 1826, issued to Johnson and a drawing of
the specifications described there (see illustration 12). The letter was
brief: "We searched our holdings of drawings and specifications for
restored patents; we were unable to identify any drawing or specification for the patent issued to Johnson on May 7, 1829. Apparently,
Johnson did not "restore" his patent after the Patent Office fire of
1836." The specifications, written in longhand, read as follows [see
the drawing which accompanies these specifications]:

> To all whom it may concern, know ye that I Israel Johnson
> Junior, of Villenova in the County of Chautauqua & state of New
> York, have made, contrived, invented, discovered and applied to
> use, a new and useful improvement in Mills or machines for

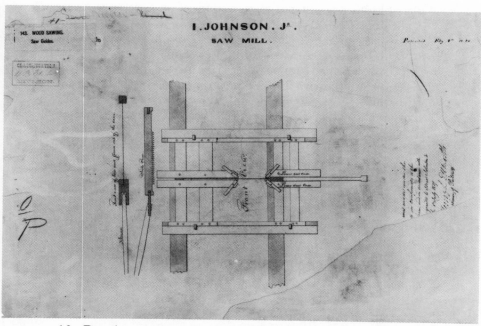

12. Drawing accompanying Johnson's patent for the mulay saw.
Courtesy of the U.S. Patent Office.

sawing boards & lumber, called a newly improved Saw Mill . . . .
In my improvement the water wheel, rag wheel, log carriage and
the machinery which move them, and all the other machinery
except the saw frame and the manner of the saws running are the
same as in ordinary saw mills. The saw in my improvement is not
strained or attached to a saw frame. It is constructed in this
manner; at the lower fender beam or other timber fitted for the
purpose, are placed & fastened two perpendicular blocks of timber
with a groove or rabbit on the inside of each, which blocks I shall
call the lower saw case. They are placed a sufficient distance from
each other to admit of the end of the pitman or shaft which reaches
from the crank of the water wheel, and on each side of the pitman
is a block fitted to the grooves in the saw case, and fastened by a
bolt reaching through them, the pitman and the end of the saw, at
the upper fender beam are placed two other perpendicular blocks
with grooves as aforesaid, which I shall call the upper saw case

placed a sufficient distance apart to admit of the saw. On each side of the upper end of the saw, and fastened to it, is a small block; fitted to the grooves in the upper case. These grooves in the saw cases, & blocks at each end of the saw cause the saw to move perpendicularly and keep it to its place. At the upper end of the lower saw case, are two slides or rollers one on each side of the saw, at the lower extermity of the upper saw case, and immediately above the log to be sawed, are two other slides or rollers one on each side of the saw as aforesaid. These rollers or slides are about the length of the width of the saw, and are fastened by bolts reaching through them, and the bolts fastened at each end by a staple or loop to the saw cases. These rollers or slides are placed there for the purpose of keeping the saw steady, and being situated immediately above and below the log to be sawed, it is impossible that the saw should run either to the right or left. The upper saw case & set of rollers or slides are so constructed, that they may be raised up or let down (so as to admit of a large or small log on the carriage) by a lever whose fulcrum is placed at the top of the upper fender beam. This improvement may be applied to any mill or machine for sawing boards or lumber with very little expense, or new mills may be constructed on this plan. It is less likely to get out of repair than the old fashioned mills, will do as much business, and make better work, and is moved with one half the power.

In writing that this is a true description and specification of my said improvement I have hereunto set my hand and seal this 16th day of January 1826.

Israel Johnson Jr.

Witnesses
Levi Benton
Ernest Muller

(patented Feb. 8, 1826)

So, in the winter of 1826, because on the frontier he could probably find neither suitable scribe nor artist for his drawing, Israel Johnson made the long trip down from western New York to Washington, D.C. If he was wined and dined out of his patent, it was done after he registered it. The books I've located make no mention of Johnson, but his saw or a descendant of it was the principle instrument for making boards for fifty years or more.

He boasted a little at the end of the long, doggedly factual description. That description, in fact, must have been largely put into his mouth by the scribes and bureaucrats at the patent office. But the little advertisement at the end, the modest boast, is as close as we come to the working of Johnson's mind, to the words he must have used when asked about it: "It is less likely to get out of repair than the old fashioned mills, will do as much business, and make better work, and is moved with one half the power." Compare that with the language Archibald McIntyre puts into his mouth in writing to Gerrit Smith: "He desires me to express to you his sincere gratitude for your kind liberality towards him." Kind liberality it may have been, but Johnson would never have used such words. Out of the darkened recesses of the Patent Office, 150 years later, came the voice of Israel Johnson: firm, plain, and confident.

8

A Young Boy from Colchester

*I*t was late November. Interlibrary Loan was having difficulty finding someone to lend an old book to me, the Patent Office was in its third week of processing my request for information about young Israel's patent, the Adirondacks were nearly a thousand miles away, and the gray weather had moved in to stay. It was on a day like this and in a mood much like it that I had a thought so obvious I nearly blushed. "If," I asked myself, "old Israel Johnson was born in 1759, how old would he have been in 1776? And what would a seventeen-year-old boy most likely have been doing that year?" The answer was obvious.

I scoured the library for some sort of publication that would list the veterans of the Revolutionary War. The only thing I could find was a printed pension roll from 1832, three years before old Israel died, but there he was under the heading, "New York, Essex County." He had been a sergeant in what was called the "Connecticut line," and he had been placed on the pension roll on April 15, 1819, at the age of sixty-one. My math made him only sixty in 1819, but that seemed close enough.

The Johnsons, then, had come from Connecticut. I wanted to dash off and look into the early records there, but I couldn't get free at the moment. I wrote the National Archives in Washington to see if they had a veteran's file on Johnson and, while waiting for an answer, started looking into Connecticut's role in the war. What was about to happen would draw me away from young Israel, but I couldn't ignore such an abundance of closely related information.

A book called *Record of Service of Connecticut Men in the Military and Naval Service During the War of the Revolution, 1775–1783,* ed., Henry P. Johnston (1889) had a complete roster of names for

114

every company that served throughout the war, plus a general sketch of each regiment's yearly service. From it I could see which unit or units Johnson had belonged to as well as follow his movements—what battles he was in, where he wintered—for as long as he served.

Old Israel's name appears in the first year of the war, 1775. The Connecticut legislature, according to Johnston, raised eight regiments that year, the second of which was commanded by colonel, later brigadier general, Joseph Spencer of East Haddam. The eighth company of this regiment was commanded by Captain Levi Wells of Colchester, and among the members of this company was Private Israel Johnson, who enlisted May 13 and was discharged December 17. Enlistments during the first two years of the war lasted only for the fighting season, roughly April through November. It wasn't until the third year of the war that enlistments were undertaken either for three full years or for the duration of the war.

Spencer's regiment "took part at Roxbury and served during the seige [of Boston] until expiration of term of service Dec. 1775. Detachments of officers and men engaged at the battle of Bunker Hill, June 17, and in Arnold's Quebec Expedition, Sept.–Dec. 1775. Adopted as Continental in July." Johnson's name does not appear in this book among those who took part at Bunker Hill or, luckily, among those who tried storming Quebec. His entire service of 1775 was in and around Roxbury where a part of the army was used to cut off the only land approach to Boston and isolate the British garrison there. The success of this seige eventually forced the British to evacuate Boston and instead make New York the headquarters of their North American military operations.

Johnston does not list Johnson as a soldier in 1776, but in 1777 he shows up in what was christened that year the "Connecticut Line." Each state had such a line, made up of several regiments, and they were all put under the command of the Continental Congress and its commander-in-chief, Washington. The state lines continued for the duration of the war, and soldiers enlisted in them either for three years or for the duration. Seventeen seventy-seven–seventy-eight was, then, the first year the American army went into winter quarters, a practice that proved nearly as demoralizing as the war itself. Valley Forge, Redding, Morristown, and other winter quarters were sites of starvation, sickness, desertion and, more than once, mutiny. Men were lured into the army on certain promises, which the state legislatures and the Congress often had difficulty meeting. Men who enlisted late in the war were offered larger incentives than those who enlisted early. Acute inflation made matters worse. In the middle of winter, soldiers often went without sufficient food and clothing. Stories are told of soldiers walking barefoot in the snow or indeed of not being able to engage the enemy because of "nakedness."

Once the standing army or the regiments of the line had been established in 1777, Private Israel Johnson found himself in the Third Regiment, Connecticut Line, commanded by Colonel Samuel Wyllys of Hartford and assigned to the company of Captain Henry Champion of Colchester. Part of this regiment helped repel Loyalist Governor William Tryon of New York in his raid on the American supply depot at Danbury late in April.

In the summer of 1778, the Third Regiment camped at White Plains with Washington's main army. It spent the next winter at Redding, Connecticut, where a mutiny flared up. The troops at Redding, three brigades in all, were considered a division. Major General Putnam, the hero of Bunker Hill, was commander. Wyllys's regiment formed a part of Parsons's brigade, but the trouble took place in the other Connecticut brigade, commanded by Jedediah Huntington.

Israel Johnson, then, was part of a regiment that considered mutiny, but, when the time came, relented. Wyllys's regiment moved from Redding in May 1779 and served in Major General Heath's wing on the east side of the Hudson in the region known as the Highlands. In November it went into winter quarters near Morristown, New Jersey. The great event of that year's campaign was the taking of Stony Point on July 15 by a force under General Anthony Wayne. Wyllys's regiment contributed one company to that force, Captain Henry Champion's. It seems likely, then, that the father of the Clear Pond millwright took part in the most impressive act of discipline displayed by the American army in the entire war. Wayne issued rum but no ammunition to the men who ran up the hill in the dark at Stony Point. They had to take the garrison with bayonets alone. Only fifteen of the twelve hundred Americans were killed. It was over in half an hour.

Johnson was made sergeant in May 1780. Early in 1781, the Connecticut Line underwent the first of several reformations, until by June of 1783, the Connecticut forces had dwindled to a single regiment, commanded by Heman Swift. Cornwallis had surrendered at Yorktown on October 19, 1781, but the war went on for another year and a half. The last battle of the Revolution was an eight-day affair in late April of 1783 at Fort Carlos III, Arkansas, in which one hundred and forty Loyalists and Indians tried to take the fort from fifty Americans. There were no casualties on either side, and the Loyalists let their eleven prisoners go when they heard about the peace treaty.

Here, then, is a rough itinerary of the military career of Israel Johnson, Esq. He joined the army from his home state, Connecticut, in the first year of the war at the age of sixteen. During that year's campaign, he served in the army's right wing under General Artemus Ward and helped keep the land approach to Boston closed to the British and Loyalists. He appears not to have signed up again in 1776, but in 1777 he enlisted for the duration, serving in one regiment or another of the Connecticut Line. For nearly seven years he seems to have traveled no father north than West Point, no father south than northern New Jersey, never much west of the Hudson, and no farther east than Danbury, Connecticut. The only engagements he might have taken part in, apparently, were Tryon's raid on the American supply depot at Danbury in late April of 1777 and "Mad" Anthony Wayne's storming of Stony Point in July of 1779. Otherwise, his service was restricted to the business of keeping the British from controlling the Hudson River. This was important because for years, at least until Burgoyne's defeat in October 1777, the British military command thought the secret to defeating the colonists was to sweep south from Montreal to New York, along Lake Champlain, Lake George, and the Hudson River, and cut the New England colonies off from the rest. Once Burgoyne had been defeated at Saratoga, trying to do just this, the Hudson was fairly quiet, the site only of occasional raids and forays.

The fat envelope finally arrived from the National Archives, and I sat down on the bottom step in the front hallway and read every word of it. The picture given by Johnston's record of Connecticut regiments had been accurate, but only generally so. Israel Johnson had served in 1776 and, in fact, had taken part in the two major battles of that year, Long Island and Harlem Heights. Also, he had been wounded during the Danbury raid.

The file contained a copy of a sworn statement by old Israel describing his service. The pension law of 1818 required that those seeking compensation make a sworn statement before a judge. This document is signed by old Israel. The bulk of the file was a month-by-month record of his service, which listed his unit and his approximate whereabouts and duties. Here there are many differences from the general history sketched out by Johnston for his unit. Also, the monthly record only starts in February 1777, when Johnson enlisted "for the war," skips immediately to July 1778, and is then complete through to his discharge at West Point on October 3, 1783, except for fourteen months in 1781 and 1782. The spottiness of Johnson's record of service is probably due to the difficulty the American army had in keeping records. Military bookkeeping went through several bad periods during the war.

The affidavit, sworn on May 7, 1818, before Daniel Ross, first judge of the Court of Common Pleas for Essex County, reads as follows:

Israel Johnson of Schroon in [word illegible] County being duly sworn [?] that in the month of May in the year of our Lord one thousand seven hundred seventy five he enlisted to serve for the period of nine months. That just before the expiration of which time he enlisted into the army of the United States to serve for the span of one year in the Company Commanded by Captain Levi Wells in the Connecticut line. which company made a part of the Regiment Commanded by Col Wyllis of Hartford in the Connecticut line that he did accordingly serve for that period faithfully and honorably—And this deponent further says that in the month of February in the year of our Lord one thousand seven hundred and seventy seven he enlisted for and during the war in the company commanded by Captain Henry Champion in the Regiment commanded by Colonel Willis and in the [Brigade?] commanded by General Parsons according to the best of his recollection And this deponent further says that in the year of our Lord one thousand seven hundred eighty three at Westpoint in the state of New York he received an honorable discharge from the army, which is lost and that at the time of receiving his discharge he was under the command of Col. Butler—And this deponent further says that on the first day of January one thousand seven hundred and eighty three he received a Sergeant's warrant which is hereunto attached—[the handwriting changes here] And this deponent further says that during his [land?] [service?] he bore a part in the battle of Long Island, in the retreat from New York, in the affair at Harliam heights—Elizabethtown point—and in the affair at Danbury he was wounded in the hand

And this deponent further says that by reason of his reduced circumstances he is in need of the assistance of his country for support and that this deponent is now in his fifty ninth year and he entered the army before he was sixteen years old and further says not—

The monthly reports of Johnson's service do not begin until July 1778, and they are suspended for all of 1781 and part of 1782. Despite such sketchiness, a sense of what he did as a soldier emerges, as do some important new details.

Johnson's first monthly report, July 1778, lists him as "On Comd. boating." "On command" meant that a soldier was away from his unit performing other essential tasks. Johnson was often on command. In July of 1778, his unit was at White Plains. Presumably, he was detached from his regiment "boating" nearby on the Hudson River. Boating must have been some sort of guard or surveillance activity, though perhaps it was maintaining and guarding a ferry service across the Hudson. It must have been necessary to keep a large number of boats ready in case the army had to move suddenly. In the retreat from Long Island, in August of 1776, the defeated American army was saved from certain capture by a huge assemblage of small boats that took them across the river in the night to Manhattan. "Every variety of craft," says Henry Johnston, the historian of the 1776 campaign, "row-boats, flat-boats, whale-boats, pettiaugers, sloops, and sail-boats" was commandeered along a thirty or forty mile stretch of the lower Hudson to ferry Washington's troops to safety. It was the Dunkirk of that war.

Johnson was "On Command East River"—probably boating— while his unit was either at New Milford or at Camp "Reading" from October 1778 to April 1779. This means that he was not in camp when Huntington's brigade attempted a mutiny. From May to July 1779, he was on command at Fishkill, so he was not at the storming of Stony Point, either. "Fishkill Landing," as it was called then, is just across the river from Newburgh on the east side of the Hudson

where, for a time, Washington had his headquarters. The word
"Landing" suggests that again Johnson was boating, either running
or guarding a ferry.

The monthly strength reports for June 1780 show that Wyllys's
regiment was in the Highlands across from West Point, but it was in
that month that Israel Johnson took part in the battle at Elizabethtown
Point. He seems to have been detached from his unit—on command,
I presume—this time for fighting. He was made sergeant on May 1.

The battle at Elizabethtown Point, right across from Staten
Island in New Jersey, took place on June 7, 1780. General Knyphausen,
the Hessian commander, was in charge in New York while his
superior, General Clinton, was off fighting in South Carolina.
Knyphausen thought it was a good time to attack New Jersey.
British intelligence had told him about the mutiny in the American
army there the previous winter and indicated as well that the country
brimmed with untapped Loyalist sentiment. It was bad information.
When he landed at Elizabethtown Point with five thousand troops,
he was stopped practically where he stood by about one thousand
New Jersey militia under General Maxwell. Knyphausen managed to
push inland a ways, but Maxwell's troops were reinforced, partly by
regulars, and he was forced to dig in near Springfield where he
thrashed about for two weeks, burned Springfield and a neighboring
village, called then Connecticut Farms (now Union), retreating to
Staten Island on June 23. Johnson was most likely one of the regulars
brought in to reinforce Maxwell on the seventh.

Johnson's monthly reports resume in March 1782, five months
after Yorktown. In July, when Lieutenant Colonel Thomas Grosvenor
took command of the First Connecticut Regiment, Johnson was sick
at New Windsor. He was sick again at New Windsor on August 8,
and in October he spent some time "In Connt. after [a] deserter." The
only other thing said of him was that on May 17, 1783, he went on
furlough for eight days. He mustered out in October 1783.

The other battles he took part in were those at Harlem Heights
and at Danbury. The fracas at Harlem Heights was simply the next
move the British made after driving the American army off Long
Island in August 1776. The Americans had slipped across the river to
Manhattan, and the British regrouped and pursued them there. They
landed at Kip's Bay on September 15, routed the outer defense forces,

mostly militiamen from Connecticut, and then engaged the whole army the next day farther north at Harlem Heights. The battle was nearly a draw.

Finally, Danbury. Danbury was a major supply depot for the American army, and General Howe, the British commander in New York, decided in early 1777 that it should be attacked. He put the Loyalist governor of New York, William Tryon, once an officer in the British army, in charge of fifteen hundred regular troops and three hundred Loyalist militia and told them to march inland and destroy the stores. Danbury was in American-held Connecticut, so the troops had to be landed from ships off the south coast of the state. They were put ashore in the late afternoon of Friday, April 25th, and at about 11:30 P.M. marched inland toward Danbury. There was almost no resistance. They reached Danbury at 4:00 P.M. where they encountered their first real resistance. Colonel Jedediah Huntington, whose brigade was to mutiny next winter in Redding, was in charge, and he had, according to a letter he wrote on the day the British arrived, "about 50 Continental troops, and as many again militia." These one hundred men retreated to the high places around the edge of Danbury and fired on the British as they came into town.

The British, of course, drove them away and then set about destroying the stores, which was no small job because it included three to four thousand barrels of pork and beef, one thousand barrels of flour, and one hundred barrels of rice. The greatest loss, though, was "upwards of 1000 Tents and some Marquis." The Americans had no industrial capacity for making tents at that time. The next day, Sunday, the twenty-seventh, the British withdrew from Danbury and, after three costly skirmishes at Ridgefield, spent a sleepless night south of that town, and on the twenty-eighth scurried to their ships and safety.

In the retreat from Danbury, the British were opposed by a hastily assembled force of militia under the command of General David Wooster. They divided into two bodies, one under Wooster to harass the British from behind, the other under the second-in-command, Colonel Benedict Arnold, who rushed ahead of the British force to challenge it from the front. This challenge took place at the village of Ridgefield, and the fighting there produced most of the one hundred and seventy-one British casualties. The first contact made was from the rear, north of Ridgefield, and in the second of these skirmishes, Wooster was mortally wounded. The British tried to avoid Arnold, who was a feared soldier even before Saratoga, but finally had to face him in the village itself.

The net result of the Danbury Raid, according to Robert McDevitt, was not as it looked on the day the British troops reboarded their ships and sailed away. The Americans had had a major supply depot raided and its stores destroyed, but they were able to recover all but the tents with relative ease. The British, on the other hand, suffered enough casualties that they never again attempted such an inland raid. Finally, it was the engagement that brought Benedict Arnold his long-deserved promotion. He was made second-in-command under General Horatio Gates in the Northern Department and so set in place for his crucial contributions to the defeat of Burgoyne six months later.

Where was the eighteen-year-old Johnson in all this? Johnson had enlisted in the Connecticut Line in February and hence was a "regular," a Continental soldier. The only mention of Continental soldiers in all that I've read about the Danbury Raid is of those fifty or so who met the British in Danbury itself. Huntington was their commander, but Huntington was also involved in the fighting around Ridgefield. Whether he was with Wooster or with Arnold, I don't know, but I assume that Johnson was with Huntington until he was wounded in the hand. All Johnson's sworn statement says is that "in the affair at Danbury [I] was wounded in the hand." Were it not that military reporting often has a generalized character due to the nature of fighting, I would assume Johnson was wounded in Danbury itself in the late afternoon of Saturday, April 26, as he and a hundred others were firing down on eighteen hundred British and Loyalists from the elevated ground outside the village. The whole four-day "affair" cost the Americans twenty lives and seventy-five men wounded. One of the wounded was the father of the, at the moment, remote subject of this narrative.

Where in Connecticut did old Israel come from? One of the last books I looked at, *Collections of the Connecticut Historical Society*, Vol. 8, says quite plainly on page 58 that Israel Johnson's "place of abode" was Colchester. That was also the town from which his first two company commanders came, Levi Wells and Henry Champion.

13. Grave of Israel Johnson, Esq. (1760–1835), with new flag.

Another door had opened. One day I would have to go to Colchester, Connecticut.

A footnote. In the summer of 1983, I spent a month in Keene Valley, and it was then that I met Paul Stapley. Paul is one of the pioneering local historians in the area. It was a copy of his survey of local cemeteries, shown me by Mrs. Dobie in North Hudson, that gave me the first hard facts to go on. I arranged to meet him one day at the county clerk's office in Elizabethtown. I had only a smattering of small questions for him, but I remember that in talking with him I learned about such half-tangible things as the way land was surveyed and sold, how people lived and moved about, what state the local records were in, and so on. Everything I knew at the time was brought down closer to the ground.

We were sitting in a back room where the employees take their coffee breaks, and at a lull in the conversation, he mentioned his interest in identifying veterans among the old settlers of the area. I said, I think I might have something that would interest you. What's that, he said. Israel Johnson, Esq., was a Revolutionary War veteran. Really! Do you have proof? I pulled the copy of old Israel's file out of my briefcase. His face lit up. May I copy it, he asked. Of course. He ran off and did so.

Since then I have pestered Paul a few times with odd questions. He always writes back right away. Except for the time I wrote and told him he was probably related to Israel Johnson. That time he called, and we talked for half an hour. But that's a story for another chapter.

At the end of that summer, as I was starting back to Indiana, I went out of my way on a hunch. I wanted to go past the DeLorme Cemetery in North Hudson. I wouldn't need to stop. All I had to do was drive past and glance at old Israel's headstone, which is not far from the road. I wanted to see if my discoveries had born any fruit. They had. I saw it right away, even going forty miles an hour: a new flag stuck in the ground next to the headstone of Israel Johnson, Esq.

9

A Trip to Connecticut

*A*s it turned out, the discovery of old Israel's war record was just the beginning of a long journey backward into Israel Johnson's ancestry. Once started, it was impossible to stop, and though it would mean for a time abandoning Johnson—the specific, loquacious, inventive millwright of Clear Pond in Essex County—it would come to mean an enlarging. What are the boundaries of a person, after all? Where does a person begin and end? The tombstones give the conventional boundaries, birth date and death date. But none of us is fooled by that. I'm Irish, the Irishman says, Potato Famine Irish, though he lives in Poughkeepsie and drives a Toyota. He not only belongs to his body but to a culture and a history. Israel Johnson is not just the man who was born in Wells Township, Rutland County, Vermont, in 1785 or 1786 and is buried, for the moment, we know not where. He is also how he came to be born there at that time, as well as what happened to him, where his work, his ideas, his flesh led to.

To my writing this book, for one thing. To my driving a thousand miles or so in March 1985, in cold, gray, blustery weather, to Hartford, Connecticut, so I could spend three days at the Connecticut State Library and a half day at the Connecticut Historical Society. I wanted to find out about Johnson's ancestry and then do a bit of snooping around Colchester. I had no reason to think I might find much, but as it happened, I had an experience something like winning a genealogical sweepstakes.

The Vital Records for the Town (meaning township) of Colchester record the birth of an Israel Johnson on February 17, 1760. The parents were John Johnson, Jr., and his wife, Anstress. No other Israel Johnson was born in Colchester at or near that time.

Other Israel Johnsons were born, though, and they, too, were the children of John and Anstress Johnson. The first was born on September 25, 1739, but died on December 31, 1741, four days after his older brother, John, died. The second Israel Johnson and his twin, John, died the month, perhaps even the day, they were born in June 1753. The Israel Johnson we know, the Revolutionary War veteran, was the third Israel that his parents tried to bring into the world. For some reason, they were determined to have a child named Israel.

They were religious people. Their names and the names of most of their family show up in the records of the First Congregational Church of Colchester, founded in 1732. Collating both town and church records, I learned that John and Anstress Johnson had no fewer than fourteen children, the first born in 1737, the last— Israel—born in 1760. Only six lived beyond childhood. A year and a half after Israel's birth, on October 27, 1761, Anstress Johnson died, age "about 44."

Anstress was born Anstress Newton, though some records spell her first name Anstis, others Austis. She was married on January 6, 1736, and was the daughter of Major Israel and Hannah Newton. This, then, is what the name Israel meant to John and Anstress Johnson. Their first child was named for the father, John. It was a patriarchy, after all. But the second (and two others) were named for the mother's father, Major Israel Newton.

John Johnson, Jr., old Israel's father, is less visible than his wife. His death is not recorded in Colchester. I presume he moved elsewhere and died there. He might have been the John Johnson who married Ann Smith on September 6, 1764, in Colchester. He might have been the John, son of John Johnson—one reason for calling him junior—born in Colchester on January 16, 1713. At his marriage, if this were so, he would have been twenty-three, at his wife's death forty-eight, at his remarriage fifty-one. I was less interested in his possible remarriage than in his parentage. How far back could the line of Israel Johnson be traced? To understand this obsession, you have to see the shaky signature on an old deed, feel the powdery paper, smell the centuries of dust, squint at the illegible words scrawled in faded brown ink, curse quietly at words that will never again be legible, reach the last vaguely remembered ancestor on a genealogical chart, the obvious guess, the tiniest fragment of memory,

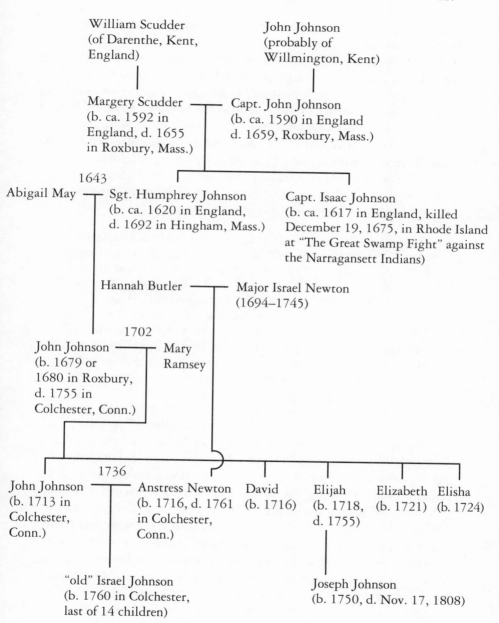

1. The Johnson genealogy from about 1590 to 1760.

probably transformed by having had it whispered down through the generations for centuries.

The records of the First Congregational Church, Colchester, say that Israel Johnson was baptized, not born, on February 17, 1760. No matter. Let us think of it as his birthday and get on with the business of reconstructing his way into the world. I was later to find two or three genealogies that took his ancestry back to England and the late sixteenth century, but first I came across a deed that those same genealogies must have based their findings on. John Johnson, Jr., old Israel's father, was called that because his father was also a John Johnson. Both names appear on a deed of 1754 in which the father passes his Colchester land on to his son.

> Two Sertain Tracts of Land Lying in ye Township of Colchester it being ye two half Lotts Laid out in ye Sequestered Commons So Call'd. Laid out on ye Right of Josiah Strong one Lot Laid out on ye East Side of ye Town Platt it is Lot No. 15. Containing 20 acres in ye whole & one half is mine & other half belongs to ye heirs of John Bulkley Esq. Late of Colchester deceased. ye one half I Convey. ye Lot being bounded out upon <u>record</u> to which I Refere. ye other half a Lott laid out on ye Right above [?] Laid out on Pye Hill so Call'd. N. 16: ye whole Lott Contains Seven acres upon record ye one half is mine ye other half belongs to Nathll. Foot.

This deed was made by "John Johnson of Colchester," and he passed all of this along to "my Son John Johnson Jun. of ye same Town County & Colony." The next year the church recorded the death of a John Johnson, "Aug. 7, 1755, AE 67." Later that year, on October 7, John Johnson—Junior no longer—was made administrator of his father's estate. Among the estate papers is an inventory of John Johnson's belongings, which gives us a good idea of the kind of life Old Israel's grandfather led. It is a list of about sixty items, including "table cloath, corn & oats, dry casks, 2 half bushels, two tubs, mortar & pestle, warming pan, Andirons Tong & Tool, sundry small books, Two Bibles, a testament, one blanket, looking glass." The animals included a mare, the most highly valued item at ten pounds. A cow, a heifer, a swine. A trunk, a box, a pocket book. Iron skillet, iron kettles, iron pot, two axes. A "great chair" and four little chairs, a table. And other items like "old curtains," "small trunk" "pork."

Everything in the house was given a value in pounds, shillings, and pence. It was a farmhouse, not lavish, but substantial.

I don't understand the legal arrangements of a probate will, but John Johnson [Jr.] and a cosignor, Samuel Sisler of Hebron, were required by such a document to give five-hundred pounds to the judge, Joseph Spencer, Esq., judge of the Court of Probate for the district of East Haddam. I assume it was necessary because old John Johnson was in debt when he died. His son was not given the land the previous year; he had to pay one hundred and fifty pounds for it. "Near the top of the list of household belongings was one pound six shillings of "paper money."

The town records for Colchester list five children of a (i.e., the only) John Johnson of Colchester [see genealogical chart]: John (b. Jan. 16, 1713, who I think is John Johnson, Jr., father of old Israel), David (b. Feb. 10, 1716), Elijah (b. Sept. 20, 1718), Elizabeth (b. Feb. 17, 1721), and Elisha (b. July 16, 1724). The early land deeds record several sales of land to and by a John "Jonson." He first bought twenty-one acres of land in Colchester from Josiah Strong. At the time he was known as "John Jonson of Roxbury," Massachusetts. Two years later this same parcel of land was sold to an Elizabeth Wilson by "John Jonson of Colchester." Thereafter, John Jonson, later Johnson, of Colchester was involved in two or three other land deals. One fact that persuades me that "John Jonson of Roxbury" is both "John Jonson of Colchester" and the grandfather of old Israel, is a 1735 deed between John Johnson "then of Roxbury . . . now of . . . Colchester" and Josiah Strong, which seems to be a rewriting of the 1710 land sale.

Everything points to the conclusion that Israel Johnson's lineal forbears came to Colchester from Roxbury, Massachusetts, in or around 1710. At this point, I spent a morning in the library of the Connecticut Historical Society and stumbled on, not one, but three or four exhaustive family genealogies of "John Johnson of Roxbury." The most reliable of these was a six hundred-page bound book by Paul Franklin Johnson called *Genealogy of Captain John Johnson of Roxbury, Massachusetts* (Los Angeles, 1948). I also found *The Colchester, Conn. Newton Family, Descendants of Thomas Newton of Fairfield, Conn. 1639* (Naperville, Illinois, 1911), compiled by Clair Alonzo Newton. In other words, I had found every known forebear of Israel

Johnson and hundreds of the descendants of his uncles and aunts. Israel himself (old Israel) is mentioned in these genealogies, but nothing was known about him except the date of his birth or baptism. The compilers had other work to do, other lives to record. Old Israel, as a newborn infant, simply hangs like a frayed thread at the edge of a large worn carpet.

Considering what we are about to discover of his ancestry, it is a wonder Johnson ever came loose from it. Did he never talk about his family to his wife and children? Was he born too late for that? His mother died when he was only one, and his father seems to have remarried, to an Ann Smith, when he (Israel) was four. Maybe the subject of family was awkward in the home of his stepmother. Or, maybe he was so caught up in the amazing events of this time that he forgot about his family. He enlisted in the army at fifteen and did not return home, if he did return, until he was twenty-three. He helped drive the British away. He spent eight years living in camps under some of the worst hardships ever known to a rabble that called itself an army. He was probably given the one-hundred acres of bounty land promised most men who enlisted. Where was it? Where did he go after the war? Did he sell it instead? He married shortly after he mustered out of the army because he was having children two years later in 1785. Who married him and where? The huge index of early marriages for the state of Connecticut at the State Library in Hartford makes no mention of it. Israel Johnson was the youngest of several children. He grew up in the house of his father and stepmother, was then uprooted by war, and afterwards set wandering with the rest of the land-hungry veterans. It is said that one-third of the people of Connecticut left it in the years immediately after the Treaty of Paris. It was only their distant descendants and the odd crank who bothered to look back. Israel Johnson was simply typical of his time. He went off in search of fresh prospects and lived his own life, not everybody else's.

Old Israel Johnson never knew his grandfather, John Johnson, but he seems to have grown up in his house, because it was deeded to his father in 1754. If that is so, Israel Johnson grew up either right in the Village of Colchester or just outside it on a place called Pye Hill. Israel never knew his other grandfather either, though he was named for him. Major Israel Newton (b. March 5, 1694) married Hannah

Butler of Hartford, and among their children was Austis, as the Newton genealogy calls her, born January 1, 1716. Major Newton was the son of Captain James Newton, one of the so-called proprietors of the Town of Colchester, founded 1698. The family came from Rhode Island and before that from Massachusetts. If Clair Alonzo Newton is right, the family can be traced back to Reginald de Neuton, a twelfth-century Lincolnshire knight. No doubt he was part of the new Norman aristocracy in England. And, as if that weren't enough of a burden to carry, a branch of the family gave the world Sir Isaac Newton, born in Woolsthorpe, a Lincolnshire hamlet.

I had to blink once or twice when I read that, but, yes, Israel Johnson of Clear Pond, the loquacious inventor, was a distant relative of the most famous scientist-philosopher in English or English-speaking history.

The military titles held by so many of the first colonists reflect the nearly constant state of warfare in early America. Part of it involved hostilities against the Indians, but much of it stemmed from the great European rivalries. Major Israel Newton was a casualty of that between England and France. He died from sickness at the siege of Fort Louisburg, Cape Breton Island. A little-known battle in an almost forgotten war, King George's War, fought between 1744 and 1748. In one way or another, the English and the French were at war for almost a hundred years before Napoleon's defeat, an event that finally made England the dominant colonial power in the world. Major Newton wouldn't have seen it this way, but he was a tiny pawn in this struggle for economic and political supremacy, a cycle of colonial domination, which I suppose it could be said his grandson fought to break.

Major Newton was prosperous and influential. He held a number of Town offices—surveyor, tax collector, justice of the peace—and he was several times deputy to the General Assembly for Colchester. He was commissioned "Captain of 1st Company or train band" in the Town of Colchester in 1730 and in February 1745 was made a major "of the forces to be raised and sent . . . in the expedition against Cape Breton." The fleet against Fort Louisburg sailed on Sunday, April 14, 1745. Fifteen hundred of these men took sick in camp around the French fort, including Major Newton, who died there on May 24. He had a premonition of this end, or perhaps just natural caution,

because on April 1 he made his will, two weeks before sailing with
the expeditionary force. It is a long and interesting document, worth
quoting in some detail. It shows what real prosperity was in mid-
eighteenth century colonial America. If John Johnson was a substantial farmer, Israel Newton bordered on great wealth. His list of
household goods and personal property fills a page and a half with
small print. The total valuation was 2,398 Pounds, 4 Shillings, 11
Pence.

The section on clothing alone is revealing: "His wearing clothes,
red coat, jacket, briches, hat, cape and wig, Duroy coat and Briches,
plate button coat, black coat, great coat, broadcloth jacket, Fustian
and briches, leather briches with plate buttons, black rosed hatt,
dark gray wig, little wig, 4 ruffled shirts, 1 Holl shirt, 5 stocks [pairs
of stockings], Holland cape, cotten stockings, purple blue stockings,
pr. gloves and cane, silver shoe buckles, knee buckles, gold butts
[buttons], silver butts."

Among the animals, including ninety-seven sheep, were "two
oxen, bull, fat cow, Cambo, brindle heifer and calf, Rose, Poosh,
Vilet, Buxom, Blackeye, Blossom, Pink, Cleary, Wells," as well as
"Asahel mare" and "Israel mare," and wedged in between cartwheels
and irons and knives and forks were "Dave, Nero, Cloe," who sound
to my ear like slaves or indentured servants.

The dispensations in the will begin, "To my beloved wife I give
and bequeath the use of the west lower room in my present dwelling
house and the use of the cellar under the cheese house for her own
benefit and advantage as long as she remains my widow—also I give
and bequeath to her one good feather bed and furniture which she
shall choose in my house, one case of draws, one iron pot, two pewter
basins, two silver spoons, one-half dozen chairs, one-half dozen plates
and tin platters, . . . two good cows such as she shall choose, one
horse kind to be chosen by her, ten sheep. All the creatures to be kept
and maintained on my farm by the person to whom I shall give the
same."

His land lay "partly in Colchester partly in East Haddam" on
both sides of the Lyme road. He gave the land on the west side of the
road as well as his "wearing apparel" to his two sons, Israel and
Asahel. To his son Asahel, he gave a "Brown Mare colt that came of

my black mare," a gesture which probably made up for the deeply symbolic final bequest to them both: "I give to my son Israel my silver hilted sword and to Asahel my other sword."

The daughters were not forgotten. The remainder of the moveable estate was to be divided equally among the five of them—"Austis, Mary, Hannah, Abigail and Miriam." Finally, "all my land lying in Colchester on the east side of the road to Lyme to be divided equally between them in quantity and quality."

So, John Johnson, Jr., married into a wealthy family in 1736. He would hardly have married for that reason, because Anstress's dowry would have been modest. The major portions of her father's estate would have gone to her brothers. Still, there would have been few, if any, more prominent families in Colchester at that time than the Newtons.

Clair Newton's family genealogy had other tantalizing information, including two photographs of the exterior of Major Israel Newton's house and one of its interior. "The home of Major Israel Newton still stands and is now known as the Pine Tree House, though the occupants in 1911 keep chickens in the lower west room." The same room where the widow Newton lived out her life.

I read about the Newtons in the morning, and that afternoon drove down to Colchester. It now seemed possible to find a few graves of people I'd come to know and to see the house where old Israel Johnson's mother, Anstress, grew up. Colchester is a small village, smaller now, I think, than it was in Israel Johnson's time. It is laid out around an obvious common. A few old buildings among newer ones lie scattered along the edges of it, but nothing looked as though it could be colonial. It isn't a self-consciously pretty town, as many towns in New England are now. It's a place where people live. It has an unofficial town historian in Barbara Brown, whose pamphlet, *Flintlocks and Barrels of Beef,* I had read the day before at the State Library. She describes Colchester's contributions to the Revolutionary War so thoroughly that she even mentions Israel Johnson. Ms. Brown not only took his name from the list of Connecticut men in the Revolution, but also sent for his war record from the National Archives. As nearly as I could tell, she sent for the war records of everyone known to have come from Colchester. Israel Johnson is only

14. Grave of Major Israel Newton (1694–1745),
Colchester, Connecticut.

mentioned in passing. Nothing is said of his ancestors and, of course, she knew nothing of the move to Vermont, the later move to Schroon, his grave in North Hudson.

I went to the library first. The only person there was the librarian, and she had never heard of the Newton House. She looked it up on a list of Colchester antiquities, but it wasn't there. She suggested I stop by the antique store and talk with the proprietor who was a local history fanatic. I asked about what the various graves' registries call the "Old Burying Ground" in Colchester. She'd never heard of it, but she took me to a window and pointed to a lot about a block away, a corner of which stuck out from behind a building.

I thanked her, walked across the street and around the building and there, without doubt, was the Old Burying Ground, overgrown with brambles and dotted with a few dozen empty bottles. The early gravestones were made of a reddish brown stone, and many of them have lost their facing. The face of one gravestone lay in a heap on the grass at the foot of the stone. I could just make out a few words and letters in the small pile of rubble. Major Israel Newton's grave will join the others in a few years. In fact, I recognized it only because I knew something about him and could piece together what was left of the inscription. Only two Johnsons were buried there. Elijah Johnson (b. Sept. 20, 1718–d. Aug. 28, 1755) was one of old Israel's uncles. Joseph Johnson, Elijah's son, born in 1750, died on November 17, 1808, when his own cart ran over him. Like Israel, Joseph fought in the Revolutionary War. Anstress Johnson's death is listed in the town records, but there is no stone for her, and was none even in 1888 when Frank E. Randall compiled his list of inscriptions from the Old Burying Ground.

I went to the antique store where I met a nice lady and told her roughly what I was doing. She offered to call Barbara Brown (who lived right across the street) and ask her where the Israel Newton house was. Ms. Brown told her that it was torn down about seventy years ago. She was kind enough to relay directions on where it stood, so I thanked the antique store owner's wife, left, and drove out to look. South out of Colchester, at the first stop sign, take the right fork. At the next stop sign, turn right on West Road and go about two miles. The road narrows, twists, and turns bumpy. It is wooded on both sides with new tract houses here and there. About two miles out on West Road, an old crumbled rock wall runs along the edge of a wood. Why would someone put a rock wall around a wood? Obviously, it had once been a farm, Major Israel Newton's.

✳

What of the rest of the Johnson lineage? It trails off into oblivion in the County of Kent at the time of Shakespeare. John Johnson, Jr., father of old Israel was seventy-seven at the time of the 1790 census.

He does not appear in the 1800 census, and, though he certainly could have been dead by then, my theory of the moment is that he and his second wife, Ann Smith, are the one male and one female "of 45 and upwards" in the Israel Johnson household in Rutland County, Vermont in 1800. Old Israel at the time was only forty.

We know a little about the father of John Johnson, Jr., already. His name, too, was John Johnson. He was born in 1679 or 1680, probably in Roxbury, Massachusetts, and he died in Colchester in 1755. He had no headstone. He and his wife, Mary Ramsey, had four children in Roxbury and five in Colchester, where, to judge from the Colchester land deeds, they moved in about 1710.

The father of John Johnson was Sergeant Humphrey Johnson. Born about 1620 in England, he died on July 24, 1692, at Hingham, Massachusetts. He also lived at Scituate and in Roxbury and is described as "a capable man in town affairs and often employed in the public business." He had, as Paul Franklin Johnson puts it, "an uncommon inclination to law suits." Deane, in his *History of Scituate*, says that "few men have left on the records of the court so many evidences of [a] litigious disposition." Humphrey Johnson married twice. With his first wife, Elinor Cheney, he had ten children. With his second, Abigail May, he had two, the first of whom was John, grandfather of old Israel Johnson. Isaac Johnson, Humphrey's older brother, was Captain of the Roxbury Company in the "expedition" against the Narragansett Indians in 1675. He was at the head of his company in what is sometimes called "The Great Swamp Fight" of December 19, the bloodiest battle in colonial history, and was killed storming the Indian fort. Humphrey was a sergeant in the same company.

Which brings us, finally, to Captain John Johnson of Roxbury (ca. 1590–1659), father of Humphrey and great, great grandfather of old Israel, who landed at Salem on June 22, 1630, in the fleet with John Winthrop. He settled in Roxbury where he was active in the business of the Massachusetts Bay Colony. For a long time he was surveyor general, which meant he had care of the arms and ammunition of the colony. He was town clerk for Roxbury and was chosen to represent the Town in the House of Deputies in 1634, the first year of that assembly, and for twenty-one years afterward. "Late in his life," says Paul Franklin Johnson, "John Johnson was granted one thousand acres of land in consideration of his great service to the Colony."

John Winthrop, in his famous history of the Massachusetts Bay Colony, called Captain John Johnson "A very industrious and faithful man in his place" and related an extraordinary incident in Johnson's life. On April 6, 1645, Johnson's house, used for storing the colony's gunpowder, exploded. Said Winthrop, it "blew up all about it, and shook the houses in Boston and Cambridge, so as men thought it had been an earthquake, and carried great pieces of timber a great way off and some rags and such light things beyond Boston meeting house."

Captain John's wife was Margery Scudder, daughter of William Scudder, "yeoman" of Darenthe in Kent, England. She was born in Darenthe in about 1592 and died in Roxbury on January 9, 1655. Captain John's father apparently came from Wilmington, Kent. His name was also John.

And there I run out of the Johnson ancestors, so far away from Israel Johnson of Clear Pond that he seems invisible. I wonder how much of all of this information he would have known. Well, not really. He probably knew none of it. What use would it have been to a man milling boards in a primitive wilderness? And yet he carried this history in his veins, making, or helping to make, what Shakespeare described in the time of his great-great-grandfather a "brave new world."

10

The Johnsons Meet
"Wellington's Invincibles"

I began work on the Battle of Plattsburgh in the summer of
1983. George Hotchkiss, the historian of lumbering in the Old
Northwest, said young Israel fought there. Through friends, I was
able to live for a month that summer in Keene Valley in a small
chalet at the edge of the woods, just off the Ausable River at the
south end of the village. The bridge to it had washed out several years
before, so I had to park near the highway side and scramble over a
make-shift arrangement of old boards and logs to get to the house. I
call it a chalet because it has that dark, peaked, gingerbreaded look I
associate with *The Sound of Music.* It was comfortable, away from
nearly everything, and just rustic enough to keep me from feeling
like a tourist. It had a wood stove and an LP gas stove, even a phone.
A spider lived in one of the front windows, so I learned a great deal
about the habits of spiders. A bat came calling once or twice at night.
Mice appeared regularly. One scurried across my hand as I lay reading
in bed, and one night I rolled over on one in my sleep. It scrambled
up my back and got away before I quite knew what was going on.
Another night, coming home from dinner at the Elm Tree Inn,
tiptoeing gingerly across the river, I heard thrashing in the brush
beside the road. The next morning I found a place where a bear had
slept beside the river, not a hundred feet from the house. Several
kinds of wildflowers grew in the meadow outside the door. I'd never
seen Deptford pinks before, so I brought some home at the end of the
summer and planted them in the front yard.

I wrote the chapter on the Iron Works that month in an old
garage out in a field about a quarter of a mile from the house. This

was also the month that I climbed Mt. Marcy, going in, of course, by way of Lake Sanford, past the ruins of the old Iron Works and the boarded-up remains of the Tahawus Club, said to include some of the original buildings of the Village of Adirondac. This was the route of the first people who climbed Mt. Marcy, those who stayed overnight at Clear Pond in 1836 and 1837. I also went back to Elizabethtown and found new—alas, legal— documents relating to both Israel Johnsons. And, I went to Albany to see what I could learn about Israel Johnson and the Battle of Plattsburgh.

To climb Marcy the way it was first climbed, you park in the lot just beyond the half-dozen buildings of the long-defunct Tahawus Club. Founded in the early part of this century, this club took over what buildings remained of the Village of Adirondac, the place Archibald McIntyre and David Henderson travelled to at least once a year to see how the mining progressed. Andrew Porteous lived here as manager, hassled by his neighbors. Robert Hunter was hired as overseer by the Works when it ceased operations in 1856. He and his family lived here by themselves for ten years or more, one of their children acting as schoolmistress to the others.

It's about three miles in, most of it horizontal, from the parking lot to what's called Flowed Lands, a shallow lake separated from Lake Colden by the Colden Dam. At the dam, I turned up along the Opalescent River. The climb up the Opalescent is rough enough in places that ladders have been built to help people over the biggest obstacles. It was in this area that the first climbers in 1836 were turned back by bad weather. The Opalescent itself is a narrow, tumbling river with many rocky falls. It takes its name, I gather, from the opalescent feldspar in the rock, which turns the water milky green. You climb for a mile or more in such a rush of water you almost have to shout to be heard by the person next to you.

The Twin Brook lean-to was taken, but off to one side, where the two brooks come together, I found a flat place among some pines and pitched my tent. Two things have happened in the Adirondacks since I was a boy scout there in the fifties. The water is no longer reliable, even in remote places, and the bears have come back. They say bears are practically harmless, but only if you give them everything you have to eat, holding nothing back for yourself. You must never keep food in the tent, no little cracker for a midnight craving, not even a

15. Theodore R. Davis's woodcut *The Deserted Village of Adirondack {sic}, Harper's Weekly,* November 21, 1868.

vacuum-sealed candy bar. So, I hung my food high, took incredibly small sips from my canteens filled at home, and lay awake most of the night listening for bears.

Up at seven, I left my pack in the lean-to and scrambled up the mountain. It was gray and overcast. Even so, a trail crew was already at work on the trail along Feldspar Brook. After a long steep climb, the trail levels almost to a plateau just before reaching Lake Tear of the Clouds. The lake is hardly big enough to be called a pond, but in the mist and silence it's an ocean of tranquility. Beyond it is what looks like a small mountain, most of it bare rock. I could hardly make it out in the rising mist. This small mountain, of course, is the summit of Marcy. In a gray stillness, alone with my breathing, I walked up it, reaching the top just before nine o'clock. I had the top and such view as there was to myself. But not for long. A piper cub blew in from the west, undoubtedly giving some tourist an early morning thrill, and passed right over my head. Not that I could have lingered. The sky was darkening, a wind was coming up, and it was eleven miles back to the car. I started down at a steady clip.

It was raining lightly before I got back to Lake Tear, and by the time I reached the lean-to and my pack, it had turned into a steady, all-day downpour. It was little more than a trudge the whole way down, broken only by a brief rest in a lean-to at Flowed Lands, where a saintly couple fixed me a cup of hot tea. When I reached the parking lot I climbed up on the front porch of one of the boarded-up buildings, undressed, wrung out my clothes and put them back on. In a state of some repair, I drove off to Long Lake for dinner.

George Hotchkiss said that young Israel had fought at Plattsburgh. I had asked, but young Israel had no service record in Washington. Did people in the area just pick up their rifles and run up to see what was going on? Was a general alarm sounded? It seemed a waste to read up on the Battle of Plattsburgh if Johnson hadn't taken part, so I drove down to the State Library in Albany one day to see if there were any state service records. I looked in various compilations before discovering that service records in the state of New York were not kept at the State Library but across town at the Bureau of War Records, Division of Military and Naval Affairs on what is called the State Campus. I was advised by a librarian to call first. Luckily, they were still open, but I was told to hurry since the office was about to close. After a fifteen-minute dash across Albany, I reached the gate and was directed to Building No. 22, the Public Security Building. There, the guard made a phone call, and within minutes I was talking with Tom Murphy, a short, slender, friendly man in rimless glasses, who came down to the lobby to meet me. He listened to my questions, then led me down to a huge, darkened storage area where ranks of filing cabinets stood guarding the military history of New York State. He found a drawer among the hundreds, opened it, flipped through the cards for a second or two, and found, not one, but two, cards with the name Israel Johnson at the top. One was for Israel Johnson, the other for Israel Johnson, Jr. Both held the rank of "matross" in Captain Russel Walker's company of Colonel Levi Cooley's regiment of artillery. The cards were pay rosters, and both Johnsons had been paid for service from September 7 to September 16, 1814. The Battle of Plattsburgh took place September 11. The only remarks were that Israel Johnson, Jr. was "On Command" and that "this Co. allowed 3 days travel home." They were both paid $2.66.

The state offices in Albany had only the pay records for New York residents fighting in the War of 1812. The National Archives, which houses all documents relating to immigration, military service, the census, government land sales and the like, had everything else. I wrote them again and hoped for better luck. In the meantime, I had proof that Israel Johnson had indeed been at the Battle of Plattsburgh, or had at least been mustered into a military unit at that time, and that his father had as well. Not many men, I imagine, were veterans of both the Revolutionary War and the War of 1812. It was one hundred twenty-five miles back to Keene Valley but worth every mile of the drive.

The large Webster's at the Keene Valley public library told me that a *matross* was an obsolete word for "a soldier next in rank below the gunner in a train of artillery who acted as a kind of assistant or mate." In the United States the term was apparently synonymous with "private of artillery." The Statutes of Massachusetts for 1793, which were still in effect in 1810, said that "Each company of Artillery shall consist of one Captain, two Lieutenants, . . . six Gunners, six Bombardiers, . . . and thirty-two privates or Matrosses."

I had the 1812 service records for both Johnsons sent to Bloomington. When they arrived, Richard Cox in his cover letter elaborated further. "A matross," he said, "was generally a gunner's mate who assisted in loading, firing, and sponging the guns." Sponging? I suppose that's how they kept guns from overheating and exploding. Men with buckets and sponges, damping down the outside of the barrel, a primitive water-cooling system. The service records for Israel Johnson and his father make it clear that Cooley's was a regiment of the New York State Militia and that both men's term of service was ten days, not enough time, as Richard Cox said, "to qualify for benefits under any of the later pension and/or bounty land acts."

Israel Johnson, Jr., was described as "On Command" during his tour of duty. He was also "present." His father, on the other hand, was "absent." Does that mean he was not at the Battle of Plattsburgh? Perhaps. Though I discovered later in one of the accounts that a detachment of "convalescents" took part in the affair. The one thing that leads me to believe that he went to Plattsburgh, aside from the fact that he was paid, and that he, too, was "On Command," is a note at the bottom of his service record: "Residence from the place of discharge 55 miles." He seems to have been discharged at "the place of discharge," which I presume was Plattsburgh.

Young Israel has a similar note on his record, though with an interesting difference: "Residence from the place of discharge 52 miles." He lived at this time three miles closer to Plattsburgh than his father, which, if it were three miles up Route 9, toward Plattsburgh, from the North Hudson cemetery, across the road from which old Israel lived, would have put him close to Weatherhead's.

Along with the service records came three different rosters for Captain Russel Walker's company, the first of which describes Levi "Cooly" as a lieutenant colonel and the commander of the Sixth Regiment in the Second Brigade of Artillery. There are forty-five names in all, one captain, three sergeants, three corporals, three gunners, three bombardiers, three musicians, and twenty-five matrosses. Both Israels were matrosses, as were Nathan F. Johnson and a Stephen Johnson. Nathan, I feel certain, was young Israel's younger brother, the one mentioned in the 1836 will deed as living in Indiana. Stephen was probably a relative, though I can't be sure of it. Elijah Woodworth was in Walker's company, as well. His wife, Elizabeth (Johnson), had died only a year and a half earlier. And Nelson Burgess, who had married or was going to marry Sally Johnson, was one of the bombardiers. He, too, migrated to Indiana a few years later.

✳

The battle itself came in two parts, the naval battle on Lake Champlain, which only took about two hours, and the land battle, called the Siege of Plattsburgh in the early accounts. The siege started north of Plattsburgh on September 6 and lasted until almost dark on the day of the naval battle, September 11, many hours after the British flagship, Confiance, had struck its colors. As Benson Lossing tells the story, the British army under Sir George Prevost was beginning to make headway against the New York Militia and the Vermont Volunteers when news reached the American soldiers that the British fleet had surrendered. The Americans cheered loudly, and Prevost and the British soldiers guessed the reason. They had apparently not been told the news. Rather than try to fight alone, far from a supply base, in an aroused enemy's wilderness (militia and volunteers were still arriving in large numbers, even on the eleventh), the British army retreated to Canada, leaving most of their baggage, all but their walking wounded, and a great many deserters behind.

Historians are still baffled by this battle. The British should have won. The Americans were more or less evenly matched against them on the lake, but the American army at Plattsburgh was made up of only fifteen-hundred regulars and roughly three-thousand New York Militia and Vermont Volunteers. Against this small, largely untrained, army came fourteen-thousand British regulars fresh from a succession of conquests against the armies of Napoleon. They were routinely called "Wellington's invincibles." General Macomb, the American military commander at Plattsburgh, in his dispatch on September 5, called the army that was then within ten miles of Plattsburgh, "the heroes of Spain, France and Portugal." It was the best-trained, best-equipped, most successful army in the world, and it outnumbered the Americans three to one.

As nearly as I can tell, the New York Militia had two skirmishes with the enemy: one north of Plattsburgh on the Beekmanstown Road on September 6; the other, on the Saranac River at what Lossing calls "Pike's cantonment," a ford three miles upstream from Plattsburgh proper and the lake. The militia was commanded by Major General Benjamin Mooers, and the Vermont Volunteers by General Strong. Mooers had sent out an urgent appeal for the entire militia force in his district to help repel the invasion. By September 4 he had about seven hundred men under his command. Macomb then ordered him to advance a few miles north of Plattsburgh to meet the invading army. Seven-hundred untrained militia were not supposed to engage fourteen-thousand experienced regulars but instead, as Lossing says, "watch the enemy, skirmish with his vanguard, break up the bridges, and obstruct the road with felled trees." The militia spent the night of the fifth in Beekmanstown. The next day half the British force, the right column, arrived, and the militia broke and ran at the first firing of weapons. They crossed into Plattsburgh at what was called the upper bridge and then destroyed it. Later, the British tried crossing there, but the militia drove them back. The siege was on.

It was the next day, September 7, that Russel Walker's company was mustered into service. If it took them three days to get home, it probably took as many days to get to Plattsburgh. It seems safe to say, then, that Israel Johnson, father and son, reached Plattsburgh the day before the battle itself. By that time, the defenses of the village were set. That part of Plattsburgh north of the Saranac River had been evacuated. To reach the American army, the British had to cross the river, and there were only three places to do it. The lower bridge was right in the village itself, at the mouth of the river. The upper bridge was a mile upstream. Both of these approaches were guarded by small forts. Three miles upstream was a natural ford. Macomb put his regulars at the two bridges, including invalid troops who were told to fight to the death. The militia and volunteers were sent to guard the ford. Apparently, Macomb was worried enough about the militia after its shaky performance at Beekmanstown that he felt he could not rely on them to stand up to the main thrust of the British army, which he expected at one or both of the recently destroyed bridges. General Orders, New York State Militia, Third Division, September 8, 1814, had this comment on the militia's performance at Beekmanstown:

> The general [Mooers] is not insensible to the merits and patriotism of those who, upon the approach of hostile forces upon this frontier, have gallantly flown to the defense of their country, and who under his command still continue steadfastly to oppose the progress of the enemy. The general regrets that there are some who lost to patriotism and to honor, after coming forward in obedience to his call, fled at the first approach of the enemy, and afterwards basely disbanded themselves and returned to their homes; thereby disgracing themselves, and furnishing to their fellow-soldiers an example that all brave men detest and abhor.

Not only that, but Mooers was "determined to have all deserters punished in the most exemplary manner." All of which was published in *The Plattsburgh Republican* on September 14, three days after the battle.

The militia and volunteers formed the left flank of the American defenses. General Robinson's brigade was sent against them, but they were apparently late in getting started. Once started, though, as John Mahon says in his recent history, "His men quickly scattered the American militia." John Stahl, on the other hand, implies that the "New Yorkers" gave ground gradually against obviously superior numbers. He also says "the retreat of the militia might have developed into a rout if the Vermonters had not arrived at this moment and steadied the nerves of their New York brethren." General Macomb's letter to the Secretary of War, the next day, said, "The militia of New York and the Volunteers of Vermont have been exceedingly serviceable, and have evinced a degree of patriotism and bravery worthy of themselves and the states to which they respectively belong." In an elaboration of the battle for *Niles Weekly Register* (October 1, 1814), Macomb went further: "At the upper ford he [the enemy] was met by the militia and volunteers, and after repeated attempts was driven back with considerable loss in killed, wounded and prisoners."

The loss was real, certainly, but the cause is not entirely clear. Mahon implies that the British were not, as Macomb says, driven back by the militia and volunteers. Instead, they were ordered by their commanding officer, Prevost, to retreat because the battle on the lake had been lost. Robinson thought he had broke the American flank, but he obeyed orders. The men were apparently sullen, but they too obeyed orders. They retreated as far as Chazy, in fact, eight miles away, before their retreat was detected. Mooers told his militia to chase after them, which they did with a will. Much booty lay about, and three hundred deserters had to be rounded up.

The battle was talked about for years afterward. Some Canadians said the British army nearly mutinied over the "bumbling of Plattsburgh." Maybe the British did bumble it, but one of the reasons has to be that the American naval force defeated the British convincingly in two short hours. If Robinson had been allowed to drive the militia back, he would have driven himself deep into hostile territory, far from supplies and replacements. Napoleon's campaign in Russia must have been fresh in the minds of all military commanders.

Cooley's regiment reached Plattsburgh, and it presumably bombarded the regiments under Robinson as they crossed or tried to cross the Saranac River at Pike's cantonment. Wrestling cannons and ammunition around in the woods must have been strenuous work. And then, because of these same cannons, the gunners, bombardiers, and matrosses probably could not go blithely off chasing a retreating army and picking up booty.

The militia fought all day on the eleventh, then chased the British army the next day or two. On the fourteenth Mooers issued orders discharging the militia. Walker's company was given three pay days to get home.

And that was the military career of Israel Johnson, Jr., of Schroon, later of Clear Pond, loquacious inventor and millwright, who afterwards told the story of his fight at the Battle of Plattsburgh, probably several times, to young James D. Lindsay, who, in the nineties, casually mentioned to George Hotchkiss in Davenport, Iowa, that Johnson "was a soldier in the war of 1812 and saw service at the battle of Plattsburgh, N.Y."

Macomb was immortalized, as they say, by having a mountain named for him. With the Dixes it forms a cluster of mountains north and east of Elk Lake. They are the nearest mountains of size to Clear Pond.

II

Israel Johnson Rediscovered

t was 1985, November, the warmest November I could remember in Bloomington. It seemed impossible, but I had been
working on this book more than four years. The book's ending had
been clear in my mind for a long time. I would not ever learn what
happened to Israel Johnson, how and where he ended his life. Last
seen in the 1855 New York census in the Town of Schroon, he would
have died before the 1860 federal census and been buried without
headstone in the same cemetery as his father. What else could I
assume? The last scene in the book was set in my mind. Then, I spent
a week at the National Archives in Washington, and all that changed.

I had reached a dead end. All sources of information I could tap
easily were exhausted, and yet large, unanswered questions remained.
Who was Joseph Frost, other than the man who bought young
Israel's land? How did General Mooers use the militia, particularly
Cooley's regiment of artillery, at the Battle of Plattsburgh? Could a
roster of Knowlton's Rangers be found? Old Israel may have been a
part of that unit at the battle of Harlem Heights in 1776. Did
bounty land records exist that would say whether old Israel took land
for his service in the Revolution? He might have gone where bounty
lands were being distributed before he moved to Vermont. Of course,
the vital records of that state would need to be looked at some day.
Finally, what happened to young Israel after 1855? I hoped eventually to find some living connection to all I had learned. Did he die, as
I assumed, before the next federal census in 1860? If so, tracing his
descendants would be impossible, though perhaps I could locate a
descendant of one of his brothers or his sister. I had no great confidence
that answers could be found to these questions, but I had to make one
serious try. So, in early November 1985, I went to Washington for a

week to use the National Archives, the single best repository of records and papers pertaining to the settlement and expansion of this country.

Years before I had spent a few nights in Washington at a small bed and breakfast hotel called the Tabard Inn. It was near Dupont Circle on the back side of a block that has the Canadian and several South American embassies on it. Small, sometimes inexpensive restaurants dotted the neighborhood. The Tabard, in fact, did a steady trade in lunches and dinners of the wine and quiche variety. There were bookstores, wineshops, a deli or two, even what used to be called greengrocers. You would sometimes pass couples talking in Italian or French. A man would be walking slowly along the street at dusk having an earnest, almost intimate, talk with someone about international banking. His coat would be draped over his shoulders as though he were walking in the Tuileries. Joggers peppered the back streets on their way to and from Rock Creek Park, a ravine where the Perrier company had set up an outdoor running and exercise path. Discreet male prostitutes lurked in selected, well-lit doorways, but only late at night. It was very sophisticated.

The Tabard was all I knew about Washington hotels, so I called to make a reservation. The Tabard was booked up, but they recommended a similar hotel four doors down the street. I had no difficulty making a reservation there. My flight arrived in Washington in the early evening, so I was fortunate to have a reservation. I came right up on the subway, checked in, and ten minutes later checked out. The Tabard does not have a great many frills, but its mattresses are not slabs of foam rubber stitched up in old sheeting, its rugs are not threadbare, nor its walls tacky with coagulated dust. And I don't remember a much-jimmied window, which opened a little too conveniently onto the fire escape right next to the bed. I left my hotel, went straight down to the Tabard and threw myself on their mercy. Luckily, they had a room. I moved in at once, breathing as I did, and went downstairs and joined the young Washington professionals waiting in line for a table. It was not really a line, of course, but a dark-paneled lounge with elegant, seedy overstuffed furniture of the kind found in chic suburban homes of the forties. People were drinking spritzers and talking about their therapists while waiting to be called for a table. I picked up a stray section of the *New York Times*, by this time of day smudged and misshapen from constant use, and eavesdropped on everyone.

Next morning, I was at the door of the Archives twenty minutes before it opened, as were about forty other people. The genealogical frenzy of recent years is such that Monday morning at the Archives is not a little like boot camp indoctrination. People are lined up, procedures explained, passes made out, briefcases searched, and the doors open precisely at 8:45. At that point, it becomes a little like a one-day close-out sale. The elevator is stormed. The quick and athletic dart for the stairway hoping to beat the elevator to the fourth floor. Everyone is headed for the microfilm reading room because the first law of genealogy is: Secure (and hold) a microfilm reader. This object is a small, self-contained projector that enables you to read microfilm. You may have come here from north Texas or eastern Washington, but if you don't get, and guard, your microfilm reader, all money spent on plane fares, hotels, subways, and meals instantly evaporates. All the rush and worry was needless, however. The National Archives has perhaps a hundred microfilm readers.

The chief attraction of the National Archives is that everything is in one place: all census reports, all military records, all bounty applications, "bounty" being the old term used to describe the government's payment—sometimes in money, more often in land—to those they lured into military service. If you cannot find there what these sorts of records reveal, the information probably does not exist. I started slowly. I thought it might be a good idea to look at old Israel's Revolutionary War record again. I had no reason to think that the copy I'd been sent two years before was incomplete, but as it turned out, it was. The whole file gave me at least one valuable new fact.

The new papers in old Israel's file concern his attempts in 1828 to put his name back on the pension roles. The original pension laws of 1818 had been revoked, and many legitimate claimants were thrown off the lists and had to reapply. New affidavits had to be sworn, and one of Johnson's, dated July 24, 1828, describes how Alexander Moses, Nathan Perry, and Gardner Stow appeared before Leander J. Lockwood, a justice of the peace in Essex County, and swore that to the best of their knowledge Israel Johnson had been a sergeant during the Revolutionary War. Treasury Department claim slips filled out the next month say further that Johnson "received a certificate for the reward of eighty dollars, provided by the resolve of the 15th of May, 1778." Since this Treasury Department form is a printed one with room only for a name, a unit, a date and the like, it would seem that thousands reenlisted in 1778 for a standard $80 bounty and not on the promise of bounty lands after the war. A search of the bounty land records confirmed this. So, after mustering out in 1783, Johnson did not travel to some remote part of the country to take up land he had earned by serving the army. He had already taken money.

The new papers also included his sergeant's warrant. It is a short but pithy "greeting" from his regimental commander at the time: "Zebulon Butler, Esqr., Col. of the 1st Connecticut Regiment in the service of the United States of America, to Israel Johnson Greeting." "Reposing special trust and confidence in your prudence and good judgement, I do by these presents appoint you a Serjeant," and so forth. It is handwritten, signed by Colonel Butler and dated "Camp, Jan. [21?] 1783." This is slightly puzzling because, as we know from other parts of his military record, he was made a sergeant on May 1, 1780. He was about to leave the army. Perhaps he wanted a record of his achievement, a kind of honorable discharge.

Though I discovered a number of things while I was in Washington, the main reason for going there was to locate a living descendant of one of the children of old Israel. I would have preferred a descendant of young Israel, but his disappearance after the 1855 New York State census made that seem unlikely. Of course, any descendant would have been welcome. The public records would bring me to the 1910 census (subsequent censuses being confidential under the new laws concerning privacy), but if I came that close, someone mentioned in that census could still be alive and might be located. And *that* person, so I hoped, might lead me to a direct descendant or the family genealogist or other valuable information.

The two will deeds for Israel Johnson, Esq., in Elizabethtown identify six beneficiaries, who I believe were his five living children and a grandchild, Nelson Woodworth. The children were William, Israel, Jr., James, Nathan, and Sally Burgess. James, Nathan, and Sally, named in one deed (April 6, 1837), were at the time all living in different counties in Indiana. William, Israel, Jr., and Nelson Woodworth are mentioned in the earlier deed (December 8, 1835); and because their place of residence is not given, I assume they lived where the deed was drawn up, namely, Essex County, New York. It was certainly true of Young Israel. Nelson Woodworth's connection to the family had become clear only after my first visit to old Israel's grave. Next to it was the shared grave of his daughter and first wife, both Elizabeths, both dead on the same day, February 8, 1813. The daughter was twenty-four at the time and wife to Elijah Woodworth; Elijah, who died in 1834, was buried next to her. Nelson, I feel certain, was the child of Elizabeth and Elijah. His wife, Nancy, and four of their children are also buried in North Hudson, next to Elijah Woodworth. Had Nelson's mother lived long enough, she would have been a beneficiary to old Israel. Nelson, I think, took her place.

My plan for finding a living relative was simple. I would go through the 1860 reel for the whole of Essex County to see if young Israel had moved into another township. I had done this once before, but it is too easy for the mind to wander while cranking microfilm. If you stop to pick a mote from the eye or squeeze the forehead in the heat of exhaustion or exasperation, your eye might easily slip down a single entry and all your effort be lost. (It is necessary, I might add, to cast oneself in these or similarly heroic roles just to endure the blinding boredom of this work.) When I was satisfied that he had truly disappeared, as I was sure I would be, my plan was then to try to trace James, William, Sally, and Nathan through the census records to see if I might find someone alive in 1910 whose children or grandchildren might be found at or near their 1910 residence. It took me an entire morning, but I satisfied myself forever that Israel Johnson, Jr., did not live in Essex County in 1860.

I started with James Johnson. The will deed said he lived in Dearborn County, Indiana. The 1820 reel for that county lists a Nathan Johnson and a Nelson Burgess, and my suspicion is that this Nathan was old Israel's son and Nelson his son-in-law, Sally's husband. I made a note of them and passed on. I was looking for Jameses. In 1830 one James Johnson shows up in Dearborn County, in Sparta Township. He is between thirty and forty years old with a wife between twenty and thirty and three boys all ten or under. I assume he is the same James who in 1840 is between forty and fifty years old and living in Laughery Township of Dearborn County. His wife is between thirty and forty, and he then had eight males living in the household, ranging in age from less than one to twenty.

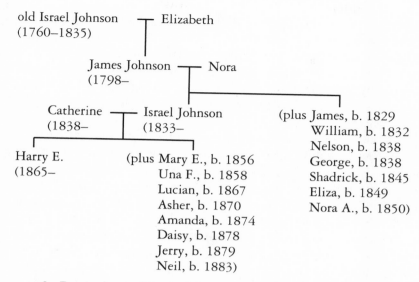

2. Descendants of James Johnson of Dearborn County, Indiana.

Starting with the 1850 census, everyone in a household was named. Age, occupation, and place of birth were also listed. It is an informational quantum leap. The only eligible James Johnson in Dearborn County lived in Clay Township. Evidence is circumstantial, but there is a lot of it. From the previous censuses, we expected him to be between fifty and sixty. He was, in fact, fifty-two and so was born in 1798. He was also a millwright, the family trade. He was born in New York. His third son's name was Israel. This Israel was sixteen in 1850, a farmer, and like his older brothers, James (twenty-one) and William (eighteen), born in Indiana. Nora, the elder James's wife, forty-three, was born in England. The fifth son was named Nelson (twelve). Too much of an echo is heard in this family of old Israel Johnson's family for this not to be his descendant. Even the two daughters, Sare Ann (eight) and Elizabeth (one), echo the Sally and Elizabeth of old Israel's household.

I go into such detail with James just to give an idea of how you must not ask too much absoluteness or factual accuracy of the census but be willing to interpret, that is, make good guesses.

Presuming I had found the right James Johnson, son of old Israel and younger brother of young Israel, it was easy to find him in later census reports (see fig. 2). In 1860 he still lived in Clay Township and was still a millwright. He was sixty-three and living with his wife, Nora, and their children George (twenty-two), Shadrick (fifteen), Eliza (eleven), and Nora A. (ten). In 1870 he was seventy-two. He called himself a farmer and lived with his wife and a woman named Nancy Johnson, aged forty-six. By 1880, old James, eighty-two, lived by himself.

The 1890 census for the whole country was lost in a fire. By that time old James would have been ninety-two anyway. So, I turned to another of old James's children, the one with the compelling name. Israel, sixteen in 1850, a farmer, had been born in Indiana. He was still living in his father's house. By 1860 he had left, but in that year an Israel Johnson, aged twenty-five, turned up in Washington Township, Dearborn County. He, too, was a farmer and had been born in Indiana. He had a wife, Catherine (twenty-two), two daughters, Mary E. (four) and Una F. (two), and an adopted son of nine named James. I would not have bet much more than a dollar that this was James's son, but I was hopeful. He was still in Washington Township in 1870. He was thirty-five, Mary was thirteen, and Una was missing. Other family members included Harry E. (five), Lucian (three), and a Sarah C. (thirty) born in Indiana, whom I suspect was the Catherine of 1860 using another of her names and cheating slightly on her age. Israel was still in Washington Township in 1880. He was forty-six, a farmer; he and his wife, now just Sarah and now thirty-four, had four new children: Asher (ten), Amanda (six), Daisy (two), and Jerry (one). What convinces me that this Israel Johnson was the son of James and Nora, is the information given about them. Israel said in 1880 that his father had been born in New York, his mother in England.

A new Israel Johnson enters these knotty pages. Son of James and grandson of old Israel, he was obviously named for his grandfather. Still alive in 1900 and still living in Washington Township, he was sixty-six at the time (born, October 1833 in Indiana) and had been married forty-five years. His wife had gone back to the name Catherine, and this time she was sixty-one. They lived with their daughter, Daisy (twenty-three), and son, Neil (seventeen).

By the 1910 census, the most recent one now available to the public, Israel had disappeared from Dearborn County. He would have been seventy-six, so it's likely that he had died.

To keep moving toward the present, I felt my best chance was to locate one of the children of Israel Johnson of Dearborn County. I chose Harry partly because he had a middle initial, E. That would limit my choices in the various census indexes. He was five in 1870, so I had a good chance of finding him alive and about thirty-five in 1900. I chose 1900 because that census is completely indexed for the whole country. I started with Indiana but found no one. I went to Illinois and Iowa. No one fit the facts I had. Kentucky, Missouri, Kansas. Which way would someone go in 1900 who was hoping to improve his chances or just looking for work? The only answer seemed to be: west. But there was nothing in Nebraska, Oklahoma, Texas, or Wisconsin. In desperation, I turned east and there in Ohio I found a Harry Johnson listed as a "roomer" in the home of Milton T. Lewis of 231 Michigan Street, Toledo. He was thirty-five, born in Indiana, where his parents were also born. He was a train dispatcher. Perhaps this was Harry, the son of Israel, but the information was too slight. I kept looking. I went through every state and territory and found only one other conceivable candidate, Harry E. Johnson (no age or place of birth given) who lived at 718 Spruce Street in Seattle as a boarder in a house with "no head shown."

It took me more than a day to seal up this dead end. The search for James Johnson and his descendants had led me to a new Israel Johnson but not beyond. That Israel Johnson, however, had lived all his life in Dearborn County, Indiana and had lived into this century, so it seemed likely that, when I returned home, I could spend some time in that county and find a descendant or two, who, if my luck continued, might know something about Israel Johnson, millwright, of Clear Pond.

At the moment, though, I was in Washington, D.C., and I had only five days to get what I came for. So, I slipped into an efficient routine. Up at seven, I had the complimentary breakfast while reading the morning paper, walked three blocks to the subway, which, with only one transfer, delivered me almost to the door of the National Archives. "Archives" is even the name of the stop. General Winfield Townley Scott sits on an iron horse above it. The Archives stayed open till ten, but after a sodden lunch at the cafeteria in the basement, gnashed down quickly because it is risky to leave your microfilm reader for long, I could only hold out till about seven before I had to leave and find dinner. This was easiest and most pleasant in one of the small restaurants around Dupont Circle. Afterwards, back at the Tabard, I showered, read for an hour, and fell asleep.

Such was my method and routine. I applied it to Sally Burgess next, but the results were far less satisfying. To begin with, I had no absolute assurance that she was born a Johnson or that she married Nelson Burgess, though the circumstantial evidence is strong. Before 1850, had she been living in her husband's household, she would not have been named. Old Israel's 1837 will deed said that Sally Burgess lived in Fayette County, Indiana. The 1840 census for that county lists a "Sarah" Burgess, forty to fifty years old, as head of a household. No male of comparable age lived with her. Is this our Sally Burgess, widowed? Possibly, especially when it turns out that Nelson Burgess lived in Indiana in 1820 (Laughery Township, Dearborn County) and in 1830 (Wayne County), but not in 1840 of thereafter.

There is little to go on here, but Indiana land records, which I found later at the State Library in Indianapolis, show that on December 22, 1817, a Nathan Johnson and a Nelson Burgess jointly "relinquished" a parcel of land in Dearborn County and that, on July 12, 1819, a Nelson Burgess and a Jonathan Johnson jointly relinquished a piece of land in the same county. The bringing together of a Nathan Johnson and a Nelson Burgess in this part of the world is further circumstantial evidence that this is the Johnson family. It also tells us how soon after the War of 1812 some of the Johnsons went west.

None of this, however, leads to a conceivable descendant of old Israel Johnson. No Sarah Burgess lived in Fayette County in 1850. And, though there was an Israel Burgess living there, a farmer, aged 28, born in Indiana, whose four-month-old child was named Sarah F., it would be folly to call Israel Burgess the son of Sarah Burgess, grandson and namesake of Israel Johnson, Esq., even though we believe it to be true.

The next road I tried stumbling down lay through the life of Nathan Johnson. Old Israel's will deed of 1837 said he came from LaPorte County, Indiana. Earlier I had found a reference to him in an old compilation of local history in the Indiana State Library. William Hacker in 1879 wrote in longhand a book called *Biographical and Historical Sketches of Shelby County*. Nathan Johnson has his own entry in it. "We can learn nothing," says Hacker, of the early history of Nathan Johnson except that he was a mill-wright by profession, and was employed by John Walker in the erection of his saw-mill on Laughery creek in Dearborn county; came to Shelby county shortly after Walker, and erected the mill for him at this place. Subsequently he purchased a mill site some seven miles up the river, and erected thereon a saw and grist mill of his own.

In the year 1833 he sold out these possessions and removed to LaPorte county, where he continued to follow his profession of erecting mills of various kinds, until perhaps in 1840, he removed to Texas, and the last we heard of him, he was still employed at his favorite pursuit. As he was advanced in age when he removed to Texas, he must, in the course of nature, soon after have passed away—but of this we have no certain knowledge.

Nathan Johnson was one of the most indefatigable men that ever resided in our county. Strictly moral and honest in every relation of life, never so happy as when doing something to aid in developing the resources of the country.

Since they were both traveling millwrights, this vignette of Nathan's life gives us a glimpse into young Israel's. Nathan was born within a year of him.

With these facts, it was not difficult to find Nathan in the census records (see fig. 3). But, as with James and Sally, the record trickles out inconclusively, this time in Fannin County, Texas. In 1850, Nathan told the census taker in Texas that he was sixty-four. So, he was born in 1786, within a year of young Israel. By 1860, Nathan had died, and his farm was taken over by his son, William (born in 1834) who lived on it till he died sometime between 1900 and 1910. In 1910, William's son, James (born in 1868), lived on the property, the address for which was "Honey Grove & Johnson Crossing." James had a new bride of twenty at the time but, as yet, no children.

Here, again, as in the case of James Johnson, the son of old Israel, I had traced descendants down through the last of the publicly available census reports. In fact, here was my best prospect yet for finding a living descendant of the Israel Johnson family. Old James's direct descendants took me to Israel Johnson of Dearborn County, Indiana, but I could not find him or his children in the 1910 census. James, Nathan's direct descendant, on the other hand, had just married in 1909 after taking over the farm his father, William, and

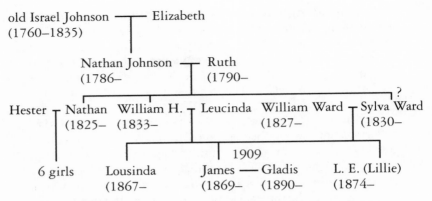

old Israel Johnson ——— Elizabeth
(1760–1835)

Nathan Johnson ——— Ruth
(1786–   (1790–

                                                              ?
Hester ┬ Nathan William H. ┬ Leucinda William Ward ┬ Sylva Ward
       │ (1825– (1833–   (1827–   (1830–

                          1909
6 girls   Lousinda   James ——— Gladis   L. E. (Lillie)
           (1867–   (1869–   (1890–   (1874–

3. Descendants of Nathan Johnson, who finally settled in
Fannin County, Texas.

grandfather, Nathan, had owned and worked for sixty years or more. He and Cladis or Gladis (I couldn't read the handwriting) probably started having children in 1911 or so. The oldest of them would be no older than my mother.

I was pleased. That was what I had come to Washington for. It was Thursday noon, though, and my flight back to Indiana did not leave till eight o'clock the next night. I called the airlines, but they were going to treble my fare if I changed my reservation. I grumbled and stayed put. I looked up a few things I could have found at home, and when the sun came out, I went outside. Buildings, broad and remote, streets like asphalt rivers, obscure generals astride immense horses, wind and sun. I decided to walk up to the Library of Congress. It was only six blocks away, behind the Capitol. It was, indeed, only six blocks, but it was also a mile or more. Past the National Gallery and its Annex, past other massive buildings, nameless and for the most part windowless and doorless, past a square pond the size of a city block. Then the Capitol and its grounds. Surely, this is the biggest building in the world, so big it obscures, by absorbing, the hill it sits on. Beyond it, the Library of Congress, where I asked a question about Vermont regional history so precise and arcane, they wrote me a stack pass right away, and I walked into the place where, I'm told, every word every written about America or in America and by Americans, plus a fair sampling of the rest of the words of the world, are kept. I just looked and flipped open occasional books and forgot all about whatever small item it was I had come there to find.

In the night, I woke and reminded myself that I was here for one more day only and that perhaps I should make some effort, I couldn't imagine what, to find Israel Johnson, Jr. At daybreak on Friday I got up and trudged back to the Archives.

I took out the 1850 census again, the last federal census in which I had seen young Israel. He was sixty-four, his wife, Polly, was sixty-seven, and his daughter, Betsey, twenty-four; and they lived in the Town of Schroon. Right above this entry (and so, right next door to them) was the family of Lewis Johnson, forty-two, his wife Freelove, thirty-one, and their children, Hollis (nine), Huldah (eight), Alexander (five), and Betsy M. (one). I had never located the William Johnson mentioned in the 1835 will deed, so I kept my eye open for William Johnsons, too. The 1850 census is indexed, so I found eight William Johnsons right away living in Essex County. Four were immediately ruled out because they were born in England, Ireland, or Canada. One was living in the Essex County Poor House, but he was fifty-five years old and at one time had been a collier. Another was a twenty-four-year-old "peddlar" living in the Town of Essex. A third, another collier, was only eighteen and lived in the Town of Chesterfield. None of these seemed promising, but the eighth had a remote, but definite, connection to the Johnson family. A William Johnson, twenty-five, lived in the Town of Schroon in the family of Alvin Bloomfield, the shoemaker, and his wife, Phila. Living in the same household were our old friend, Nelson Woodworth, his wife, Nancy, and their two children, Mary and Marvin. Nelson had been named in old Israel's will, and it seems likely that this William Johnson, though he would have been ten at the time of the will and was probably not the William mentioned, was at least a member of the family.

I still hadn't traced young Israel beyond the 1850 census, except to the 1855 New York census which had him still living in Schroon. Then I had a thought. I went back to the 1850 census to Lewis Johnson. I had no way to relate these two Johnsons, Israel and Lewis, but they apparently lived next door to one another, since, as genealogists say, next entry means next door. Let us assume for the moment, I said, that they are related and see what happens. Given their ages in

1850, Israel (sixty-four) and Lewis (forty-two), they might have been father and son. Maybe Lewis will be my ticket into the present, I thought. I looked him up in the 1860 census. No luck. I found a Lyman Johnson (fifty), though, in the Town of Schroon, but this was just more new information, which I did not want at this moment, so I let it go.

The Lewis Johnson trail, as the guidebooks say, turned cold. Then I thought, let's try that trick that led me to old Israel's Revolutionary War record. I looked at the 1850 information on Lewis Johnson's family to see if any of the sons would have been the right age to serve in the Civil War. The thing the National Archives does best is preserve and index war records and pension claims. Hollis was nine in 1850 and would have been an ideal age for soldiering in 1861. The General Index to Union Civil War Pensions listed four Hollis Johnsons. Only one served in a New York military unit. I called up the file, and indeed this was Hollis, son of the Lewis who had lived in the Town of Schroon in 1850. But Lewis, as the bulky file gradually revealed, with its sworn statements from him and at least twenty of his friends and acquaintances, had moved from the Town of Schroon, Essex County, over the county line into the Town of Horicon, Warren County. It was no more than twenty or thirty miles away, but if you're searching by census report and someone moves out of a county, they can move anywhere. The next county is as far away as Australia.

Civil War pension records are not on microfilm, and it takes an hour to call them up. It was almost noon when they arrived, so I scanned the Hollis Johnson file well enough to learn the basic story of Hollis's service and Lewis's appeal for pension funds and to know which of the hundred or so pages to have xeroxed, all so I could get back to the microfilm reader and chase Lewis and his descendants into the present. My plane left in about four hours.

Hollis and his brother, Irwin, enlisted in 1862 in the 118th Regiment of New York Volunteers, an infantry regiment. Hollis caught typhoid and died in July of 1863, and not until sixteen years later did Lewis petition the government for a pension. By that time, he had lost his wife, was crippled by rheumatism, and had to rely on the charity of a friend for his room and board. His story is part of this story, but I must now follow the odd, spurty unravelling of these events to their strangest and most miraculous revelation yet.

I went back to the census records. In 1860, in the Town of Horicon, Warren County, New York, Lewis Johnson, carpenter and joiner, lived with his wife, Freelove, and their five children. He was fifty-one, she forty-one. Alexander, fifteen, was now called "Irwin A." The newest child was George W., five years old. Sixteen dwellings away lived a William H. Johnson, thirty-four, a farmer, with his wife, Susan, twenty-seven, and their two children, Eugene H., two, and John H., almost one. There was also a boarder, John B. Jackson, sixty-eight and a carpenter, plus an elderly couple. This couple was Israel and Molly Johnson, seventy-six and seventy-eight respectively. He called himself a "basket maker," and she did housework. He said he was born in New York rather than Vermont (it must be easy at seventy-six to forget or to slur one's words), she in New Hampshire. Ten years later, in the same county, in the same household, three new children appear, one named Hollis, born in 1865, two years after another Hollis Johnson, the son of the man who lived only sixteen houses away, had died of typhoid in the huge military hospital in Portsmouth, Virginia. Israel Johnson was still there. He was eighty-six and this time called himself a carpenter. He got his place of birth right this time, as well: Vermont. Molly (or Polly) was gone. In 1880, though the William H. Johnson family still had all five children at home on the farm in the Town of Horicon, Israel was gone.

Israel Johnson of Clear Pond, for this can be no other Israel Johnson, son of Israel Johnson, Esq., of Schroon, moved to the Town of Horicon between 1855 and 1860 and lived in the family of William H. Johnson, probably his son, until he died, sometime between 1870 and 1880.

The darkened room full of microfilm readers at the National Archives is an intense, quiet place. People behave almost as though they were in church. The pressure of boredom and want in that room is almost stifling. Fingers run down interminable lists of names. Sighs rise occasionally above the rip and squeal of the microfilm readers. But there also happens in that place sometimes an unpreventable shriek or squawk, something almost like a yell, which, stifled as quickly as it comes up, produces a sound like few heard outside a zoo. On the Friday afternoon of which we have been speaking, in early November 1985, a short noise of this sort burst forth. When this happens, people look up and sometimes smile before bending again—with renewed hope—to the task of cranking another mile of microfilm.

Hollis and his brother, Irwin, went to Chestertown from their home in Adirondack and enlisted in the 118th Regiment of New York Volunteers on August 8, 1862. This was Adirondack in Horicon Township, Warren County, on the east shore of Schroon Lake, not the village where the old Iron Works flourished in Essex County. In 1862, the Works had been shut down for six years. What the inducement was for Hollis and Irwin, other than the cash bounty, I don't know. Both enlisted for three years or "during the war." Hollis left his wife of almost sixteen months and a small farm on which he had recently put twenty-one dollars down. It was about to give him his first crop. The unit mustered in Plattsburgh on August 30, and the boys went off to war. Irwin came back about three years later, but Hollis was admitted with typhoid fever to Balfour General Hospital, a military hospital in Portsmouth, Virginia, on July 9, 1863. He died a week later.

His father, Lewis, was a self-employed carpenter and joiner who never had any steady work. His wife died in 1867, and he went to live in the home of a friend, Benjamin T. Wells, in Adirondack. In 1878 he became persuaded that as the poor father of a veteran who had died in wartime, he was entitled to a pension. He applied but must have met with great scepticism because, over the course of two or three years, he called on at least twenty people to swear affidavits before one justice of the peace or another and reassure the government that he was indeed who he said he was, that his son had served, and that he was destitute. Even the daughter of the minister who married him swore an affidavit. Ruth A. Clark said her father, John H. Barker, "a minister of the Gospel," married Lewis Johnson to Freelove Montgomery on September 22, 1839, in the Town of Schroon. The claim was denied at first but seems to have succeeded finally because the file has a U.S. Pension Agency certificate, dated October 4, 1899, saying that Lewis's death had been reported to them as September 24, 1899. He would have been ninety.

Of all the affidavits sworn to awaken and loosen the government's charity, Lewis Johnson's tells most. Not his first one (April 3, 1878) or his second (February 21, 1879), but the long, five-page outpouring of his life, dated October 7, 1879, delivered, one can sense clearly, by an astonished citizen to his disbelieving government.

I was married to Freelove Montgomery in the year 1839 and had five children, as follows: Date of marriage Sept. 22, 1839.

Hollis A.   born November 22, 1840—married about summer of 1861. His wife died September 20, 1862 [20 days after he joined his unit in Plattsburgh].

Huldah   born Jany. 31, 1842. Married.

Irwin   "   Dec. 9, 1843

Elizabeth   "   Feby 8, 1849

George   "   July 20, 1855

A long narrative follows describing how Hollis's farm had to be "surrendered" to the original owner since he, Lewis, had no money to continue payments on it, how he supported himself by doing odd jobs as a carpenter, never earning more than $150 a year, how he was taken in on a more or less charitable basis by a friend, Benjamin T. Wells, and allowed to live in Wells's house. "I have never owned any real estate in my life," he said, "and my personal property consisted only of ordinary household furniture and wearing apparel, but no money invested in stocks, bonds or any other securities. I am now and have been since the death of my wife without any means of support excepting from the proceeds of my own manual labor."

Wells's own sworn statement tells the same story, adding only that during the early sixties, he let Johnson and his family live rent free in the house next to his own. "From 1861," said Wells, "until his wife, in 1867, died, his earnings were barely sufficient to comfortably support the family . . . . I doubt very much if they ever had a week's provisions in the house ahead . . . . After [his wife's] death he came to live with me." Another of the sworn statements says that Lewis Johnson moved from "Schroon, Essex," where he was married in 1839, to "Adirondack Warren County" in 1855. That is probably the year when Israel and Polly Johnson also moved to the same town to live with William H. Johnson.

But, who was William H. Johnson? He must have been a relative of some sort. That he would name one of his children Hollis, two years after the death of a neighbor's son with the same last name (and so the same complete name) also suggests that William and Lewis were related. Israel, to presume for the moment that he was Lewis's father, did not move in with Lewis probably because he was so poor. In 1860 William's real estate was valued at $700 and his personal estate at $500. Lewis had no real estate, and his personal estate was worth only $185. William was also just starting out in life. He would have been twenty-nine in 1855 and was either just married or soon to be married. Grandparents would be useful in a house with infants and young children. Let me make another guess and say that this William was probably the same as the one living in Schroon with the shoemaker, Alvin Bloomfield, in 1850. He was twenty-five then and called himself a laborer.

We must stay with this William, though, whoever he was, because he is the closest thing we have to a direct descendant of young Israel's (see fig. 4). If nothing else, his house was, so it seems, the last house Israel Johnson lived in. William was still alive in 1910 and still living in Horicon Township. In 1880 he and Susan had five children: Eugene H. (twenty-two), John H. (twenty), Henry H. (fourteen), Archibald H. (thirteen), and Robin L. (ten). In 1870 Henry H. had been called Hollis. If this seems odd, Robin's name in that year, the year of his birth, was Goodman. In 1900 William, seventy-four, had two sons still at home, Hollis H. (thirty-four) and Robert L. (thirty), both of whom had changed their names again. His wife, Susan, was sixty-nine. By 1910 she had died, but Robert, now thirty-nine, had married a woman named Lena (thirty-two), and they had a ten-month-old daughter, Marion. Hollis was forty-four, single, and still living on the farm. Old William was a widower and eighty-five.

The last thing I was able to do before dashing across Washington for my plane was to see what happened to the sons of William Johnson—Eugene, John, and Archibald—who had moved away from Adirondack. The 1900 index listed no Eugene H. Johnson in the whole of New York State. It listed nine John H. Johnsons, some living in places like New York City, Buffalo, and Albany. Of the two Archibald Johnsons in New York in 1900, one lived in Oneida County, the other about thirty miles south of Adirondack in the Town of Queensbury, Warren County. He was the right age, thirty-three. His mother and father were born in the right places, New York and Vermont. And, a reason not to be dismissed, he lived nearby. Archibald's wife, Julia S. was twenty-three. They had been married four years and had two sons, Earnest (three), born in November 1897, and Clifford (one), born in February 1899. Archibald was an "hostler."

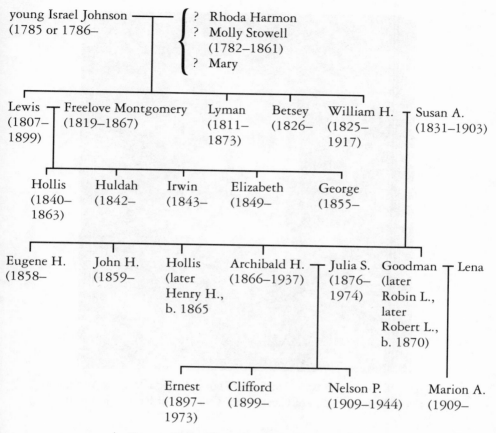

4. Descendants of Israel Johnson of Clear Pond,
Essex County, New York.

When I think that I almost took a flight home Thursday evening because I had found all that I thought could be found, my palms turn sticky. For two or three years, I had been certain that young Israel died between 1855 and 1860 and that he was so poor he could not afford a headstone. He was buried, I was sure, in the same cemetery as his father, up at the north end in the field where there are no headstones. Human life may be mysterious, but it is also predictable. There were no nursing homes or welfare agencies in the nineteenth century, only the poorhouse and the madhouse. A family was all a person had for old age and hard times. Little wonder they bred so

16. William Johnson (1825–1917) of Adirondack, New York,
son of Israel Johnson of Clear Pond. Courtesy of Robert Johnson.

many women into early graves. And yet for all the procreating and
clinging to families, all the hard clearing of land and the tilling,
what a restless brood. Nathan Johnson would have gone to Tasmania
to build mills if his health had held out.

    And I think of Harry Johnson, who spoke to no one and came
from nowhere, interrupted in his drifting by the census taker in 1900
in a Seattle flophouse. A great grandson of Israel Johnson, Esq.? A
remote cousin of Isaac Newton? It's an amazing world.

12

"Hardships, Troubles, and Treachery"

Nineteen eighty-three was the summer I spent a month in Keene Valley. I wrote the chapter on the Iron Works in the little garage-converted-to-summer-cabin next to the overgrown tennis court at the far end of the Kaufman's field. It was also the summer I climbed Mt. Marcy, the summer I met Paul Stapley, and the summer I started work on Joseph Frost.

Frost was the man who bought Israel Johnson's land at Clear Pond in 1846. I felt certain that knowing something about him would tell me more about Johnson, in particular why he lost his land. Though I started my search for Frost in 1983, I couldn't finish it until two years later. For the sake of clarity, I lump it here together as a single piece.

I was at such a stage in all these matters in 1983—still afraid I might have missed something—that one day I drove over to Elizabethtown to take a last look at the grantees' and grantors' lists for Essex County. As soon as I walked into the county clerk's office, I recognized Philip Sullivan, the man who had helped me two years before. He asked what I was here for this time, and when I mentioned Israel Johnson, he remembered the name. In fact the name had been stuck in his mind for some reason. Ten minutes after we'd parted, he came up to me and said it had come back to him. He'd seen the name recently on what is called the "General Index to Miscellaneous Papers Filed or Recorded—Essex County, N.Y."

The grantees' and grantor's lists were getting me nowhere again, so I thanked him and went off looking for the index to miscellaneous papers. I'd never heard of these papers, so if I hadn't run into Philip

Sullivan that day in August of 1983, I would never have learned, for
instance, that old Israel ran an inn or that Joseph Frost had sued
young Israel. The sale of Johnson's land to Frost began to take on a
new look.

First, the new information about old Israel. He had sold his
sawmill on the Schroon River in 1816. What he had done for the rest
of his life had never been clear. Many people logged land and then
spent the rest of their lives farming it. Among the miscellaneous
papers of Essex County are two documents with his name on them,
dated 1818 and 1819, which it took me two or three readings to
realize were tavern licenses. For $125 deposited with a justice of the
peace, Johnson was allowed to run an inn in his house. Under certain
conditions, though: "that he shall not during the time he shall keep
an inn or tavern keep a disorderly inn or tavern or suffer or permit any
cock fighting gaming or playing with cards or dice or keep any
billiard table or other gaming table or shuffle board within the inn or
tavern by him to be kept or within any outhouse or yard or garden
belonging thereunto." This, for all its color and extravagance, was
the standard declaration sworn to by all who opened taverns in their
homes. I happened on several more, including one in 1818 for
Randall Farr, Johnson's friend and neighbor.

Israel Johnson, Esq., it would appear, gave up milling in 1816 for
tavern keeping, and when old Peter Smith said in his 1822 diary that
he spent the night at Esquire Johnson's, he was in fact putting up at
a local inn. Considering who Peter Smith was, it was probably a well-
run and highly recommended inn for that time and place.

Two years later, looking into the early history of Vermont, I
discovered one reason why old Israel might have turned to tavern-
keeping. H. P. Smith published histories of Addison and Rutland
counties in 1886, and in both he tells the story of 1816:

> The "cold summer of 1816," as it is known, but really of two
> summers, 1816 and 1817, blighted nearly all crops in many parts
> of the State and caused great loss and considerable suffering . . . .
> On the 17th of May, 1816, there was snow on the ground and the
> earth was frozen hard enough to bear the weight of a man . . . the
> 6th [of June], says an old diary, was "very cold with snow-

squalls." . . . On the morning of the 10th ice half an inch thick was found in some localities. On the 29th of July the ground was covered with frost.

In his 1885 history of Essex County, Smith says, "After the farmers had planted their potatoes in the spring of 1817, the suffering was so great in some instances that they dug up the seed potatoes and ate them." Winslow Watson tells how in 1816 people in Essex County were hungry enough that many, gathering from "miles about a [grist] mill, would crave the privilege of collecting its sweepings." It might have been a smart thing for an old man to sell his mill that year. Innkeepers are less vulnerable to the hardships of the climate than either millers or farmers.

I also discovered the most plausible reason for the deaths of old Israel's first wife and oldest daughter. Abby Maria Hemenway says in her history of Addison County, Vermont, "This [1813] was the most mortal year; 50 died of the prevailing [typhoid] epidemic." Addison County is just across Lake Champlain from Essex County, the two then connected by a ferry at Crown Point. Eighteen twelve-thirteen was the first year of the War of 1812, and with all the men going to war and carrying various camp epidemics around the land, particularly in this frontier between the United States and the British in Canada, it is little wonder that many died, including, I feel certain, the two Elizabeths—Johnson and Woodworth, mother and daughter—who died the same day, February 8, 1813, and were buried under the same headstone in North Hudson.

I was lucky to be staying in Keene Valley. My friend there, Emily Neville, is a lawyer, and only a lawyer could make sense to me of the suits involving the two Israel Johnsons. For instance, one document, ten pages long, concerns a William Joiner as plaintiff and James Green, Jr., Titus Walker, Randall Farr, and Israel Johnson [Esq.] as defendants. It is written in a hasty, illegible twitch, but appears to involve the attempts of the defendants to rid their community in 1824 of a man they described as "indolent," "infamous," "contemptible," and otherwise "to have been worth nothing." Mr. Joiner seems to have bristled at this view taken of him, so he filed what looks like a libel suit. So earnest was he in the defense of his good name that he took the case as far as the Supreme Court of New York State. At this point, however, he relented. The case was called several times, each time requiring that the charge be written out again in the hasty scrawl, but Mr. Joiner seems to have departed the area and sought out new prospects and new, unlucky neighbors.

That leaves us with two judgments against young Israel, one in 1842, the other in 1846. The 1840s were troubled years for Johnson. Archibald McIntyre described him to Gerrit Smith as "poor old Israel Johnson" in October of 1843, a man who could "scrape together" only $32 of the $50 he owed Smith at the time. "Allow me to plead for the poor old Pioneer," said McIntyre. Smith relented and Johnson was allowed to stay on his land. Of course, Johnson lost the land three years later. What Johnson's problems were we may never know, but on February 26, 1842, a judgment was recorded against him for $89.74 plus costs. The plaintiff, Beriah Sprague, brought suit on September 3, 1841. A judgment, as I understand, is, or was, the record of a grievance, not necessarily taken to trial, but to be brought up against the accused should he ever come before a judge. I don't know what Beriah Sprague thought was worth $89.74 to him, but where there's steam, there's apt to be boiling water.

The second document seems to be a full-fledged suit. The grievance and disposition are clear, or would be if we knew nothing else about the parties involved. It is the case of *Joseph Frost v. Israel Johnson and Constant S. Myrick.*

> 1846. March 2d. [word unclear] personally served on C. S. Myrick only by Alvin S. Bloomfield Constable his fee $1.50.
> 1846. March 14.   Plaintiff & Constant S. Myrick one of the defendants appeared. Defendant Israel Johnson did not appear—Plaintiff declared for Goods Wares & Merchandizes sold & delivered the defendants. Labour & Services performed for said defendants. Moneys had & received, lent & advanced, paid laid out & expended. All at Defendants request—Said Goods consisting of Pork & other provisions, tea, tobacco Melasses & common Store goods delivered at defendants residence at Clear Pond in West Moriah in the month of February 1844. . . .
>   Cause adjourned on motion of the defendants to the 21st day of March 1846 at Justices Office

1846. March 21. Plaintiff appeared pursuant to adjournment and
tried cause. Defendants did not appear—
    Witness sworn on the part of the plaintiff William John-
son
1846. March 21st. Judgement rendered against the defendants for
the sum of one hundred dollars damages and for two dollars
and ninety seven cents costs . . .
    I certify that the above is a transcript from my
Docket   Dated March 23d 1846

Chauncey Fenton Justice of Peace

On the reverse side is the single word *paid*. Chauncey Fenton was for
years a justice of the peace in Crown Point. The case was heard there
and later recorded in Elizabethtown.

The issue seems clear. Joseph Frost was not paid for his services.
But who was Constant Myrick? He was not just a co-defendant; he
lived in the same house as Israel Johnson. And why did Israel
Johnson never show up after being summoned? Was William Johnson the man he ended up living with in Horicon Township about ten
years later? If so, why would he act as witness "on the part of the
plaintiff" and against his father? The biggest question was, what did
all this have to do with Frost's finally buying the Clear Pond property
from Smith? A definite though complicated connection existed between these things, but I had to wait two years to find it out.

It took me that long to find the time to go the Arents Library at
Syracuse University. The two best sources of information about land
sales in this area are the county clerk's office in Elizabethtown and the
Gerrit Smith papers at Syracuse. If these papers contained all the
information Mr. Lyon had found a few years earlier about Johnson's
dealings with Smith, they might also say something about Joseph
Frost. Frost could not have bought land from Smith without ex-
changing several letters, and Smith saved everything. So, one day in
the middle of March 1985, during spring break, I drove up the hill to
the Arents Research Library. It was cold and rainy. Piles of blackened
snow lay shoved against the curb. A nasty wind blew down from the
great Canadian waste. Syracuse had been eliminated from the NCAA

basketball tournament the night before. Life seemed insupportable. Mud lay everywhere. I wanted to say to the despondent undergraduate leaning against a trashed telephone booth outside the student union, whose hair seemed to be torn, "Don't worry." But she would have hit me with her rucksack and told me to go away. I went away on my own.

I spent the entire day turning over letters, notes, and deeds. I had only one day, so I threw my eyes down hundreds of pages of cramped, chocolate-brown handwriting looking for words like *Israel* and *Johnson* and *Frost* and *Clear Pond*. If I found one of these words, I read whatever it was. Otherwise, I raced on.

It had been exciting finding the low dike at the outlet of Clear Pond in 1981. I had looked a long time in—was it 1982 or 1983—with something like awe, at Johnson's xeroxed signature on the agreement he made with Gerrit Smith. A dozen other close brushes with this man had picked up my heart rate. But nothing equalled finding two letters written by him, as I did that day in Syracuse. It made the mud in Syracuse shine.

Other things turned up, as well. A pencilled copy of Kiersted's map of Township 44 showing what parts had been sold, with "IJ" written over subdivisions one and three of lot twelve. A note by Smith speculating on how his father, Peter, purchased the land in the first place: "My father & Jno. Kiersted bought their interest in Township No. 44 at tax sales in 1826 I believe." A letter from R. D. Lindsay to Smith, dated "Schroon March 8, 1835," concerning his and Increase Wyman's interest in buying subdivisions 6 and 9 of Lot 12. Two years earlier, these two had, with Johnson, bought the whole of Lot 13, to the north of Clear Pond. The Smith papers also had several letters from Joseph Frost.

The first of these letters, 4 December 1839, makes no mention of Johnson, but it says a great deal about Frost's relation to Smith. The letter comes from a place called Bridport, which it took me a long time to realize was Bridport in Addison County, Vermont, right across Lake Champlain from Crown Point. Also, if it wasn't already apparent from the suit brought against Johnson, Frost ran a store there, Joseph Frost & Co. In this first letter to Smith, it is clear that Frost acted as an agent for Smith in this area. He collected mortgage payments for him and saw that they were deposited in Smith's name at the State Bank in Albany. Much of this letter describes the difficulty two of Smith's mortgagees were having selling timber in a depressed market, so it seems Frost was something of a "double agent," also, often speaking to Smith on behalf of his beleaguered debtors.

He appears to have played this role for Israel Johnson. The next item is a letter from Frost to Johnson. It has no date, but it has been filed in the Smith papers in a box marked "1840 Jan–Apr. " The letter starts, "Uncle Johnson Sir." For a time I thought Frost might have been related to Johnson, but "Uncle" is probably just a salutation of friendship. "I want you should do Rite to Gerit Smith Stating the facts of your Contract being out of your Possession & the Treachery of Mirick & his advisors You say to Smith that you want him to take good note Sutch as will be sure & that you want to get a deed—I think that the best way to get over this Job is to get a deed Rite out any thing you want in this way I will doo for you that I can in Rite Yours J. Frost[.]" Johnson and Frost, it appears, had discussed this matter before. At the very least, Johnson had explained Myrick's treachery, whatever that was, and asked Frost to intervene for him with Smith. The next document explains how Johnson's deed came to be out of his possession.

This Indenture made this Seventh day of August one thousand Eight hundred and forty three between Israel Johnson and Constant S Merick witnesseth that I the said Israel assign over all my right and title to the premises which I now hold in possession Except the water priviledge on condition that said Constant maintains me and my wife through our Lives in a becoming manner and after my death the water works are at his command.

Copy of the originall   Signd Israel Johnson

                                             Constant S Merick

Indenture, indeed. Johnson handed himself and his wife over to another person. But why? Also, this is careful, legal language. Johnson or Myrick or both hired a lawyer. This curious act was done deliberately and with mutual consent. With treachery, too, however, as the following letter from R. D. Lindsay to Smith begins to explain.

Schroon River Jany. 15, 1845

Dear Sir

I hav ben Requested to inform you that the Contract you give
Israel that is to Say for lots at Clear poond the mony was obtaind
from Mr. Frost & Mr. McIntyre for the benefit of Johnson now it
appears that Johnson has made a partial assignment to Merick a
Soninlaw of Johnson for wich he expected him from his a greement
with Merick that he was to live with him Johnson & Carry on the
place but it apears that Since he has the asignment that he is a
Going to Sell it for a minor Trifel but if I hav ben Correctly
informed the assignment is not good for much as their is neither
Date nor Consideration as I understand the matter & it will be
wished by the large Part of Comunity that you due in this Case all
you Can for Mr. Johnson Please inform me as soon as possible

Yours Truly
R D Lindsay

So, Constant—unfortunate name—Myrick was married to one of
Israel Johnson's daughters. He lived in Johnson's house, which explains why he and Johnson were said to live at the same residence in
the suit Frost brought against them. Johnson naturally thought he
had good reason to put his and his wife's fortunes in the hands of this
man. Their daughter had. But, let's let Johnson tell the story. He
wrote it out in a letter to Smith.

Clear Pond   January 1845

Mr. Smith this is to inform you the trouble I am in concerning
my land my not being able to carry on my farm and mill alone I
took my Son-in law to assist me, signed over the article to him in
the following manner [here follows a short version of the "indenture"] soon as he got the article in his hands he appeared to posess
a diferent Spirit, grew indolent neglecting his business, taking
what money we received from travelors frequenting the Taverns
which were eight and nine miles from us, he has done no plowing
this fall, sold his team spent the money likewise sold the article of
the Land for one hundred Dollars, and calculated to clear and leave
me in the streets this appears to be because I talked to him for his
conduct. But as my Friend Frost by Accident found out the

treachery, he broke up the bargain before the money was paid He soon came and informed me, See my son-in-law, Counciled him to restore me the article take up his agreement and settle the affair but he refused to give up the article. When I received my son-in-law into my family he had a pair of young cattle his bed and Beding, wife and one child he had no provisions I have furnished my self and him provisions for the year past and have got to furnish my self an family for all time to come, for he has raised but six bushels of oats, one bushel of rye, one bushel and a peck of wheat, twelve bushels of india wheat, and not potatoes enough to last us through the season.

Now Friend Smith after you have considered the hardships troubles and treachery I have met with you are willing to grant me a deed, as my Friend Frost think is the best and surest way to avoid being further imposed upon by my son-in-law. I will inclos in this letter the line Mr. Frost sent me on wednes last his Council and wilingness to assist me the Bearer of Mr. Frost's letter told me that Mr. Frost said he would Deposit notes to your satisfaction in Albany Bank for to grant me the deed.

Sir please write me what you will do, and the sum now due . . .

Yours with Respect

I Johnson

Smith wrote back from Peterboro on January 27 saying he was "pained to hear of [his] severe trials" but claiming he had no legal right to give him a deed. He advised Johnson to "continue in possession" of the land but make no payments for two or three years. "Then if in the mean time your son in law has not paid on it, it will be safe therefore for me to think it an invalid contract & to deed you the land on your paying the sum due me on it."

Frost had never written to Smith about the matter, but he did so within a few months. Though dated "Bridport 25 1846" it comes from the box of papers marked "1846 Mar.–May." "I Rite to you by Partickular Request of Jonson & some other Persons whoo Reg[r]et to see the old man go to the County Poor House." Frost describes the difficulty and then transcribes the "indenture" into his letter. He continues: "I understand this Contract [the indenture] has bin Presented to you by Myrick Sturdefent or Messrs. Frink & Safford of Saratoga wishing you to take it & give a new one Referring to some other Person not Jonson Sir it is all Rong no other object than to cheat Jonson out of a living Myrick never has furnishd one shilling to feed or clothe Jonson or Wife—it has bin apertaind by Running the line between Jonson & Big Lot [#13] ownd by Frink & Safford that there is 4 or 500 good Pine Logs whitch makes all the trouble."

In 1840 Isaac Frink and Truman Safford had bought from Gerrit Smith Great Lot 13, the one immediately north of Clear Pond. This was the lot that Increase Wyman, Israel Johnson, and R. D. Lindsay started making payments on together in August 1833. Smith sold to Frink and Safford presumably because Johnson and the others were no longer interested in the land. I had assumed they were local people, friends or acquaintances of Johnson's. It now seems that they were partners in a Saratoga lumber firm, and considering what was going on in 1845 with Johnson's homestead at Clear Pond, it might be that they had their eyes on the 500 good pine logs still left on Johnson's property. Had they, in fact, snatched lot 13 from Johnson and his friends in 1840, and were they about to do the same in 1845? But Frost has more to say.

> Mr. Israel Johnson is a very simple Singular man, all castles & no foundations Still he is a Perfect honest man He and his Friends has Aplyed to me for help . . .
>
> Myrick is a Poor Miserable Fellow trying to sell the Contract for 25 or $50 I hope sir at last that you will not make a deed to anyone but Jonson or Myrick . . .

> Yours Very Truly
Joseph Frost
Addison County Vt

> P.S. You will find Plenty of good men Ready & Willing to state to you the facts in Schroon when you Pass there to your Land Sale next summer

As we know from Smith's land records, Johnson owed $320.29 on the land in April of 1846. Joseph Frost's offer to buy the land for Johnson in that year seems an act of uncommon generosity. $320 was a great deal of money then, more than the ordinary store owner would have to give in charity. But it is at exactly this time, March of 1846, that Frost brought suit against Johnson and Myrick. Can the man offering to buy land for Johnson be the same man who brought a suit for damages against him? Perhaps the point of the suit was to discredit Myrick, though some sort of chicanery by Frost can't be ruled out. When the dust finally settled in November of 1846, Joseph Frost was the clear and sole owner of Johnson's Clear Pond property.

Frost wrote Smith again in June:

> Sir I am sorry to give you so mutch trouble in this Business of Israel Jonson Still his Health & Condition urges me to doo so He did not meet me at Albany to go & see you as Agreed in the Spring in Consideration of Poor Health his Health is yet Bad, the Inside Sheet is handed me by R. D. Lindsay whitch I Anex these lines too if you grant his Request & Make the deed in my name I ask the favor to hav you send it to Archibald McIntire of Albany with Direction to hand me when I hand him a note at 6 months for twoo hundred Dollars

The "inside sheet," dated June 16, 1846, is a short letter from Johnson to Smith stating his desire to have Frost acquire title to his land. It is also signed by Johnson's friend, R. D. Lindsay, and said by him to be Johnson's voluntary act. "I hav on Reflection made up my mind to hav Joseph Frost as he is a going to pay the mony to git the title git the deed in his own nam from you as he has this Day given me a Contract to let me hav Six years to pay the a mount of the purches mony & I hav sums and Judgments that air unjust for me to pay & to bring all in to Consideration You will doo a favor to Deede to him." Those "sums and Judgements" probably include the one brought by Frost himself. Johnson seems to be asking Smith to deed his land to a man who has brought a judgement against him, one he considers to be "unjust." The water seems distinctly murky.

A note about R. D. Lindsay. He was more than a friend. H. P. Smith said in 1885 that a Robert D. Lindsay married old Israel's daughter. This would have made him young Israel's brother-in-law. The census shows that in 1840 Robert D. Lindsay lived in the Town of Schroon. But, he and his wife were between thirty and forty years

17. Letter from Israel Johnson to Gerrit Smith, dated
"Bridport, June 16, 1846." Courtesy of Syracuse University Library.

old, which means that both were anywhere from fifteen to twenty-five years younger than young Israel. Old Israel did have a daughter in 1810 who was between ten and sixteen, but I wonder if it wasn't young Israel's daughter he married, the one who was under ten in 1810.

Johnson's letter was written in Bridport, almost certainly at Frost's store. This letter is also less literate than his other letter, and the two hands are different. My hunch is that the Bridport letter was dictated. The hand of that letter resembles Lindsay's, though the signature is Johnson's.

Frost, it would seem, did not buy Johnson's land out of charity. All that happened was that Johnson's mortgage was transferred from Smith to Frost. Unlike Smith, Frost bound him to pay it off in a certain amount of time, six years. This whole business has made me wonder about Gerrit Smith's land dealings. His generosity and leniency can't be disputed, but he was also a practical man. Evidence suggests that he left himself open to higher offers on land that was already under contract. Frink and Safford of Saratoga eventually bought land (lot 13) that Johnson and his two friends had made payments on, and according to Frost they were about to do it again in 1846 with the land Johnson was living on. Frost and others were friendly enough with Johnson not to want to see that happen, and that is presumably why Frost bought the land at Clear Pond.

Yet there was a moment when Frost proposed paying off Johnson's mortgage and having the deed made out to Johnson. What happened to that idea? All Johnson says, and he says it in a letter written for him at Joseph Frost's store in Bridport, is that "on Reflection" he thinks it best to hand over the land, deed and all, to Joseph Frost. Is there something a little off here, or are the two of them just being realistic? Perhaps Frost's suit against Johnson should be looked at in a different light. It was brought only three months before Johnson asked Smith to sell his land to Frost. Is this how the one hundred dollars damages in the suit was paid? And what about Frost's assessment of Johnson's character, "all castles & no foundations?" A "simple, Singular man" and a "Perfect honest" one, as well. I feel like a lawyer in a court, defending a dead client from ghosts.

Gerrit Smith's response to Frost and Johnson's proposal was to agree to it, which he did by letter on August 12, 1846.

All that remains of this extraordinary business are two short letters, one from Frost to Smith (November 18, 1846) describing the details of the final transaction and the other from Archibald McIntyre, who, even at the end, played a role in the disposition of Johnson's affairs. "My dear sir," McIntyre wrote Smith on November 28, "I rec'd on the 26th your letter of the 23rd with your deed to Joseph Frost. I immediately notified his agent here of the fact, and this day he deposited to your credit in the State Bank $335.08, the consideration for the land conveyed."

November 23 was the date recorded in Smith's book when the Clear Pond property was conveyed by warranty deed to Joseph Frost. The contract Johnson made with Frost in 1846, to pay the land off in six years, does not survive, as far as I know. By the time of the 1850 census, Johnson had moved out of the Town of Moriah—or North Hudson, as it became in 1848—and back into the Town of Schroon. He and Polly lived alone with their daughter, Betsey. Was it Betsey, I wonder, who had the bad luck to be married to Constant Myrick? She was twenty-four in 1850.

✳

As the census shows, dozens of Frosts and Myricks lived in Vermont in the early and middle eighteen hundreds. In 1830 twelve Frosts were listed as head of household in Vermont, ten of them in Addison County. The 1850 Vermont census listed thirteen Myricks as head of household, seven in Addison County. A Myrick became Secretary of State for Vermont in the 1930s.

I assume Constant Myrick came from this Vermont clutch, though I was never able to find him in the census records. He is not listed in the 1850 census index for either Vermont or New York, and I didn't look any further, considering it perhaps appropriate that he and his infamy should disappear entirely.

With Joseph Frost it is a different matter. For one thing, his purchase of the land at Clear Pond is recorded in Elizabethtown, dated November 23, 1846, as is the sale of that land by his heirs in 1870. Frost was born in 1793, and when he first appeared in the census records, in 1820, he was living in Bridport with his wife and had no declared occupation. By 1830 his household had mushroomed.

He was thirty-seven, and nine people lived in the household, including another male, aged thirty to forty, two aged twenty to thirty, and one aged fifteen to twenty. I assume none of these males was his child, since none was in the household in 1820. I don't know when he opened his store, so I don't know whether these other males were employed by him or were just roomers. The females included his wife, one person aged fifteen to twenty and two girls between five and ten. Most likely, these girls were his children. In 1870 his heirs were three women.

Frost's occupation was listed for the first time in 1840. Two of the people in his household of eight engaged in commerce. Joseph was forty-seven, his wife between forty and fifty. Other household members included two males (twenty to thirty) and one (fifteen to twenty), two females (twenty to thirty) and another (five to ten). By 1850, when the census records started naming everyone, Joseph Frost had given up his store. He was fifty-seven, living in Bridport in the house of William Moore, twenty-eight, an innkeeper, and he called himself a farmer. Next door to this inn was the household of Darwin Rider, twenty-seven, a merchant, whose wife, Miranda Rider, twenty-eight, was later listed as one of Frost's heirs. The Clear Pond property was deeded to her and two other women after Frost's death on June 22, 1863. Other members of the Rider household in 1850 included Lydia Rider, forty-four, probably Darwin's mother, Betsey L. Frost, forty-six, perhaps Joseph's sister, Marietta Frost, twenty-seven, and Betsey J. Frost, sixteen. The last two were two of Joseph's daughters and eventual heirs. In 1860, they were still living in Darwin Rider's household, except they were then called Mary E. Frost (thirty-six) and June B. Frost (twenty-five). It was as Miranda S. Rider, Mary E. Birchard, and Jane B. Frost that these three women inherited land from their father in 1870 that had once been homesteaded by Israel Johnson.

I could not find Joseph Frost in the 1860 Vermont census, though I know he died in 1863. It seems that he turned his store over to his son-in-law, Darwin Rider, who fortunately was not another Constant Myrick. As for the town he lived in, Brookes's *Universal Gazetteer* (1823) describes Bridport as a "post town and township of Addison county, Vermont, on Lake Champlain, near Crownpoint, 15 miles S from Vergennes, and 5 W from Middleburg." In 1854, according to *A New and Complete Gazeteer of the United States,* the population was 1393. Joseph Frost & Co. may have been in the post town of Bridport, but Henry Perry Smith, in his *History of Addison County Vermont* (1886), mentions a "West Bridport" with "a beautiful location on the lake shore. It was originally called Catlin's Ferry, and subsequently went by the name of Frost's Landing. There has been a store and settlement here for many years." I assume this store had once been Joseph Frost's. One end of the Champlain Bridge touches down there now.

The heirs of Joseph Frost (Miranda S. Rider, Mary E. Birchard, and Jane B. Frost) on December 20, 1870, did, for $400, deed all of the original 195 acres that Israel Johnson began making payments on in 1831 to Orson Richards of Sandy Hill, Washington County, New York. Orson Richards, a land speculator, in 1875 deeded this and numerous parcels of land in several New York counties to a Dean Sage of Brooklyn. It seemed fruitless to chase this phantom further. It was undoubtedly passed around among land and lumber speculators, used and discarded, bought at tax sales, until Finch, Pruyn of Glens Falls bought it sometime in this century and in our own time sold it to those who have made it a part of the Elk Lake and Clear Pond forest preserve.

Joseph Frost bought Johnson's land in November, 1846. In July of that year, J. T. Headley, author of *The Adirondack; or Life in the Woods* (1849), passed by the property on his way into the Iron Works. "At length we emerged into a clearing," he says, and there he met a teamster he had hired earlier to take him the rest of the way. The teamster sat "in a log hut . . . quietly eating his breakfast." No mention of Johnson or a sawmill, though it was most likely Mrs. Johnson who made the man his breakfast. Alfred B. Street, in *The Indian Pass* (1869) describes getting lost near Clear Pond. He was trying to make his way from Roots's Schroon River Hotel to Indian Pass, and, reaching Clear Pond, he called it "a pretty sheet, a mile long and half a mile wide, with no islands. There is quite a farm cleared at the pond, but I looked in vain for the customary homestead." Verplanck Colvin, the famous surveyor, passed "Johnson's Clear Pond,"

as he called it, in August of 1871 without comment. (See the *Albany Evening Journal* for Saturday, August 26, 1871.) Colvin knew about Johnson's connection with Clear Pond, even twenty-five years after Johnson had left it, or he knew that someone named Johnson had been connected with it in some way. The intriguing comment is Street's, however: "I looked in vain for the customary homestead." By the late 1860s, twenty years or so after Frost purchased the land and while his three daughters still owned it, the house, the sawmill, the barn, and perhaps other buildings had all come down.

So, I wonder, again, about the photograph in Pete Sanders's office. Could it be that old? If not, what was that building and who were those people?

13

"No Heaven—No Hell"

*O*nce I knew that I was writing a book about Israel Johnson, sometime in late 1981 or early 1982, the question was: Is this a book about Israel Johnson or is it about my finding Israel Johnson? Put more simply, am I writing about Johnson or myself? I tossed this question back and forth for a long time and even talked with friends about it. "Oh, make it about your search," some urged. Others said exactly the opposite. "Stick with Johnson. Reconstruct his life."

Obviously, I've taken the first option, but I didn't do it easily and not until the late spring of 1983 after classes had ended and I could spend two weeks away from home at a writers' colony—Ragdale, in northern Illinois. Once I started writing, though, it happened as naturally as leaves.

Biographies, I'm sure, are always about their authors. Boswell wrote about Boswell in his life of that other Johnson, Samuel. Discrete, thorough, sensible, astonished Boswell, not a little taken with his own good fortune at being admitted to the feast of eighteenth-century British colonial supremacy as marked in its crowded London coffee shops, its eccentric genius, brilliant talk, its new energies in prose—the essay, the novel, the biography—its hideous poverty and gin-splashed depravity. I, too, wanted to write about things that mattered to me, but the poet in me did not want to look too closely at motives and intentions. After all, I'd been telling students for years, "Show, don't tell." In other words, don't explain yourself. Let someone else be the critic. Get down where the feelings swim around with their big teeth looking for something to eat.

And yet, you can't put the mind to sleep. Whales have to come up for air.

I had grown up in the Adirondacks. That's a start. Actually, I had lived there, just outside Saranac Lake, from 1946 to 1955. That's not a long time, really. I've lived longer in Indiana. In fact, I've now lived longer in Indiana than I've lived anywhere. Why am I not writing about that? Or, because I probably am, how is this disconnected tale of my search for an ordinary person who had, for all intents and purposes, been lost to human memory, the story of my own life or the story my life had become? I suppose it was to avoid direct answers to this question, indeed to avoid asking the question in the first place, that I became absorbed in the minutiae of a place that was near, but not quite, the place where I felt I had originally come from and belonged, a place so far away from me in the 1980s that I felt in some way I had come loose from the universe.

And it would turn into a tale, not of finding the lost home of the soul, but of finding the inevitable, the historically verifiable, opposite, the homelessness of everyone. This tale took place in a forest, a primitive forest that was cut down in the name of human progress but then came back very nearly to erase the memory of those first settlers. It seemed almost exact for the story of "my" life to be the story of my finding a few scattered allusions to a person I was not related to in any way and could not find. Except in the deep way of human anonymity. The way a life can sink so far down into the ponds and underground rivers that it can clarify itself, steep itself in the earth, wander in sunless chambers and sluices, emerging who knows how many years later as a kind of water, a clear pure blood, of which the scientists say we are mostly made.

This hopping from one corner of Johnson's life to another, this focusing now on him, now on his father, now on John Winthrop, now on me, is, in fact, as perfect a record as I can make of the smooth, seamless working out of a problem in my mind.

I had known for years that old Israel Johnson had moved to Essex County from Rutland County, Vermont, in 1803, but it wasn't until 1986 that I was able to go there to look through the vital records and land deeds. I did some reading before I went, and though little can be found in books that relates directly to the Johnsons, certain large episodes in Vermont's history tell how and probably why old Israel went there and why he left.

I am less interested in the political machinations that made Vermont's early history turbulent than I am in what made that part of the world suddenly appealing to its pioneer settlers. It is interesting to know that much of the land was simultaneously claimed by New Hampshire and New York or that there was a moment during and shortly after the Revolution when powerful factions in the state negotiated secretly with the British to have Vermont restored to the Crown. But these matters probably had little to do with the reasons why twenty-three-year-old Israel Johnson, newly discharged from the army, left his home in Colchester (to presume he returned to it) and moved into a primitive wilderness.

In 1790 and 1800, the years of the first two censuses, Johnson lived in the Town of Wells in Rutland County. He must have moved to Vermont sometime after he mustered out of the army in October 1783 and before young Israel was born in 1785 or 1786. It's doubtful that he married while he was in the army, since no children arrived before young Israel. His wife Elizabeth's maiden name and home town remain a mystery. It would seem natural for her to have come from Colchester, but their marriage is not mentioned in Connecticut's records.

Settlement was slow in Vermont because it was part of the no-man's-land between the warring superpowers, Great Britain and France. They were at war with one another, off and on, for nearly a hundred years. Each side enlisted the loyalty of certain Indian tribes, and life along what is now the Canadian border was risky until the French were finally defeated on the Plains of Abraham, and the Treaty of Paris was signed in 1763. The French and Indian War drove the French government from North America for good. The same war also introduced large numbers of English colonial troops, men born in Massachusetts, Connecticut, Rhode Island, and New York, to this unspoiled wilderness. As soon as it was safe to live in what is now Vermont, men moved there in swarms, traveling along the same roads they had built for the army. The principle road, called the Crown Point Road and later the Great Road, began At Wentworth's Ferry on the Connecticut River, near present-day Springfield, and ended at Chimney Point on Lake Champlain, later called Frost's

Landing, opposite Crown Point. It passed within twenty miles of the Town of Wells.

Migration to Vermont after the French and Indian War was cut short, however. The Revolutionary War made it a no-man's land again, this time between the Americans and the British. Not until that war was over did migration start in earnest. Israel Johnson, Esq., was part of this crowd. The historians of early Vermont all say that two kinds of people moved there, one to the east of the Green Mountains, one to the west. The group to the east came generally from the settled communities of eastern Connecticut, and being conservative, they quickly set up towns and villages like the ones they had come from. They were Congregationalists, mostly, and they brought their Congregationalism with them. Those who settled west of the Green Mountains, says Frank Bryan in *Yankee Politics in Rural Vermont*, "were far different from those who populated the river towns. Many were adventurers who remembered the fertile lands of Vermont from their travels . . . during the French and Indian War; others were escapees from New England Congregationalism, and a large number were land speculators . . . . The people west of the mountains, more radical and warlike, were more apt to be land speculators, adventurers, or religious outcasts than ministers and landed gentry." Chilton Williamson, in *Vermont in Quandry: 1763–1825*, quotes some loyalists in 1782 complaining that "the common people" of that region "are the hottest rebels they have ever seen." As we will see, Johnson's land dealings in the Town of Wells suggest that he was not just a millwright but something of a land speculator as well. His eight years in the army would have made him familiar with land speculators, adventurers, religious outcasts, and hot rebels.

Nathan Perkins of Hartford, a Congregationalist minister, made a tour through this region in 1789—"my mission to ye New Settlements" is what he called it—and in his journal he said, half the people "would choose to have no Sabbath no ministers—no religion—no heaven—no hell—no morality." Reverend Perkins no doubt observed correctly on this matter, but luckily he observed other things. For all his shocked sensibilities and outraged spirituality, he saw how people lived, admired their strength, and sympathized with their misery.

Words cannot describe ye hardships I undergo . . . got lost twice in
ye woods already—heard ye horrible howling of ye wolves. Far
absent—in ye wilderness—among all strangers—all alone—among
log-huts—people nasty—poor—low-lived—indelicate—and
miserable cooks. All sadly parsimonious—many, profane—yet
cheerful & much more contented than in Hartford—and the
women more contented than ye men—turned tawny by ye smoke
of ye log-huts—dress coarse, & mean, & nasty, & ragged.—Some
very clever women & men—serious & sensible. Scarcely any po-
liteness in ye State.

In 1789 Israel Johnson probably lived no differently or better than
the people Perkins described.

When I go from hut to hut, from town to town, in ye Wilderness,
ye people nothing to eat,—to drink,—or wear,—all work, & yet ye
women quiet,—serene,—peaceable,—contented, loving their
husbands,—their home,—wanting never to return,—nor any dressy
clothes; I think how strange!—I ask myself are these women of ye
same species with our fine Ladies? Tough are they, brawny their
limbs,—their young girls unpolished—& will bear work as well as
mules. Woods make people love one another & kind & obliging
and good natured. They set much more by one another than in ye
old settlements. Leave their doors unbarred. Sleep quietly <u>amid
flees—bed-buggs—dirt & rags.</u>

Johnson may have heard Perkins preach. An undated entry says,
"Wednesday afternoon rode to Wells and preached to a listening
congregation." Unless, of course, old Israel was a hot rebel and a hater
of religion.

Perkins's diary shows that Vermont was once thickly forested, so
the first business of settlement was lumbering. As a millwright,
Johnson would never have been idle. Once it was cleared, the land
was farmed. The soil was fertile, but it was quickly abused and
depleted. Even Reverend Perkins was able to see in 1789 that
"Vermont will not be a grain Country after a few years." The population exploded from 30,000 in 1781 to 154,000 in 1800, but then
leveled off quickly. Population rose 150 percent between 1781 and

1790 and only three-tenths of one percent between 1850 and 1860. Two-thirds of the people in 1800 were twenty-six years old or younger. Most of the original towns were named for towns in Connecticut, and for a while in the early days, the region was called "New Connecticut."

The first civilians to reach Vermont were the land speculators. Either individuals or companies of men purchased large tracts of land, had them surveyed, and then set about inducing the young and adventurous to buy lots and move onto the land. The advertising techniques of the late eighteenth century may seem crude by our standards, but they worked. Ads appeared regularly in local newspapers—usually weeklies—in places like Connecticut and Massachusetts. They promised cheap, rich, easily cleared land ("sawmill and School now under construction," as one ad put it). Land bills were posted in prominent places, and they were even read from the pulpit. This in a day when it was compulsory to attend church. Special deals were often struck. It was common for land agents to take a token down payment, sometimes none at all, and not come knocking on the door for several years. By which time, many had picked up and moved a state or two west. Such people were called "birds of passage." A common inducement was to offer special rates, even free land, to the first people to arrive. Mills were needed almost at once, both sawmills and gristmills, and some land companies offered free land to the man who would build a mill. John Goodrich reports that "the proprietors of Arlington [VT] offered fifty acres to the man who would set up a grist mill at a place designated, by such a day, then fifteen months distant."

Israel Johnson, Esq., went to Vermont after his discharge from the army because it was the most sensible of his options. He was the youngest child of a large family, so his prospects in Colchester were probably slim. Cheap land was suddenly available to the north, and thousands of people from Connecticut were going there, including, no doubt, many of his friends and neighbors. Millwrights were needed right away. Some land companies were giving land to millwrights. As for the hardiness required, he had just spent eight years living in camps on terrible food, in smoky huts, with one blanket to keep warm, and, if he was lucky, one well-patched pair of pants. He was twenty-three and had just completed the best training available for frontier life, eight years in America's rag-tag army.

Land records in Vermont are kept by township clerks, not county clerks, which means that township records for Wells are kept in the Village of Wells. So it was that I found myself in March of 1986 parked in front of Hopson's Store in a light so blinding I could barely squint my way through it. Everything was white. The houses were white, the picket fences, the church, the steeple (and, yes, the people), even the salt on the road. Whatever wasn't white was covered with snow, and the snow, which often isn't, was also white. I staggered into the store and asked the man stocking the shelves with toilet paper (white) if he knew who the town clerk was and where his office might be. He pointed to the man behind the counter.

The Hopsons have been in Wells a long time, probably since the beginning, but Lance Hopson is no withdrawn village patrician guarding his town against the coming of the twentieth century. He is pleasant and helpful, with a trace of the generic north New England accent. He runs the only store in the village, a general store with high ceiling and wooden counter. In a room at the back he keeps the township records and collects its taxes.

The Wells's land records are not indexed, so Mr. Hopson pored over the books for me, found eight deeds that mentioned old Israel as buyer or seller, xeroxed them on the tiny machine on his desk, splaying the old eighteenth-century ledgers flat on the glass, and I went away humming with accomplishment. My trip that March could only last a week, so I was on the fly the whole time, driving from Montpelier to Albany to Elizabethtown to Wells, with quick stops in Crown Point, Brant Lake, Adirondack, Fort Edward, and one or two places I'm forgetting. This was to be my last trip, I thought, an assembling of the last scattered details.

When I got back to Bloomington, about three days later, I finally read the eight land deeds word for word. Something was missing. The deeds showed that Johnson altogether bought seventy-four acres of land in Wells and sold 305 acres. I called Mr. Hopson. He made another search while I waited on the phone and found two more deeds. Israel Johnson, Esq., then, as far as can be known, bought four parcels of land, totaling $217^{1}/_{4}$ acres, and sold five parcels, totaling 305 acres. Obviously, he bought another $87^{3}/_{4}$ acres, but the sale or sales were not recorded. Unless, of course, he was given this land because he was willing to build and run a sawmill.

The first of the ten deeds is dated April 5, 1791; the last, January 10, 1803. In all but the first, Johnson is described as Israel Johnson of Wells, Rutland County. The first deed describes him as Israel Johnson "of Granville in Washington County and State of New York." That was news. In 1790, as the census reported, he had been in Wells. By 1791 he had apparently moved to Granville, New York, which is right on the Vermont border, only four miles from Wells. Later that week I went to the Washington County offices in Fort Edward and looked for some mention of Johnson in their records, but I found none. By the time of the second Wells' deed, October 5, 1791, he was again Israel Johnson of Wells, Rutland County. The purchase in April had brought him back into Wells township, and it made him the owner of a sawmill. Johnson may have started as a millwright by purchasing someone else's mill, though it's possible that Johnson built the mill on Lathrop's property and bought it later. It stood next door to another sawmill, one owned by John Law.

In October 1791, Johnson bought another thirty-seven acres, this time from John Law and Samuel Broughton, "bounding," says the deed, "as followeth beginning at white oak tree on the south end of Single Hill about twenty chains northerly from Israel Johnson Mill then Running west to goodsell Brook then running down the Brook to the great Brook to take enough from the East end of our Lot South of the Mill Brook to Contain thirty Seven Acres." Johnson, by then, was known as a mill owner, and the deed tantalizes us with the thought that, if the white oak were still there, we might find where the mill stood.

The details of these deeds, except where they say something specific about Johnson, are less important than their bulk and frequency. In a twelve-year period, he made at least ten land contracts. By my math, he spent £149 and $1,332 purchasing land and made £65 and $2,950 selling it. This must be how he came to have $1200 to buy 300 acres from Zephaniah Platt in Essex County, New York, in 1803. The period of Johnson's land dealings in Vermont, 1791–1803, coincides almost exactly with the period Lewis Stillwell, in

Migration From Vermont, says was the most prosperous in that state's history. Land values in Vermont rose 170 per cent between 1791 and 1806. "One farmer in Brandon," says Stillwell, "bought fifty acres for 50 pounds in 1787 and sold the same for 600 pounds eleven years later."

At that point, genealogical disaster struck. Following a stray, worrisome thought, I consulted the 1790 census for Washington County, New York, and there found what I did not want to find: another Israel Johnson. He was more than sixteen years old and lived with a woman of similar age and three other females under sixteen. "My" Israel Johnson, "old Israel" of Schroon, who then lived in the Town of Wells, Vermont, had a household with one male and three females older than sixteen and two males under sixteen. These were not, so it seemed, two entries for the same household. If Israel Johnson of Washington County, New York, moved to Wells in 1791 and bought property there, we would have a pretty mess on our hands. A quick check of the census indexes, however, turned up no other Israel Johnson as head of household in the entire United States in 1800 except "my" Israel in Vermont and one each in Connecticut and New Hampshire. Both of the latter, however, lived in the same counties and townships they had lived in in 1790, which means that the Israel Johnson of Washington County, New York, had disappeared by 1800.

Despite the sudden confusion, I have little reason not to conclude that Israel Johnson, Esq., was a millwright, landowner and small-time land speculator in Wells. The township records show that an Israel Johnson was also a Town official. In 1795 and 1796 he was voted a selectman for the Town of Wells. "My" Israel Johnson was later to hold several offices in the Town of Schroon, but he seems to have come to those jobs with experience. In one of his land transactions in Wells, Johnson bought some land jointly with a Joseph Button, Esq. They bought it in 1800 and sold it two years later. I mention this because in the Vital Records for Vermont, I found that in 1805—no date given—"Israel Jonson, Jr.," married Rhoda Harmon. The groom lived in Wells. No age, occupation, or parents were listed for the groom and none for the bride. The "name of the party officiating" was Joseph Button, justice of the peace.

This is puzzling. I have assumed that young Israel came to Schroon with his father in 1803. The first certain reference to him there is in the 1810 federal census. It could be, however, that Israel either stayed behind in Wells for a few years when his father and mother moved to New York or came back to marry his childhood sweetheart. The real puzzle, of course, was the name. Is Polly or Molly a nickname for Rhoda? Hardly. When young Israel's wife's name is finally given in the census reports, which is not till 1850, it is Polly. It now looks as though she was his second wife. Suddenly, all my assumptions about young Israel's family suffered a slight tremor.

Another fact surfaced. I spent some time in Vermont reading old newspapers to see what the land ads looked like. I wanted to know what sorts of places people were being lured to in the early 1800s and by what arguments. I stumbled on a notice in *Spooner's Vermont Journal* for September 28, 1802, that a parcel of land called Minehead in Essex County, Vermont, was going to be sold at public auction if the proprietors and landowners did not each pay the $16.25 back taxes required of them. The list of delinquents is long, but it includes an Israel Johnson.

Old Israel, then, as nearly as we can know, moved to Wells township between 1783 and 1785. He was part of a large migration of people from Connecticut looking for better prospects. The number of his land transactions suggests that he worked as hard at land speculating as he did at milling boards. He became prominent, perhaps even prosperous, and the voters made him a selectman in 1795 and 1796. He stayed in Wells until he decided to buy land in New York in 1803. Land values rose rapidly as people moved into Vermont. Most men, Johnson among them, looked to the land market for sustenance and prosperity. Just before buying the land in New York, Johnson seems to have signed on with a land scheme in northern Vermont, and then backed out of it. When he moved to the Town of Schroon, it looks as though he left his son Israel behind. "Israel Jonson, Jr.," of Wells married Rhoda Harmon in Wells in 1805, but by 1810 he, too, had moved into the Town of Schroon. Vermont's prosperity had peaked. Its forests were disappearing fast, and to a young millwright with a flash of genius in him, large nearby tracts of unbroken wilderness must have looked very tempting.

Old Israel's move to New York was part of another general migration. People kept pressing into frontier areas like Vermont. Population rose swiftly. Between 1800 and 1812, people migrated either deeper into Vermont or just across Lake Champlain into New York. As Lewis Stillwell describes it, a large "overflow took place into northern New York" at this time:

> In a day when winter traveling predominated, it was a simple task to cross the ice of Lake Champlain and to include northern New York as, for all intents and purposes, a part of the Vermont frontier. Thus it came to pass that the first settlement in town after town in the New York counties of Essex, Clinton, Franklin, St. Lawrence and Jefferson was made by Vermonters. In principal centers like Potsdam and Malone, Vermonters were predominant. There was a Vermontville in Franklin County, and a "Vermont Settlement" in St. Lawrence County. Rutland in Jefferson County was christened after Rutland in Vermont. . . . Indeed, if any region in America deserves the name of New Vermont, it is the northern counties of New York State. . . .
>
> The Vermonters pushed across the lake, threaded the wilderness, selected and bought a good farmsite, cleared the land, came back to get the family, loaded a big sled with household goods, and went to stay on the New York frontier.

The realities of emigration were far different from the simple stroll into the woods suggested by the usual phrases of the land ads: "pleasant situation, healthy climate, good water and excellent soil." Recall Reverend Perkins's shock and disbelief. Roads, if there were any, were only crude pathways broken by stumps, slash and bog holes. The land was covered with thick forest. Swamps were common. Rivers flooded in the spring and fall and were often dangerous to cross. Winters were long and cold. Much of the land was rocky, and the soil was thin. Disease and death greeted the first settlers heartily. As though that weren't enough, settlers often had to cope with unscrupulous land agents. "Every species of foul play is practiced against us," wrote Nathan Ford to Colonel Samuel Ogden in 1805. "I have thought it good policy to send a man (who is very well qualified) to that part of Vermont from whence the greatest emigration to this country comes, to make a true statement of the country, and lessen the force of misrepresentation, by exposing the fraud practiced upon the credulity of those who seek a better country."

Israel Johnson moved to Essex County in 1803, built a sawmill on the Schroon River, lost his wife to typhoid in 1813, sold his mill in 1816, remarried, turned innkeeper, held various offices for the township, added "Esq." to his name, died in 1835, and had himself buried across the road from his house. He never went back to Vermont, as far as I know, and Connecticut must have become a foreign country to him. When he last lived there, the United States of America did not exist, and the place he was to die in, the Adirondacks, was described as a "broken unpracticable tract."

14

The Grave of Israel Johnson

*M*y diary for March 15, 1986, says, "Here I am in a motel somewhere southeast of Cleveland on my way to meet a man who may be the great grandson of Israel Johnson of Clear Pond. Me, with my five years of looking and my cardboard box full of papers. What will he make of it? What will I?" The complete truth is that I was already 400 miles from home, and I still had not written or called to see if it was all right to stop by and see this man. I was afraid he might say he wasn't interested. Maybe I would sound to him like an IRS investigator. I thought, if he's going to tell me please not to bother him, I would rather he told me to my face. What was the point of doing all this if it couldn't be brought down out of the windowless libraries and attached somehow to the world? Someone must be related to Israel Johnson, I had been telling myself. Of the probable hundreds, I had found one.

The man was Clifford Johnson, and though he wasn't entirely sure when I talked with him on the eighteenth, I was able to prove later that he is, indeed, Israel Johnson's great grandson. He is the Clifford, son of Archibald, grandson of William H., whom I had found on a census reel on my last day at the National Archives in November of 1985. Not only that, but he also lives in the same village young Israel Johnson did at the end of his life, Adirondack, on the east side of Schroon Lake. Where, I was hoping, young Israel's gravestone might be found.

My trip to the east in March 1986 was to have been my last. I had found everything it seemed possible to find. Six or seven details had to be checked on, no more. After that, all I had to do was write it up. Or finish writing it up. I had been writing the story of my looking for

Israel Johnson since 1983. The first installment, in fact, was about to appear in *Blueline,* a literary magazine edited at the time by Alice Gilborn in Blue Mountain Lake.

When I found Clifford Johnson's name on a 1910 census reel in Washington, he was one of many people I had found who were related to Israel Johnson, all of whom, of course, might have been dead by 1985. All I could be sure of after the trip to Washington was that Israel Johnson had spent his last years in Adirondack. So, two or three weeks before making my "last" trip east, I called the Warren county clerk's office and asked for the name and phone number of the Horicon town historian. Whoever it was would probably know something about Johnsons in the area, and once I had a few names, I could make some phone calls to see if any of them had ever heard of Israel Johnson.

The town historian, Colleen Murtaugh, is from Brant Lake. Adirondack and Brant Lake are the only towns shown on my road atlas in the whole township. Both are very small. When I had explained myself to her, Colleen Murtaugh said right away that a Clifford Johnson lived in Adirondack. I said that it was a name I had run across. She had a graves list, too, for the two cemeteries in Adirondack. Flipping through it quickly, she found the names of several Johnsons, including two Williams, one Hollis, Freelove Montgomery Johnson, and others, but no Israel. She said she would ask around and get in touch with me by mail. Her letter came just before I left on the fifteenth. "After our phone conversation this afternoon I spoke with Mr. Clifford Johnson. He *is* Archibald Johnson's son. Israel Johnson *is* William Johnson's father (making Israel Clifford's great grandfather). He doesn't know a great deal about Israel, but does remember his father speaking of him. Clifford is under the impression that Israel is buried in the Adirondack cemetery."

I found the courage to call Clifford Johnson from Syracuse, about seven hundred miles from home. I explained myself and asked if I might talk with him the next day. He said he'd be happy to have me stop by. "I don't know very much," he said, "but sure." I was too stunned to pay attention to anything but the facts. Things were suddenly coming to a head. I had found, as far as I could tell, a direct descendant of the man whose life I had spent five years reconstructing. Five years' work, and here he was on the phone, where I should have been catching the rhythm of his speech, his habits of thought, characteristic verbal gestures, the dreams locked in his words. But all I could do was get the facts, make an appointment (ten o'clock the next morning), say thank you, hang up and stand there like someone who went to New York City once and thought he saw Dustin Hoffman in a coffee shop.

I like to set out in vague directions. That must be obvious, I suppose. The world always has a good idea if you let it come to you. I take walks at night. Not very far from home, but I never plan where I'm going. I never know where I'll spend the night when I'm on the road. I look for a motel when I'm tired. I love to knock on doors unannounced, which may be the real reason I drove seven hundred miles before I called Clifford Johnson. I finally couldn't do it, but for years I had daydreamed of knocking on a total stranger's door. I wanted to see the first look of astonishment.

Looking for Israel Johnson doesn't mean that you find him. I never thought I'd catch more than a glimpse, anyway. What you find, though, is more astonishing than anything you imagined.

Adirondack is a tiny village on the east side of Schroon Lake, across from Pottersville and the Village of Schroon Lake and all the traffic that passes through them, or used to pass through them, on Route 9. Route 9 hasn't moved, but in this stretch of the trough dug for travel between Albany and Montreal, the Northway—free, divided, and four lanes wide—is only a few hundred yards to the west of it. In fact, in one of the cruellest calculations, the Northway rises up and skims across Pottersville itself, passing no more than 150 feet from the second story windows of its ancient and slightly run-down hotel, The Wells House, in the center of the village. Now forever the shadow of the wing of progress hovers above Pottersville like a hawk above a stripped field.

I had to ask twice, and it cost me a beer in both places, before the people of Pottersville could make me see on the maps they drew in the air just where, north of town, the turnoff to Adirondack was. When I found it, I drove slowly around the bottom of Schroon Lake and up along its east side, lined with boarded-up summer homes. It was still the seventeenth, though late in the afternoon. My appointment with Clifford Johnson was the next day, but I couldn't wait till then to see the town. After five miles or so, the road took a sharp bend to the east, and there it was, a dozen or two houses and a church clustered around a general store. A sign on one of the houses said it was for sale by the Bump Real Estate Agency. In the 1870s a Dennis Bump swore an affidavit to help his friend, Lewis Johnson, both residents of this village, convince the United States government to give the latter a pension.

In two blocks, I had left the village, and there at the back of it was the graveyard. I thought it was a field at first. Two or three feet of snow lay on the ground, but at the far end of the field, I could see the tops of a dozen headstones poking up through the snow. Perhaps this is the moment, I thought. I will stop the car, get out, walk into that field of snow and find the words, "Israel Johnson," carved on one of the stones. And it will all be over. "Sunset, overcast sky, Monday, March 17, 1986, reached Johnson's grave after five years." I stopped the car and climbed up the snowbank over the fence. The snow had a hard crust on it, strong enough to hold me if I walked carefully. The headstones were fifty yards away. I took several steps. The snow held. I will be there soon, I said. Then, my foot broke through and I went down to the middle of my thigh. I had to lift hard with the other leg to get myself out, but the force of lifting drove the second leg down through the crust. An old piece of boy scout wisdom came back to me. If you break through ice, lie down. Distribute your weight. I lay down on the snow and crawled forward to free my legs from the deep holes. I rolled up on both feet again and stood still. The crust held. When I stepped forward with my left foot, for a fraction of a second all my weight was thrown to my right foot, and I sank again. I lay myself out on the snow again, and I looked at myself lying on the snow in a graveyard in a town where I knew no one, trying to get across to the stones on the other side. I could only smile. This is not the moment, I thought. This is some other moment. I scrambled out of that field and drove away.

The next day was bright and clear. This time when I drove up the east side of Schroon Lake (I had spent the night in a tiny room at the Panther Mountain House in Chestertown), melted snow streaked across the road. It would reach fifty degrees. Clifford Johnson's house is right behind the general store. Actually, it is right next to the

18. Clifford Johnson, center, of Adirondack, New York, a great-grandson
of Israel Johnson of Clear Pond. Courtesy of Clifford Johnson.

vacant lot behind the general store, where, he told me later, his
mother once ran a summer boarding house. A white picket fence funs
along the road in front of the house.

I waited a long time after I knocked. Clifford Johnson was
eighty-seven in February, "last February," he called it, and the way
his house is laid out, he had to come downstairs from the main part of
the house and through a kind of storage area to reach the door. He
said hello and I came in. No explanations were needed. He led me
back through the storage area, up the stairs and into his living or
sitting room. He told me to watch my head. A recliner sits next to
the picture window and from it he can look out at the road and as far
down it as the store.

He lives alone. For someone eighty-seven years old, he moves
about with ease. He has a long face, rounded under the eyes, speaks
calmly, and to all my questions, he gave careful answers. I sat on the

couch next to the recliner and asked if he would mind if I took notes while we talked. He said no, not at all. I tried to explain what I was doing and why, but I couldn't very well, so I got straight to the questions.

He said he "never kept track of things," but his grandfather, William, "came from Vermont." William's wife, Adelia Isham, was known in the family as "Aunt Del" (pronounced "deal"). Clifford's father was Archibald, Archy, people called him, and he moved to Adirondack from Glens Falls in 1902, when Clifford was two. Archy was seventy-six when he died of cancer of the stomach. Clifford's mother was born a Johnson in Blue Ridge. Her maiden name was Julia S. Johnson. Charles Johnson of Blue Ridge was her father and Samuel Johnson her uncle. William, Clifford's grandfather, died in 1917 at the age of ninety-six, and half the farm went to his son Hollis, half to his son Robert. Hollis, though, seems to have been the one who ran the place. The farmhouse burned sometime in the thirties. Hollis was living there at the time. When he died, half the 160-acre farm went to Clifford and half to his brother, Earnest. Where was the farm, I asked. About a mile east of town, he said. The old barn is still there, right beside the road. Who owns it now? It's all broken up and sold, he said. People from downstate. One of them is a priest. Why did people move here in the first place? The tannery. It made sole leather but went out of business in the 1870s.

When I asked about him, he said that except for his first two years, he had always lived in Adirondack. For fifty years he had been caretaker of Camp Red Wing, a girls' camp a short way up the lake from the village. He married in 1939 when he was forty. His wife was twenty-eight. They were too old to have children, he said, so they adopted a son. The son lives in Virginia, and Clifford was about to go there for a visit. When World War II came along, Clifford joined the air force, and after six months of that, he went to work in a defense plant on Long Island for two years. After returning to Adirondack, he built his own house, the one we were sitting in.

I asked what he knew about his ancestors, those further back than his grandfather. Someone in the family, he said, once tried to prove we came from Sir William Johnson. Johnson was the Crown's representative to the Iroquois nation in the last days of British colonial rule. Did they prove it?, I asked. I don't think so, he said. What about Israel? Did you ever hear your grandfather speak of his father? He wasn't absolutely sure who his great grandfather was, but he believed it might have been Israel and, further, he thought Israel was buried in the Adirondack cemetery. At that point he tried to tell me a story that used to be told in his family. He hadn't heard it or told it in years, so he had trouble remembering exactly what or who it was about. There was a man in the family who was, as he said, "brilliant." For some reason "brilliant" did not seem to be Clifford's word, so much as the one he had heard when the story was told. This man and his wife "traveled around the country building sawmills." The man was gifted and clever, but when Clifford tried to recall what he had done, he couldn't remember exactly. One story involved a mill with what he called a "walking beam." What this was exactly or what it did, he couldn't explain. Or, I couldn't understand. Two people "walked" it, and this walking made the milling easier or more efficient in some way.

This is the moment, I thought. Indeed, this may be the real grave of Israel Johnson. An old man groping among his and his family's recollections toward a person he never saw and does not know the name of. You're describing Israel Johnson, I said. Am I? I'd bet a hundred dollars on it. He smiled faintly. I mentioned I had looked up the family's genealogy. I showed him the name of his great great grandfather on my xerox of the Johnson genealogy. This man fought in the Revolution. He's buried in North Hudson. Clifford nodded his head. He said he should probably go up there and see it. But it seemed to have little to do with him. He was the person he was, and these new facts, even though they belonged to him, were not quite a part of him. Not yet, that is. He was Clifford Johnson of Adirondack. He lived alone in a house he had built himself. His father was Archibald, who had died of cancer. His grandfather, William, lived to be ninety-six. The old people told stories, but he couldn't remember them well. Few do. He remembered the telling, though. Mother, Uncle Hollis, some others, sitting on the front porch of the boarding house in the summer, remembering. He remembered them remembering.

I'd been there almost an hour. He must be tiring, I thought. He lived by himself and was used to that. I could imagine days went by without a phone call or a knock on the door. I had broken that concentration. He was gracious in letting me do that, but my time was up. I asked a few last questions. Did he remember the names of his grandfather William's brothers and sisters. No. He didn't know he had any. Did he have any relatives in Indiana? Not to his knowledge. Did he have relatives named Harmon? Again, not to his knowledge. I thanked him and told him I'd better be off. He rose and walked me downstairs, telling me again to watch my head. I may come back in the summer, I said. May I stop and say hello? Yes, he said, smiling. We said good-bye, shook hands, and he shut the door.

※

For the next two days I drove from one government office to another looking for records of births, deaths, marriages, wills, and land sales involving any of the major figures—Archibald, William, Israel, and Polly. Vital records for the state of New York don't start until 1880, so neither the Warren county clerk nor the state office in Albany had any record of Israel or Polly's death. Warren County land records show that William H. Johnson bought lot 191 of the Brant Lake Tract, a 160-acre plot "more or less," from a Joseph P. Baldwin on July 1, 1876. William must have lived on that land and made payments for twenty years or so before the land was his. The Warren county clerk also had a copy of the 1865 New York State census. William Johnson and family still lived in Adirondack. Their frame house was worth $300. William said to the census taker that he was born in Genesee County, not Vermont, in 1825. That made two of Israel's children who were born there, William and Betsey. Others in the household in 1865 included S. A. Johnson, thirty-four, William's wife, born in Vermont, two male children, E. H. Johnson (seven) and J. H. Johnson (five), and a person named Smith (fifteen), female, who, if I decipher the handwriting correctly, had been a slave and was now adopted into the family. The astonishing thing, of course, was the absence of Israel Johnson. There in 1860 and again in 1870; in 1865 he was gone.

The Johnson farm in Adirondack bustled in 1865. The farm itself was worth $1,000, the stock $500. Eighteen acres were put aside in pasture, fourteen in meadow. The previous year the farm had produced ten tons of hay. Fifteen acres were sowed in oats (90 bushes

19. Old barn on what used to be the William Johnson farm in
Adirondack, New York.

harvested), two acres in corn (60 bushels harvested), three acres in
potatoes (650 bushels harvested). They made 250 pounds of maple
sugar, 180 pounds of butter (from three cows), 700 pounds of pork
from an undisclosed number of pigs. And the fifteen lambs on the
place gave them 60 pounds of wool.

Finally, at the Bureau of Vital Records, Department of Health,
Empire State Plaza, Corning Tower, Albany, where I had to make an
appointment three hours in advance to use one of their microfilm
readers, I found the death certificate for William H. Johnson of
Adirondack, Town of Horicon, Warren County. Born October 16,
1825, died February 14, 1917. Whose father was "Isreal [*sic*] Johnson," birthplace "not known," and whose mother's maiden name was
"Stowel," birthplace again "not known." It was thus I came to know
that Clifford Johnson was, without doubt, Israel Johnson's direct

20. Old farm machinery on what used to be the William Johnson farm
in Adirondack, New York.

descendant and that Israel's wife's name was Polly or Molly Stowel or
Stowell. I called Clifford from Bloomington after I returned, and he
said there had been some Stowells in South Schroon, halfway between
Pottersville and Schroon Lake, but they had moved away long ago.
He had no idea if he was related to them.

When I left Clifford Johnson's that day in March, the first thing
I did was to drive east and south on a gravel road into the hilly
country away from the lake. I was looking for an old barn close to the
road across from a mobile home. It was not hard to find. The barn is
about the size of a two-car garage, with a plain pitched roof. Tin
roofing has been nailed over old wooden shingles. In two or three
places, the tin has been torn off. The sides of the barn had been tar-
papered at one time, but most of that was torn off. Underneath, it
looked like stucco, broken up by something like Tudor half-timbering.
The barn was locked. Down in the field across the snow, about two

21. The William H. Johnson farmhouse, Adirondack, New York, from a photograph taken in 1923 or 1924. The farmhouse, which burned down in the 1930s, was right across the road from the barn (see illustration 19). Courtesy of Clifford Johnson.

hundred yards away, a wide, low, deck-draped vacation home, boarded up, spread its palm on the ground. Off to the right about fifty feet stood a shrine with the Virgin Mary in the middle of it wearing a blue robe.

Back in the village, Clifford Johnson clings to a life I didn't even think to ask about. Father Whoever-he-is from somewhere downstate comes here in the summer to relax and pray in a field where Israel Johnson may have died and may even be buried. He brings his complicated memory, his wants and hopes, his theology, and lays them like a great cloth over the past. Not unlike snow in a graveyard.

15

Letting Go

I did go back to Adirondack that August. By that time I had found graves registries in Albany for the Town of Horicon, and though I knew I would find no stone for Israel there, I had to look. Here were Archie H. Johnson (1866–1937) and Julia S. Johnson (1876–1974), Clifford's father and mother, and Ernest, his brother (1897–1973), a veteran of World War I. William H. Johnson (young Israel's son), born October 16, 1825, died February 14, 1917, and his wife, Adelia Isham ("Aunt Del"), born March 28, 1831, died April 6, 1903, are buried under one stone. Nearby is a stone for "William N., Son of W. H. & S. A. Johnson, aged," but the rest of the inscription is underground. A Private Nelson P. Johnson (1909–1944) has a stone near Archie and Julia. It says, "109th Inf. at Luxembourg, Killed in Action, Buried on Foreign Soil, Son." Clifford's younger brother. Here, too, are Freelove Montgomery, wife of Lewis Johnson, born November 9, 1818, died May 7, 1867, and, under one stone, Hollis A. Johnson, Lewis's son, who "died at Ball farm [*sic*] Hospital, Va., July 16, 1863, AE 22 years & 8 mos." and his wife, Loraine L., who died September 20, 1862, at the age of twenty, just 43 days after her husband joined the army. I didn't stop to say hello to Clifford that day. I wanted to, but I felt I might be imposing on him.

The time had come to test what I was doing. I was far from finished with this book, but it seemed that the first chapter might stand on its own and perhaps prompt some comment. I wanted to see if this sort of thing might interest other people. I was hoping, too, that someone might read it who could give me more information. Exactly that happened. The first chapter appeared in two parts, in the two 1986 issues of *Blueline*. A few letters came in the summer from people who read the first half of the chapter, but after the second half came a small landslide. It came mostly from three people, Paul Stapley, Miss Mary Kays of Olmstedville, and Mrs. Ethel Bissell of Newcomb, all three indefatigable local historians. They have added many details and significant new information to the heap assembled here, and two of them are—or very likely are—related to Israel Johnson. I kept a log of this correspondence. The log alone is two and a half pages long. Between September 22 and December 9, 1986, I received an inch and a half of paper from the Adirondacks, all of which I read and reread several times.

It started when Miss Mary Kays wrote Alice Gilborn at *Blueline* and asked for copies of the issues containing my piece, "Looking for Israel Johnson." She had heard of the publication from her friend, Mrs. Ethel Bissell. Miss Kays's particular interest was in the Cedar Point Road, but she mentioned that Mrs. Bissell was "descended from a North Hudson Johnson." Alice knew I would be interested in possible descendants of Israel, so she sent me the letter. My first debt to Miss Kays is for writing to *Blueline*. She introduced me to Ethel Bissell.

I called Ethel Bissell right away. She told me she was the daughter of John Howland Johnson, the granddaughter of Samuel Johnson, the Civil War veteran, and the great granddaughter of Lyman Johnson. I had heard of Samuel and Lyman. Frieda Provoncha, I recalled, was the granddaughter of a Samuel Johnson. Mrs. Bissell didn't know, but she thought it likely that Lyman was young Israel's son. I told her I had run into the name now and then but had no reason to think he was related to Israel Johnson and so had paid little attention to him. I urged her to ask around in her family to see what she might learn while I went through my notes again.

Two days later she wrote out her Johnson genealogy in longhand and sent it to me (see fig. 5). It started with Lyman Johnson, born April 11, 1811, at Schroon Lake, died November 10, 1873, at Blue Ridge. He married Harriet Turner on June 24, 1838. Their children were Nathan T., born 1839 at North Hudson (if Lyman were young Israel's child, this child would have been named for his uncle), died 1842 at the same place; Phoebe, born 1841 at North Hudson, died 1842 at Schroon Lake; Samuel T., born 1843 in Chester[town],

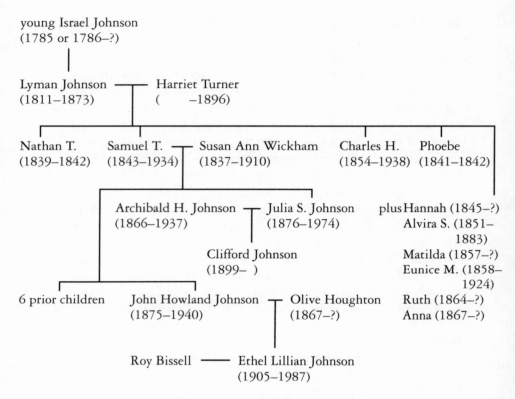

young Israel Johnson
(1785 or 1786–?)

Lyman Johnson ——— Harriet Turner
(1811–1873)   (–1896)

Nathan T.   Samuel T. ——— Susan Ann Wickham   Charles H.   Phoebe
(1839–1842)   (1843–1934)   (1837–1910)   (1854–1938)   (1841–1842)

Archibald H. Johnson ——— Julia S. Johnson   plus Hannah (1845–?)
(1866–1937)   (1876–1974)   Alvira S. (1851–
                                                                  1883)
                 Clifford Johnson   Matilda (1857–?)
                 (1899–)   Eunice M. (1858–
                                                                  1924)
6 prior children   John Howland Johnson ——— Olive Houghton   Ruth (1864–?)
                    (1875–1940)   (1867–?)   Anna (1867–?)

                 Roy Bissell ——— Ethel Lillian Johnson
                                  (1905–1987)

5. Descendants of Lyman Johnson of Blue Ridge,
Essex County, New York.

died 1934 at Blue Ridge; Hannah J., born 1845 in Chester[town], death unrecorded; Alvira S., born 1851 in North Hudson, died 1883 in Blue Ridge; Charles H., born 1854 in North Hudson, died 1938 in Gansevoort, New York; Eunice M., born 1858 in Schroon Lake, died 1924 in Saratoga Springs; Ruth (no record). Charles H. Johnson was the father of Julia S. Johnson, Clifford's mother. If Lyman was, in fact, Israel's son, Clifford is doubly descended from Israel, through his mother and his father.

Samuel Johnson (1843–1934) had been a private in Company B, 192nd Regiment, New York Infantry, during the Civil War. He and his wife, Susan Ann Wickham (1837–1910), had seven children, the seventh of whom, John Howland Johnson (1875–1940), was Mrs. Bissell's father. When Samuel died, he had thirty grandchildren, seventy-three great grandchildren, and four great great grandchildren. Mrs. Bissell was born Ethel Lillian Johnson in 1905.

Mrs. Bissell said she had never heard of Israel Johnson before Mary Kays mentioned him. Another debt to Mary Kays. But, she said, "my grandfather Johnson and my dad were both millwrights and maybe they inherited it from Israel Johnson."

It was thus that Ethel Bissell and I began a long correspondence. "I asked my grandfather, Samuel T. Johnson," she said in one letter, "what nationality he was and he said, 'Oh! I am a Yankee.' I never heard him speak of his father or grandfather. I never heard of Clear Pond until you mentioned it." I told her about old Israel's grave in North Hudson, and in early October she and her daughter, Sharon, went over to look at it. "I do not know where Lyman Johnson is buried," she said.

As soon as I learned that Lyman's first child was called Nathan, I knew I had to make a trip to Indianapolis. Nathan was the name of young Israel's near twin, so it was likely that Lyman was related to them. I spent two days in the State Library looking for Lyman Johnsons in the census records. The one I was interested in was born in 1811. He was not visible in 1830, but at nineteen he was probably living with his parents or in someone else's home as a hired hand or apprentice. I now knew that he had married Harriet Turner in 1838 and that they had had a child, Nathan, on March 16, 1839. So, it was no surprise to find in the 1840 census a Lyman Johnson, between twenty and thirty (he was twenty-nine), living with a woman, also between twenty and thirty, and one child, male, aged zero to five. What raised my eyebrows, though, was that this Lyman Johnson family lived in the Town of Moriah next door to young Israel Johnson. Of course, next door in this part of the world might have meant nine miles away. Lyman told the census taker he was employed in "manufactures and trade," perhaps the manufacture of sawed pine boards at his father's sawmill.

This is not conclusive, of course, but it suggests that young Israel and Lyman were related. These are the years when Israel, to use Andrew Porteous's phrase, was beginning to be disappointed. Constant Myrick loomed on the horizon. Beriah Sprague and Joseph Frost would soon bring their suits against him. Having a son nearby would not hurt. Look at the birth places of Lyman's children, though, and the story they tell of his unsettled life: Nathan, 1839, North Hudson [this would probably be the early community of North Hudson, about four miles north of Schroon River, near Weatherhead's Tavern]; Phoebe, 1841, North Hudson; Samuel, 1843, Chestertown; Hannah, 1845, Chestertown; Alvira 1851, North Hudson. Lyman Johnson was not easy to find in the 1850 census because his name was spelled "Lymun Jonson," but he was living then in the new township of North Hudson. He was thirty-eight, a "sawyer," and born, so it says, in Illinois. Must we rule him out for having been born in so odd a place? I think not. Illinois must be a mistake. Few people were born there in 1811. Also, his wife was named Harriet and his two children were Hannah and Samuel, all names from Mrs. Bissell's genealogy. It's true, their ages were reversed. Despite all the confusion in this entry, too much of the information is right for it not to be our Lyman Johnson.

Lyman moved away from Israel's neighborhood at about the same time that Constant Myrick showed up. For a while it looked as though Israel had his and his wife's old age taken care of. Lyman perhaps felt freer to look around for work. He seems to have moved to Chestertown for a few years. By 1850, though, he was living in the Township of North Hudson. Israel had moved away from Clear Pond by that time into the Town of Schroon. Clear Pond had moved, as it were, from Moriah to North Hudson. Had Lyman perhaps gone to be a "sawyer" at his father's old mill? The air is heavy, too heavy I'm afraid, with conjecture.

By 1860 Lyman and his family had moved into the Town of Schroon. He was fifty, called himself a laborer, this time was born where he should have been, New York, and was living with Harriet and their children, Samuel, Hannah, Louisa A., and Charles H. (Clifford Johnson's maternal grandfather). In 1870 Lyman and his family were again living in the Town of North Hudson. He was a laborer, fifty-nine and could not read or write. Harriet was fifty-two, and the children still at home were Charles (sixteen), who also could not read or write, Matilda (thirteen), Ruth (six), and Anna (three). Ruth, of whom there is mention but no record in the family papers, and Matilda and Anna, of whom there is no mention at all. Lyman died at Blue Ridge, in the Town of North Hudson, on November 10, 1873.

Was Lyman Johnson the son of Israel Johnson of Clear Pond? Is Ethel Lillian Johnson Bissell of Newcomb the great great grand-daughter of the same? The Romantic in me says, of course, The Skeptic says, we can't be sure. Together they say something like "probably."

One day in late October a letter came from Miss Mary Kays of Olmstedville. "I am going to get into the act," she said. I had not bothered her with my problems because she was not, as far as I knew, related to the Johnsons. It was a long, friendly letter, full of facts and information mostly about the Cedar Point Road, but in it, almost buried in an aside, was this astonishing observation: "If the second wife [of Israel Johnson] was a Stowell, must be a forbear of wife of Paul Stapley, new Schroon Historian. She was Hester Stowell." Ethel Bissell had obviously, and fortunately, been sharing my letters to her with Mary Kays. I wrote Paul right away.

Paul was so astonished he called me on the phone. It was November 4, about 10:00 P.M. "I don't know why I never tumbled to it, but I've known for years that Molly Stowell went to live with Israel Johnson." "Lived with? What does that mean," I asked. He didn't know exactly, but in his wife's family it was known—even today—that Molly Stowell "went to live with" Israel Johnson. He did not know when, but he clung to that phrase. He had a bound book in front of him, *The Stowell Genealogy*, published in Rutland in 1922, and he read some of it. Molly was born in 1782 in Walpole, New Hampshire, the third child of David Stoel or Stowell (born in Willington, Connecticut, 1757, died in Brandon, Vermont, 1849) and Molly Hodgkins (1755–1788). Both of these Mollys were christened Molly; it was not a nickname. Young Molly died on September 10, 1861, at Mill Brook, aged seventy-nine. I interrupted. "Where's Mill Brook?" "That's Adirondack!," he shouted. "You're related to Israel Johnson!," I shouted back. "It looks that way."

He had already driven down to Adirondack to look for Israel's grave. Snow had fallen the night before, so he had to give that up till spring. A week later a large envelope came in the mail. He had been to Elizabethtown and rooted through the census and legal records there. "My Stowell book never mentioned Molly's being married," he

wrote. The envelope contained a list of old Israel's heirs longer than
the list I had and from a source he couldn't recall. I had questioned
him rather closely on his knowledge of Molly's marital status, so in a
later letter he cited his "source" for his knowledge of Molly's domestic
arrangements: "My reference for Molly Stowell 'going to live with
Israel Johnson' has come from several Stowell family members." He
had also found William Johnson, young Israel's son, in the 1875 New
York State census, and Israel Johnson was not a part of that household.
It would seem reasonable to conclude, then, that Israel died between
1870 and 1875, probably in Adirondack. William said at the time
that he had been born in 1825 in Cataraugus County, making it the
third county in western New York where we know young Israel to
have lived in the 1820s. As Clifford had said, his "brilliant" ancestor
had been a traveling millwright. Paul said he had "heard about some
odd [grave]stones back of Mill Brook [the actual name of the brook
at Adirondack] near what was once known as Gregoryville." But it
was mid-November and the snow was too deep.

The mail kept pouring in, and pouring out. Every time a letter
arrived—and they were rarely short—a letter went back. I had once
again made contact with local memory, and between the four of us,
we were beginning to put some flesh on the statistical bones of this
narrative. At the very least, Israel Johnson's private life was more
visible. Mary Kays thought that perhaps the word, "family," had
been left off the phrase, "gone to live with Israel Johnson," but I
suspect not. People don't usually make that kind of mistake.

In late November, Ethel Bissell sent me a copy of her typed
Johnson genealogy, beginning with Lyman. The letter had a P.S.:
"Since I wrote this I got information that Philander Johnson & wife,
Lucy, lived on the north side of Rich Lake in Newcomb. Then the
info says . . . he lived on the 'old military road' or 'Chester to Canton
road' in Newcomb in 1858 . . . . Now I never heard of these Johnsons
[nor had I] & surely never heard of any Johnsons living on Rich Lake.
This Johnson deal gets more confusing as time goes by. Before Lucy
died she requested to be buried at Long Lake. I will check into that
info, now with the Long Lake historian and later in the spring I will
go to the Long Lake cemetery."

This was new, unattached information, but since the name was
Johnson, I thought it unwise to ignore it. Her source was an old

friend, Bill Roden, from Diamond Point, whose column, "Adirondack Sportsman," is printed in several upstate papers. Roden owns the files of an early Adirondack historian, Leslie N. Rist, and he had gone through these files and sent what he had to Mrs. Bissell. "I've included copy of another Johnson," he said. "Don't know whether she is of the family or not." "She" was Lucy A. Johnson, wife of Philander. Rist had also found a census entry for Lucy Johnson. It was for the Town of Newcomb in 1860. Lucy Johnson, forty-seven, born in New York, lived in a household with her husband, Philander, fifty-six, also born in New York, and an eighty-seven-year-old woman named Rhoda Johnson.

Here, for the second time only, was the name Rhoda. An "Israel Johnson, Jr." had married a Rhoda Harmon in the Town of Wells, Vermont, in 1805. I had found that fact on a four-by-six file card in an office in Montpelier on a bright cold day in March 1986, and here, in a letter from Ethel Bissell, from a letter written to her by Bill Roden, from records compiled by someone else, now dead, came the second mention of this mysterious figure. Could these two Rhodas be the same person? Was this the first wife of Israel Johnson? Or, as we must say at the moment, was this *the* wife of Israel Johnson, since it appears that Molly only went to live with him?

Back to Indianapolis and the census reels. I looked everywhere it made sense to, for Rhoda Harmons and Rhoda Johnsons but found nothing. So, I turned to Philander. There he was, of course, in 1860 in Newcomb, living with Lucy and Rhoda. Rhoda said she was born in Massachusetts. I couldn't find Philander in 1850, so I looked under "Jonson." Lyman Johnson's name had been spelled "Jonson" in 1850; and, as it turned out, so was Philander's. He lived in the Town of Crown Point that year. He was forty-four and Lucy was thirty-five. Both were born in Vermont. The two children, Betsey (six) and Henry (three) were born in New York. Philander's and Lucy's ages were off by two years from the 1860 census reports. In 1840 I made some small contact with other Johnsons. Philander (thirty to forty) and his wife (twenty to thirty), with a boy (five to ten) and a girl (zero to five), lived sixty-five dwellings away from Lyman and Israel Johnson in the Town of Moriah.

This is thin ice to skate on, but it does seem as though Philander might have been related to Israel. If so, and if this Rhoda was Israel's

wife, she was thirty-two when she married him and he just nineteen
or twenty. Stranger things have happened. The name Philander—
unusual even in that day—comes from the Greek, *philandros*, meaning love of mankind. When the word is not capitalized, it means
something else: "To make love, esp. triflingly; to flirt with a woman."
A scandalous thought to have, perhaps, but when a thirty-two-year-
old woman marries a nineteen-year-old boy one year after their first
child is born, whom they then name Philander, what can one think?
One thing is that this was the American frontier and not a Victorian
English parlor. People did not stand much on ceremony. In fact, a
good many of the marriages, either for lack of a minister or lack of
interest, were common-law marriages. Other things one can think: A
thirty-two-year-old woman in that day was dangerously close to
being permanently unwed. And, permanently dependent on the
charity of her relatives, if she had any, or on the meager beneficence of
the county. Then there was Israel. "All castles and no foundations,"
Joseph Frost said of him. A man willing to take risks, perhaps
indifferent to convention.

One last piece of information. Death certificates say little, but if
we had one for each of the principals in this story, we would know a
great deal more than we do. New York only started keeping them in
1880, however. Lyman Johnson, in other words, missed having his
death recorded by seven years. A great shame that, since death
certificates name the mother and father of the deceased. But for those
seven years, Ethel Bissell would know with certainty whether she is
Israel Johnson's great great granddaughter. "I will probably have to
die without finding out," she said in one of her letters. Death
certificates also tell where the dead are buried, and even if they have
no stone, we can say, here so-and-so is buried. Israel Johnson missed
having a death certificate by no more than ten years.

Lewis Johnson did not, however. He died in 1899. And Philander might have died after 1880. I wrote the New York Department
of Health and asked for copies of the death certificates for both. They
found only Lewis Johnson's. And yes, his father's name was Israel and
his father's birthplace, Vermont. He died on September 24, 1899,
aged ninety one years, nine months and twenty-seven days, which
means he was born on November 28, 1807. At the time of his death,
he was living in Newcomb. He was buried there two days later. I

don't know when Lewis left the Village of Adirondack, but I stumbled on him one day in the 1870 census living in North Hudson in the home of Russell Root. Root, seventy-one, was the man who started the well-known hotel in what is now the Village of North Hudson. He was the one the Iron Works often contracted with to haul in supplies in the 1830s and 1840s. By 1870 he had turned his business, the "Schroon River Hotel," over to his son, A. F. Root, and retired, a prosperous man, to farming. Lewis, sixty-two at the time, with a personal estate worth only $100, lived in his household as a "laborer." The death certificate, of course, calls him a carpenter.

The real news was that Lewis Johnson's mother was called Mary, not Rhoda or Molly or Polly, and she was born in Vermont, not Massachusetts or New Hampshire. If "our" young Israel married a Rhoda Harmon in 1805, something happened almost at once to that arrangement, since by November 1807 he had had a son by a woman named Mary. Then, toward the end of his life, there was the woman, Molly Stowell, who went to live with him and changed her name to Johnson. When did she do that? Old Israel's will deed of December 1835 calls young Israel's "wife" Molly, and every subsequent mention of her, except one, repeats that name. I say "wife," as does the will deed, but Paul Stapley insists that Molly did not, in fact, marry Israel. She was a common-law wife. Polly, I believe, was simply a mispronunciation or a mishearing of or perhaps a familiar toying with the word, "Molly." Polly was Molly, in other words. For Molly Stowell to have been called Israel's wife in a legal document in December 1835 probably means that their union—whatever it was— was not new at the time. And the more I rake these few coals over, the more plausible it becomes that young Israel's return from the Genesee sometime between 1826 and 1829 might have had something to do with Mary's death there. In 1830, young Israel—back in Essex County—had one male under five (probably William) and three females between five and ten in his household of eleven. By 1840 there were only five in the household, none of whom was younger than ten. I think he came back from western New York shortly after his wife, Mary, died there, and with three young children in the house and new property to clear and prosperity in the offing, he took Molly Stowell into his life to bring up his children, run the household, including the hosteling business, and in exchange she would call herself his wife and a Johnson. They had no children, but Johnson thought of her as his wife and, as in the business with Constant Myrick, called her such and looked out as best he could for her welfare.

The one problem with this theory is that William H. Johnson's death certificate says that his mother's maiden name was Stowell. He was born in 1825 in Cataraugus County, which would seem to put Molly in western New York at that time, to say nothing about it identifying Molly as his mother. That is certainly possible, but it is equally possible that Molly Stowell took over the job of mothering William early enough in his life that he always thought of her as his mother, even though, biologically, she may not have been.

Or, just to complicate matters, it is possible that the person who made out Lewis Johnson's death certificate, having been told Lewis's mother's name was Molly, assumed it was a nickname for Mary—as it is—and wrote it down so.

And there I must leave it. With Israel Johnson's grave still unfound, with Ethel Bissell's connection to him still not clarified, with a thousand questions left unanswered and, no doubt, many unasked. After six years and several thousand miles, Israel Johnson is little more than a ghost. What did he look like? How tall was he? What was his favorite food, his pet expression? Did he smoke?

Yet, he is a real ghost. Only real ghosts yoke a bull and a cow together or give their life's savings to a ne'er-do-well. I remember seeing my first mummy. There under the glass was the skin of a man 3,500 years old. Not the bones, which are quite plentiful in the graveyards hereabouts, but the skin. The skin of the face. Not all of that either, but most of it, drawn tightly over the cheekbones, the mouth open but pinched, the lips thin as a leaf. I probably knew less about that man than about anyone ever born, but there he was, some tangible sense of that particular assemblage of biology and history held out to me on the frail drumhead of his cheek. I could see him, his last pained vacuousness of breath. In some like way, I see a man equal to that nameless pharaoh or pharaoh's functionary, and I see the hard, joyful life he knew. His name was Israel Johnson.

Epilogue

*B*y the summer of 1987, this book was finished. Or so I thought. I had typed it, corrected it, retyped it, asked a friend to read it, retyped it again, and made a xerox copy of it. It was done, a thick white brick of words. I walked around the house with it for several days, put it down, picked it up again. Books, even unpublished books, are sensuous objects. When I open a new book, the first thing I'm apt to do is smell it.

I had planned to spend three weeks during August in Keene Valley. I wanted to visit some of the people who had helped me, partly to say thank you, partly to show them the tidy, rectangular fruit of my labor. I wanted to see Paul Stapley again, I had never met either Mary Kays or Ethel Bissell, and I still owed Clifford Johnson a visit. I wrote and made plans to visit them. Then, about two weeks before I left for the Adirondacks, Mary Kays wrote to say that Ethel Bissell had died. It was a shock. Part of the reason for visiting Ethel Bissell was to give her a copy of the chapter that described Israel Johnson's ancestry and mentioned his distant relation to Isaac Newton. I had never given her all the details. And now she was dead. The best I could do was stop at the store in Newcomb on my way to Keene Valley and introduce myself to her daughter, Sharon, and her son, Marvin. I was sorry not to have met her, I said. She had been a lively, interesting correspondent.

It was all on one day that I arranged to see Mary Kays at her farmhouse in Olmstedville (pronounced *Um*stedville, with a heavy stress on the *Um*), Paul Stapley at his home near Paradox Lake, and Clifford Johnson in Adirondack. Mary Kays offered lunch, but I had such a tight schedule I couldn't accept. I played with several kittens, instead, and traded stories about deeds and graves registries. Paul

219

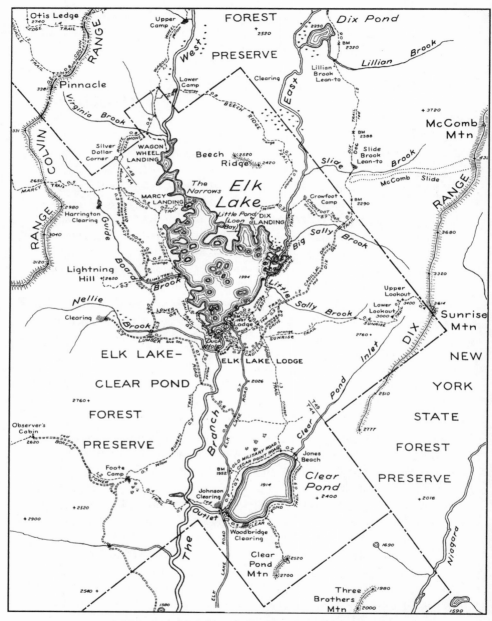

3. Topographic map of the Clear Pond Region.

Stapley took me into his kitchen out of the sun. The summer of 1987 was hot in the Adirondacks, some days hotter than in southern Indiana. I spent most of an hour talking with Paul, in the course of which he persuaded me to go to Brandon, Vermont, to look for the grave of Molly Stowell. He thought she might have been taken back to be buried with her family in 1861. I drove over a week later but found nothing.

Finally, I went to Adirondack. Clifford Johnson was still as hale and spry as he had been in March of 1986. Eighty-eight the previous February, he had no trouble getting up and down stairs. He was pleased to see me, and soon we were sitting upstairs in the living room talking about how the winter had been, what birds came to his feeder, the state of the yard and so on. I pulled out the xerox copy of the manuscript and told him I thought I was finished. I think I've found all I can find, I said. I was looking for an agent. An agent and then a publisher would probably have a good bit to say about the eventual shape of the book. It was my way of telling him that I was reluctant to give him a copy of the book right then,. Though I did give him a copy of chapter ten.

He was pleased. He started talking about some of his memories, one of which concerned two or three people in Adirondack who once, thirty or forty years ago, asked him if the Israel Johnson buried in the Adirondack cemetery was related to him. I bent forward. This was news. In March 1986, he had said only that he thought Israel was buried there. The statement was too conjectural. Now he was recalling a specific conversation, which mentioned a specific grave. Did these people mention the name, Israel Johnson, I asked? Was he sure it was the main cemetery in Adirondack? Clifford said yes to both questions. It seemed, then, that Israel Johnson had in fact been buried there. Where, exactly, we would never know. Whatever stone had been erected for him was gone.

We talked for a while longer. He showed me pictures of his wife, Caroline, and his son, Bob. I gathered from a remark he made that he had not been a widower more than a few years. Outside, he showed me the flower garden planted by his wife. Along one side was a wide bank of purple phlox in full bloom. His wife had come from Germany originally. Shortly before she died, she told him that these last forty years were the happiest of her life. It was a reluctant good-bye we

22. Probable site of the now unmarked grave of Israel Johnson
in Adirondack, New York, next to that of his son, William,
and his daughter-in-law, Adelia.

bade each other. A week or so later, driving home to Indiana, in the
midst of one of my vast transcontinental silences, I said out loud,
send Clifford a copy of the book no matter what shape it's in.

Right after leaving Clifford, however, I had a more practical
thought. I had already been through the cemetery twice, but Clifford's
story made one more trip necessary. I knew I would find nothing, but
I had to look anyway. I drove back the two blocks or so, and stone by
stone, word by word, both front and back, looked at everything
there. As expected, I found nothing.

It was hot. I was hungry and thirsty. Disappointed, too. I turned
and walked back to the car and leaned against it, looking off in the
other direction, into some trees across the road. It had been hot all
summer. And dry. The grass was already turning brown. I might as
well go, I thought, but for some reason I walked back across the
cemetery again. I wasn't looking for anything in particular, but right
next to the joint grave of William H. and Adelia Isham Johnson, the
son and daughter-in-law of young Israel, the ground sank slightly,

perhaps two or three inches. You wouldn't have noticed it unless you were looking for it. It was rectangular, about six feet long and three feet wide. And, for some reason—perhaps because it was a slight depression and so caught and pooled whatever rain fell—the grass in it was green. That's a grave, I said. It must be.

The other Johnsons, with stones, were all nearby. Clifford's memory made it almost certain that Israel Johnson had been buried in this cemetery, and what more logical place for his grave than next to that of the son in whose house he lived his last years.

It has taken several years and more guessing than made me comfortable, but this was, I felt certain, the day I found the grave of Israel Johnson. For the record, it was Wednesday, August 12, 1987, a little before noon.

Appendix

The Israel Johnson Family as Seen in Selected Federal and State Census Reports, 1790–1910

1790: Vermont, Rutland County, Town of Wells
  Israel Johnson [Esq.]
      1 male 16 yrs. and over [old Israel Johnson, 1760–1835]
      2 males under 16 [young Israel, b. 1785 or 86, and
          Nathan, b. 1786]
      3 females [Elizabeth, old Israel's wife, 1760–1813,
          Elizabeth, their daughter, 1789–1813, and perhaps
          Sally, later Sally Burgess]

1800: Vermont, Rutland County, Town of Wells
  Israel Johnson [Esq.]
      2 males under 10 [prob. James, b. 1798, and William]
      1 male 10 to 16 [Nathan]
      1 male 16 to 26 [young Israel]
      1 male 26 to 45 [old Israel]
      1 male over 45 [parent or in-law?]
      2 females under 10 [Sally and ?]
      1 female 10 to 16 [Elizabeth]
      1 female 26 to 45 [Elizabeth, old Israel's wife]
      1 female over 45 [parent or in-law?]

1810: New York, Essex County, Town of Schroon
  Israel Johnson [Esq.]
      1 male under 10 [William?]
      2 males 10 to 16 [James and Nathan?]
      1 male 16 to 26 [Elijah Woodworth?]

225

1 male over 45 [old Israel]
1 female 10 to 16
1 female 16 to 26
1 female over 45 [Elizabeth, old Israel's wife]
[Neither Nathan Johnson nor Elijah Woodworth had their
    own household in 1810. They were most likely
    part of old Israel's household.]
Israel Johnson Jr. [young Israel]
    2 males under 10 [Lewis, b. 1807, and ?]
    1 male 26 to 45 [young Israel]
    1 female under 10
    1 female 26 to 45 [young Israel's wife: Mary?]

1820: New York, Essex County, Town of Schroon
Israel Johnson [Esq.]
    1 male 10 to 16 [Nelson Woodworth?]
    1 male 16 to 18 [William?]
    1 male 16 to 26 [James, now 22]
    1 male over 45 [old Israel]
    1 female 10 to 16
    1 female over 45 [Elizabeth, old Israel's second wife]
1820: New York, Genesee County, Town of Alexander
Israel Johnson [Jr.]
    1 male under 10 [Lyman?]
    2 males 10 to 16 [Lewis and ?]
    1 male 26 to 45 [young Israel]
    3 females under 10
    1 female 10 to 16
    1 female 26 to 45 [wife, most likely Mary]

1830: New York, Essex County, Town of Schroon
Israel Johnson [Esq.]
    1 male between 70 and 80 [old Israel]
    1 female between 60 and 70 [Elizabeth, the second wife]
1830: New York, Essex County, Town of Moriah
Israel Johnson Jr.
    1 male under 5 [William H.]
    1 male 15 to 20 [Lyman?]
    2 males 20 to 30 [Lewis and ?]
    1 male 40 to 50 [young Israel]

3 females 5 to 10 [Betsey and ?]
1 female 10 to 15
1 female 15 to 20
1 female 40 to 50 [Molly Stowell, now Molly Johnson,
      young Israel's common-law wife]

1840: New York, Essex County, Town of Moriah
    Israel Johnson
        1 male 10 to 15 [William H., now 15]
        1 male 50 to 60 [young Israel]
        2 females 15 to 20 [Betsey and ?]
        1 female 50 to 60 [Molly, Israel's wife]
    Lyman Johnson
        1 male under 5 [Nathan T., 1839–1842]
        1 male 20 to 30 [Lyman]
        1 female 20 to 30 [Harriet]

1850: New York, Essex County, Town of Schroon
    Israel Johnson, 64
        Polly J. Johnson, 67 [This is Molly Stowell Johnson]
        Betsey J. Johnson, 24
    [next family recorded in census list]
    Lewis Johnson, 42
        Freelove Johnson, 31
        Hollis Johnson, 9
        Hulday [Huldah] M. Johnson, 8
        Alexander I[rwin]. Johnson, 5
        Betsy M. Johnson, 1
    Alvin Bloomfield, 55
        Phila Bloomfield, 56
        John Bloomfield, 14
        Emily Bloomfield, 11
        Prentice Bloomfield, 8
        Ellen Bloomfield, 5
        Nelson Woodworth, 28
        Nancy Woodworth, 29
        Mary A. Woodworth, 3
        Marvin Woodworth, 3 nd 1/2 [sic]
        William Johnson, 25 [prob. William H. Johnson, b. 1825,
            son of young Israel]

1850: New York, Essex County, Town of North Hudson
    Lymun Jonson [*sic*], 38
        Harriet Johnson, 30
        Hannah Johnson, 7 [Hannah was 5 in 1850]
        Samuel Johnson, 3 [Samuel was 7 in 1850]

1855: New York State Census, Essex County, Town of Schroon
    Israel Johnson, 70
        Molly Johnson, 73
        Betsey Johnson, 31

1860: New York, Essex County, Town of Schroon
    Lyman Johnson, 50
        Harriet Johnson, 63
        Samuel Johnson, 16
        Hannah Johnson, 14
        Louisa A. Johnson, 8
        Charles H. Johnson, 6
1860: New York, Warren County, Town of Horicon
    William H. Johnson, 34
        Susan A. Johnson, 27
        Eugene H. Johnson, 2
        John H. Johnson, 11/12
        Israel Johnson, 76
        Molly Johnson, 78 [who died the next year]
        John B. Jackson
    Lewis Johnson, 51
        Freelove Johnson, 41
        Hollis Johnson, 19
        Huldah Johnson, 17
        Irwin A. Johnson, 15
        Betsey [Elizabeth] Johnson, 11
        George W. Johnson, 5

1865: New York State Census, Warren County, Town of Horicon
    William Johnson, 40
        S. A. Johnson, 34
        E. H. Johnson, 7
        J. H. Johnson, 5
        —— Smith [?slave], 15, female, [?adopted]

Lewis Johnson, 57
    Freelove Johnson, 46
    Huldah Johnson, 22
    Betsey Johnson, 16
    George Johnson, 10
    Edwin [Irwin?] Johnson, 20

1870: New York, Warren County, Town of Horicon
    William Johnson, 44
        Delia [sic] Johnson, 37
        Eugene Johnson, 12
        John Johnson, 10
        Hollis Johnson, 5
        Archibald Johnson, 3
        Goodman Johnson, 7/12
        Rachel Howe, 19
        Israel Johnson, 86
1870: New York, Essex County, Town of North Hudson
    Lyman Johnson, 59
        Harriet Johnson, 52
        Charles Johnson, 16
        Matilda Johnson, 13
        Ruth Johnson, 6
        Anna Johnson, 3

1875: New York States Census, Warren County, Town of Horicon
    William H. Johnson, 50
        Susan A. Johnson, 44
        Eugene H. Johnson, 17
        Hollis H. Johnson, 10
        Archibald H. Johnson, 8
        Robbin S. Johnson, 5 [originally Goodman]
        John H. Johnson, 15

1880: New York, Warren County, Town of Horicon
    Benjamin T. Wells, 70
        Thankful Wells, 65
        Lewis Johnson, 72
    William H. Johnson, 55
        Susan A. Johnson, 50

Eugene H. Johnson, 22
John H. Johnson, 20
Henry H[ollis]. Johnson, 14
Archibald H. Johnson, 13
Robin L. Johnson, 10 [originally Goodman]

1900: New York, Warren County, Town of Horicon
William H. Johnson, 74
Susan A. Johnson, 69
Hollis H. Johnson, 34
Robert L. Johnson, 30 [originally Goodman, later Robin]
1900: New York, Warren County, Town of Queensbury
Archibald Johnson, 33
Julia S. Johnson, 23
Earnest Johnson, 3
Clifford Johnson, 1

1910: New York, Warren County, Town of Horicon
William H. Johnson, 85
Hollis Johnson, 44
Robert Johnson, 39
Lena Johnson, 32 [Robert's wife]
Marion A. Johnson, 10/12 [Robert and Lena's daughter]
Archie Johnson, 43
Julia Johnson, 33
Ernest Johnson, 13
Clifford Johnson, 11
Nelson Johnson, 4/12

Clear Pond

was composed in 12 on 13 Garamond #3 on a Linotronic L-300
by Partners Composition;
with display type set in Caslon #471
by Dix Type, Inc.;
printed by sheet-fed offset on 50-pound, acid-free Glatfelter Natural Hi Bulk,
Smyth-sewn and bound over binder's boards in Holliston Roxite B,
and with dust jackets printed in 2 colors
by Braun-Brumfield, Inc.;
and published by

SYRACUSE UNIVERSITY PRESS
SYRACUSE, NEW YORK 13244-5160